North Carolina Wesleyan College

WISDOM AND COURAGE THROUGH CHRISTIAN EDUCATION

1956

ROCKY MOUNT, N.C.

My Life

AND AN ERA

$\mathcal{M}$Y LIFE AND AN ERA

The Autobiography *of* Buck Colbert Franklin

Edited by

JOHN HOPE FRANKLIN *and*
JOHN WHITTINGTON FRANKLIN

LOUISIANA STATE UNIVERSITY PRESS
BATON ROUGE AND LONDON

Copyright © 1997 by Louisiana State University Press

All rights reserved

Manufactured in the United States of America

First Printing

06 05 04 03 02 01 00 99 98 97   5 4 3 2 1

Designer: Laura Roubique Gleason
Typeface: Janson Text with Trajan and Hampton Script display
Typesetter: Impressions Book and Journal Services, Inc.
Printer and binder: Thomson-Shore, Inc.

Library of Congress Cataloging-in-Publication Data

Franklin, Buck Colbert, 1879–1960.
   My life and an era : the autobiography of Buck Colbert Franklin /
Buck Colbert Franklin ; edited by John Hope Franklin and John
Whittington Franklin.
      p.   cm.
   Includes index.
   ISBN 0-8071-2213-0 (alk. paper)
   1. Franklin, Buck Colbert, 1879–1960.   2. Afro-American lawyers—
Oklahoma—Biography.   I. Franklin, John Hope, 1915–   .
II. Franklin, John Whittington, 1943–   .   III. Title.
KF373.F745A3   1997
340'.92—dc21
[B]   97-24771
                                                              CIP

CONTENTS

ILLUSTRATIONS

EDITORS' PREFACE

*T*he several features that impressed us as we began to work through this autobiography were the author's unswerving determination to complete it, his great anxiety to pay tribute to his mother and his wife by dedicating it to them, and his firm belief that he had something of importance to pass on to later generations. In preparing this volume for publication, we have respected to the letter the things that seemed to be of the greatest importance to the author. We have included his dedication just as he wrote it. And, believing that he had something to say, we have retained to every extent possible the spirit and the letter of his message.

Buck Colbert Franklin was no ordinary mortal. He believed to the very end that he had a destiny to fulfill. The high standards he maintained in the practice of law, his numerous efforts to serve, in a variety of ways, the communities in which he lived and worked, and his strong belief in a Power greater than any that he could behold drove him to pursue the highest and noblest goals to which he could aspire.

His writing of "My Life and an Era" would seem to confirm his belief that he had something to say that was worth saying. He wrote with meticulous care, as if clarity of thought and precision of expression would contribute to a better understanding of what he was saying, as was, indeed, the case. He could summon up the most remarkable detail, assisted in part by a diary, which he kept only occasionally. His memory was unusual, but it was reinforced by conversations during his lifetime with siblings, other relatives, and friends. The result was an account of a life and times that he deemed worth sharing with others. His offspring who have undertaken the pleasant task of preparing it not only agree with his objectives but are also pleased and honored to facilitate his aspirations.

Although there were times when he seemed to regard his prose as divinely dictated and thus not subject to any revision whatever, that was clearly not the case, ultimately. In the months before his death his flexibility was so great that he welcomed any suggestions for improvement. His words were no longer precious, and he almost too willingly acceded to any suggestions for improvement. There was sufficient agreement regarding the nature of the improvements as to encourage such modifications even after his death. This was done with the most meticulous care so that it would in no way detract from the spirit or the general arguments set forth in his autobiography.

In preparing this manuscript for publication, one important question arose with the editors and, indeed, with the publisher. This had to do with the propriety of reproducing the simulated conversations, just as the author provided, when it was quite clear that the time lapse made accurate reproduction of such "conversations" impossible. We, however, suggest that the author was attempting to convey, by using this method, what actually transpired, and we concluded that the construction of the conversations as straightforward narratives of what people talked about would be no closer to the truth than the simulated conversations. Indeed, by permitting the author's account to stand, it gave him the opportunity to provide the words and flavor of the experience which had, in turn, a flavor and value of its own.

We have sought to keep notations and explanations to a minimum. This is Buck Colbert Franklin's book, not ours. We have attempted, through a limited number of notes, to assist the author in making clear to the reader what he was saying or describing. The photographs, extending from the late 1890s to 1959, the year before his death, are themselves a statement about his life and times.

Many people have assisted us in this effort. Some, like Ruby Graham, were persistent in inquiring about its "impending" publication. Unfortunately, Ruby did not live to see the completed work. Bob Blackburn of the Oklahoma Historical Society was generous in his time and wise in his suggestions, as were other members of his staff. Daniel Gibbs, reference librarian of the Ardmore Public Library, and other members of his staff were likewise helpful. Ernestine Clark of the Oklahoma City Metropolitan Library System put us in touch with several important sources. Robert Powers of the Tulsa Historical Society provided photographs of early Tulsa and important information regarding residents of the city. Our nephew and niece (cousin) shared with us materials on Buck Colbert Franklin in their possession. Walter Hill of the National Archives and Record Service assisted us greatly in locating relevant sources in the Archives, as did Christine Louton of the National Park Service and Tim Good of the Lincoln Home National Historic Site. Our son and brother, Bouna S. Ndiaye, assisted in numerous ways, including retrieving materials from various libraries, during which he was ably assisted by members of the staffs of the libraries of North Carolina Central University and Duke University. Margaret Fitzsimmons typed the entire manuscript and lent enormously valuable editorial assistance. Nishani Frazier typed the Introduction, Appreciation, and other matters in the final stages. We are most grateful to all who have assisted us. Our wives, Aurelia and Karen, were long suffering and encouraging, for which we are grateful, but they do not share the errors and failings, which are ours alone.

John Hope Franklin
John Whittington Franklin

BUCK COLBERT FRANKLIN: AN APPRECIATION

*A*fter my father suffered a cerebral vascular accident in 1956, he refused to accept the limitations placed on him by his inability to use his right side, including the hand with which he wrote. He had many tasks to do, he insisted, among them the writing of his autobiography. He had long been a frustrated and unfulfilled writer; and I am convinced that if he could have eked out a living as an essayist, novelist, or columnist, he would have gladly done so. With several rejected manuscripts and some unfinished ones in his files, he abandoned them; and with a determination born of the realization that his time was limited, he began to write about his own life. Once he had recovered sufficient strength to maneuver his own body, he began to write his story and thus to fulfill a dream. Day after day after day, he sat before his manual typewriter carefully and precisely typing out, with the index finger of his left hand, the story of his life.

He began, "I was born on the sixth day of May, 1879, near Homer, a small country village in what was then Pickens County, Chickasaw Nation, Indian Territory." And to him, and indeed, to me as I later learned, this was an auspicious beginning. It was not quite "In the beginning was the word," but it was something akin to it, not only to him, but also to his son who would read and listen to his father's voice some thirty-odd years later. As he wrote and wrote, he was impatient to get his emerging manuscript published, and frequently he implored me to help him. He believed that with my connections in the publishing world, I could knock on any door and it would be opened to receive "My Life and an Era." Even with the several books I had written and edited, my connections in the world of publication were not as solid as he thought. Perhaps I could have exerted myself considerably more than I did.

As I now reflect on the matter, I failed to respond to my father's supplications for what I thought were good reasons. At the time, I was chairman of the Department of History at Brooklyn College, and that was a very demanding position. Having just published *The Militant South*, I was, moreover, very much preoccupied with the next stage of my own research on several exciting projects. From my point of view, there was plenty of time to deal with my father's autobiography. From his point of view, however, time was running out, and he wanted to see it published before it was too late. Unhappily, I did not fulfill his wishes, and I shall always regret this dereliction. That is not to say that I did nothing with the manuscript. From time to time, whenever I visited him and during the intervals between visits, I worked with him on various aspects of it. He was overjoyed whenever I showed some interest by working on it, and he was depressed whenever he believed that I had pushed it aside.

I would not have been so bold as to criticize my father's writing had we not had a long-established practice of exchanging views on a variety of subjects in the most candid manner. Indeed, the exchange between us became so heated at times that a bystander would have thought we were filled with anger and bitterness. That was not true and could not have been true. We loved to debate, but the debating never interfered with our respect and love for each other. For example, we had a practice of exchanging predictions on presidential elections every four years. In 1948, he sent to me his prediction that Harry Truman would win. I responded by telling him that he should stop predicting with his heart and begin using his head. When I added to this remonstrance the certainty that Thomas Dewey would win, he countered by reminding me that elections were not won or lost in newspaper predictions, but in polling booths, about which it was obvious that I knew little, if anything. I dined on crow on that Wednesday after the first Tuesday in November, 1948.

He never argued with me about his manuscript, however. He was so pleased whenever I discussed it with him or wrote to him about it that he withheld any disagreement he might have had with what I said. He was willing to be amenable to my observations and corrections if it would move his work a bit closer to publication. He also seemed to believe that my training in language usage, style, and organization of materials and ideas was more up-to-date than his, and he was willing to go with almost anything that I suggested. Peace reigned whenever "My Life and an Era" was being discussed.

Looking back on those final years of my father's life, I am touched by the manner in which he "pulled his punches," believing that the fewer the debates the sooner the edited manuscript would be completed. He must have winced whenever I told him that his writing style was excessively romantic or that his digressions were too numerous and too long. And, as I warmed up to the subject, I told him that his readers did not wish to know his views on, say, Thomas Jefferson or on reincarnation. That was not the kindest thing to say to an eighty-year-old disabled father who had received his share of rejection slips from publishers who did not like his essays or novels. He took it, nevertheless, because that was the way we always took each other's criticisms, however biting or cruel, and because he was utterly dependent on me to manage his autobiography all the way to publication.

The long hiatus between my father's death and my resumption of the final stage of preparing his autobiography for publication, now joined in this task by my son, did not diminish my fascination for what he had to say and how he said it. Nor did it change my view that what he said was of great importance. If anything, this lapse in time served to increase my admiration for what he wrote and, indeed, the manner in which he wrote. There were not many young African Americans living in the Indian Territory at the close of the nineteenth century who could provide posterity with a vivid account of their experiences and that of their compatriots. In addition to his setting forth the significant aspects of his life on that unlikely frontier for a person of African descent, the richness of detail and his firm grasp on reality made his narration both credible and compelling for me. Consequently, as I resumed work on the manuscript, an urgency not unlike that which gripped my father in 1959 took control of me and did not release its hold until my son and I had completed the manuscript and sent it to the Press.

It was not until several years after his death that I came to appreciate fully how committed my father was to being a writer. Apparently, he had always sought to reach a stage in life when he could spend the major portion of his time in that pursuit. I knew, of course, that he had attempted, unsuccessfully, to launch a weekly paper, the Rentiesville *News*, when I was not much beyond the infant stage. Later, he would write an occasional piece that appeared in Tulsa's African American weekly, the *Oklahoma Eagle*. By the time

I was in high school, I believed that his nightly habit of reading and writing was, somehow, related to his work as a lawyer. When I began to write and publish, he neither sought my assistance nor even shared with me his abiding interest in writing and publishing. Looking back on these years, and now looking at his numerous unpublished pieces, I can imagine that he hoped someday to speak quite casually of the forthcoming publication of his novel or volume of essays or short stories.

In going through his papers I found the draft of a novel, "The Trail of Tears," based on the removal of Native Americans and their African American compatriots—slaves and kinspeople—to the Indian Territory. As he told the story that was more fact than fiction, it was a tragic and inhumane uprooting of a people whose claim to the land they were leaving was much greater than those who were replacing them. There were also numerous essays on a variety of subjects such as "Thomas Jefferson," "The Negro and the New Deal," "The Negro and Communism," "Lifting as We Climb," etc. As I read through these and many more, I began to entertain the possibility of assembling "A Buck Colbert Franklin Reader." Such a work would contain the seasoned opinions, philosophies, wisdom, and observations of a sagacious man.

An important by-product of working on this manuscript was a new and wonderful appreciation of my father's life and work. The jocular tone of the debates and arguments that we enjoyed over the years obscured, if only temporarily, my high regard for all the things for which he stood. Now, without the customary range of grudging concessions of points in our arguments and with few if any reasons to remain inflexible, it was possible to appreciate him for what he was, a sincere, earnest, lovable, trusting, and trustworthy human being. As I have reflected on his life and work, I have more than once remarked to myself and to my son that we would have few if any problems if the world were entirely peopled by the likes of my father.

Another very important outcome of working on the manuscript is a reinforced appreciation for the importance of preserving and making available the recorded experiences of people of every condition, stratum of society, and outlook of life. My father's life represented many layers of the human experience—freedman and Native American, farmer and rancher, rural educator and urban professional. I learned to appreciate his struggles to become the first member of his family to attain a degree in higher education, and I learned what it meant to practice law in an environment where equal justice under the law meant that a black lawyer had to overcome overwhelming odds in securing that justice. I also learned how it took all that my mother and father had to rise above the hostility of the all-black village where I was born, a town that was under the control of members of one religious denomination who had no interest in the well-being or, indeed, the fate of those, such as my family, with other religious affiliations. I came to learn that our poverty resulted not from poor management but from the inability of my father to convince would-be clients that a black lawyer could prevail in a court of law regardless of the deep-seated prejudices of those who administered justice. He was unable to convince them often enough to make it possible for him to earn a comfortable living for his family. Sad to say, the would-be clients were realists who did not want to risk their fate in the hands of one for whom the judge and jurors might have little or no respect.

If there ever had been any doubt that my father was a man of high principle, my reading of this manuscript and my own review of his life removed it. I know of no one who hated racial segregation more than he did. Some aspects of it he had to endure, such as sitting in the Jim Crow railroad car when he traveled from Rentiesville to court in Eufaula, the county seat. But neither he nor my mother, although flexible enough to acquiesce to my going to hear the Chicago Civic Opera Company perform before a segregated audience, would ever demean themselves by voluntarily doing such a thing. I have reproached myself many times for not following their stellar example. On still another example of steadfast principle, he was so deeply committed to maintaining family stability that he often urged couples who sought a divorce to remain together and to try to work out their differences. He did so even when he was not collecting enough fees to support his own family and pay his own bills.

There are a few very significant omissions in my father's account of his own remarkable life. I am not certain why they were not included. Perhaps he had no recollection of them, perhaps the retelling would be too unpleasant, or perhaps they represented a side of the community that was so dark that they should best be forgotten. One of those was an incident that occurred shortly after he began the practice of law in Ardmore, Oklahoma. He had a client who was involved in a case in Shreveport, Louisiana. The two of them went to court there, and when his client's case was called, my father stood. The judge asked him why he was standing. He replied that he was

xviii / An Appreciation

representing his client in the case, whereupon the judge shook his head and declared that no "nigger" could represent anyone in his court. He then ordered my father to leave the courtroom. It was that searing experience that contributed to his decision to move to the all-black town of Rentiesville. In his autobiography, he says that there were two reasons for moving to Rentiesville. He gives only one reason, that the all-black village was an attractive place to live with new and inviting opportunities for rewarding work. I am inclined to believe that the experience in Shreveport, which underscored the virulence of racism, was the second reason for relocating.

Another omission was of an event that occurred in 1918 or 1919, and which I can recall distinctly, although at the time I was only three or four years old. In Rentiesville the antipathy against our family was so great that it was not unusual, I later learned, for my father to receive threats of death if he did not move away promptly. The most powerful leader in the village was the pastor of the Baptist church. He smarted under the fact that although my father had attended Roger Williams University, a Baptist college in Nashville, and Atlanta Baptist College (now Morehouse College), he was still a lifelong Methodist. This religious waywardness, together with my father's commitment to ecumenical principles, drove the followers of this Baptist minister to fight my father with all the resources they could muster. Frequently, his opponents ordered him to leave town, promising dire consequences if he ignored their threats. It was after one such threat—disregarded of course—that hooligans shot into our home, where we lived unarmed. It was the scene the following morning that remains vivid in my mind more than seventy-five years later. I felt most uneasy as I watched my father and a friend pick buckshot from the buttocks of Old Nelly, our only horse. I know nothing of the effect the experience had on my father, mother, or siblings. I can only say that my abhorrence of firearms in all forms dates from that early morning many years ago.

Nor did he explain why, during his entire adult life, he always used the initials "B. C." instead of his given name, Buck Colbert. Though the reason is omitted from the manuscript, the answer was as simple as it was characteristic of him. He did not want white people to address him by first name when it was obvious that they attached to such usage an implication of subordination or inferiority. He told me that this kind of expression was so seldom a demonstration of warmth or familiarity on the basis of equality that

African Americans had various ways to avoid it. Some parents named their children "Mister" or "Major" or "Colonel," thereby creating a problem for whites who intended to degrade blacks by withholding from them all titles of respect. His parents were not sensitized to the matter, so as he approached the status of an adult and as whites who did not know him persisted in calling him "Buck," he decided to use only the initials of his given name. It did not always work, however, for many whites were so certain of the origins of his name that they regularly referred to him as Ben Franklin.

During his lifetime, my father had little in the way of material comforts, and there were many disappointments in his professional life. He was consistently generous to his colleagues, especially younger ones who sought his advice about many things ranging from how to draw up a contract to making a will. He seldom complained, but from time to time he would tell me about colleagues who had acted unscrupulously in attempting, sometimes with success, to take his clients from him. His pride and sense of professionalism were such that he would never confront them or register a complaint against them with the bar association. When I suggested to him that he should make public their unprofessional conduct, he would brush off the suggestion with the remark that it was not for him to pass final judgment on his adversaries and that, after all, the truth would someday find the light. It was because of his persistent optimism and his strong belief that in the end everything would come out all right that I placed on his gravestone his favorite saying, *"The eternal verities will prevail."*

My father's moments of happiness were limited, and there were many times when I felt that he deserved more. One of his minor passions was motion pictures, especially if they dealt with the West. On Saturday afternoon, when he was not in his office, virtually anyone who wanted to see him knew that he was sitting on the last row in the Dreamland Theater a few doors down. Occasionally we would have a picnic in Berry's Park, which was built by African Americans who later sold it to the city. He was an avid reader with wide-ranging interests. He was at home in Greek and Roman history, in Shakespeare, in United States history, and in American literature. He read regularly the great thinkers in American constitutional law, such as John Marshall and Joseph Story. Although he had reservations about some technological advancements, he was enthusiastic about the radio; and I remember quite vividly the joy we shared in the purchase of our Atwater Kent radio to replace our first one, which I had built in school. He took television in his stride, but it never had the fascination for him that radio had.

When my mother died in 1936 he was fifty-seven, and although he took her death with his customary stoicism, I still believe that he was devastated. Believing as he did that one man was meant for one woman, he never considered remarrying, as far as I know. For the remainder of his life he lived with my older sister, Mozella, and her husband, Waldo Jones, who practiced law with him. Later, in 1947, his other son, his namesake, died at the age of thirty-nine. The loss was indescribable for the entire family, especially for me, who now had the sole responsibility for carrying on the family name. My brother died in a veterans' hospital in Virginia, and I did not know how bitter my father was about his treatment in the United States Army until the physicians asked his permission to perform an autopsy. My father withheld permission and replied calmly but sharply that his son had already been butchered enough by the military and that only in death had he escaped them and found peace.

One of the most delightful times I spent with my father was when he visited us in the summer of 1943. He had received his fee in the Lete Kolvin case and was, for the first time in history, well above the poverty level. My wife, Aurelia, and I were both teaching for six weeks at Alabama State College in Montgomery, and my brother was stationed at Camp Dothan, also in Alabama. My father met us in Montgomery, and the three of us went to Dothan to visit my brother and his wife, Bessye. He had never been in that part of the country, and he enjoyed every sight, including the capitol and other public buildings in Montgomery, as well as Booker T. Washington's Tuskegee Institute in the Alabama black belt. He also came with us to Durham, where he was delighted to visit several colleges and universities in the area.

The truly exciting moments during that summer, however, were reserved for the trip to New York. To protect him from any possible racial humiliations such as I had experienced in Manhattan, we stayed in the Theresa Hotel in Harlem. He, Aurelia, and I roamed the city seeing the sights and savoring a wide variety of foods. He was almost like a young boy enjoying every new adventure. Later, he visited us several times in Washington. He arrived, for example, four days after our son, John Whittington, was born. It was on this visit that he suggested that we should call our son "Whit" to avoid any confusion with me. He enjoyed all those visits to Washington, but none of them reached the level of sheer delight that we experienced on the grand tour in the summer of 1943.

A few honors came to my father, but not nearly as many as he deserved. It was the esteem of his colleagues at the bar that gave him the greatest satisfaction. In his autobiography he tells of the pleasure he had in introducing me to the judges and lawyers at the Tulsa County Courthouse. He does not relate how the judges and lawyers invariably turned to me and remarked that *I* should be proud of *him* because of his superior abilities and his steadfast adherence to the highest principles in the practice of law. He does tell of one occasion in 1928 in which a dispute emerged in an African American church between the members and their pastor. The judge in the case appointed my father master in chancery to hear the dispute. Since this was the first time in the South that an African American had presided over such a judicial proceeding, it attracted national attention. The matter was settled peacefully when the pastor resigned as it became clear that the congregation would, in any case, vote him out of office.

Although my father doubted that he would ever actually argue a case before the United States Supreme Court, he had a strong desire to be admitted to practice before the highest court of the land. This would, in a sense, be a validation of his right to represent his clients before any court of jurisdiction despite the refusal of one Louisiana judge to permit him to argue a case in his court. On one of his visits to us when we lived in Washington, a Tulsa friend and legal colleague, Roy St. Louis, moved for my father's admission to practice before the United States Supreme Court. On January 31, 1949, Aurelia and I accompanied him to the Court, and we were filled with pride and happiness as Chief Justice Fred M. Vinson, based upon the motion by St. Louis, nodded his approval and welcomed my father to practice before that august body. For my father, an unswerving professional and a dedicated practitioner, this was a crowning recognition, and the ultimate answer to earlier unsavory experiences in courts of law.

In the year before his death, he was tendered a large civic reception and dinner about which he tells in his autobiography. Those of us who were present and saw him struggling to control his emotions during the numerous expressions of respect, esteem, and affection discovered anew how a lifetime of dedicated service has its own reward. One of the greatest tributes to my father came posthumously when the city of Tulsa named a new park in his honor. At the dedication services, the mayor of Tulsa and the president of Morehouse College, Dr. Hugh Gloster, were among those who paid tribute to him. He would have enjoyed the program, the reception, and most of all the T-shirts on which were emblazoned "B. C. Franklin Park" and which scores of young boys and girls wore with obvious delight.

It is now well into the fourth decade since my father died on September 24, 1960. Without some great or momentous act on his part or on his behalf by his contemporaries who knew him well, it is unlikely that any clear and lasting impression of his life and work will survive. And yet a strong argument can be made for the nurturing of his memory. Out of the Chickasaw Nation in the Indian Territory this youngster emerged with sufficient mental powers to impress his superiors and to justify a program of advanced study that was unusual for that time and place. His work in college and his performance on the state bar examination more than fulfilled the confidence that his early mentors had in him. His half century of arduous and creative practice before the Oklahoma bar and his numerous efforts to elevate the civic and religious life of his community placed his contemporaries deeply in his debt. If one were to pause and reflect on his life and work, it would be logical to laud him for the valuable things he did and the memorable contributions he made to the well-being and improvement of his fellows.

In this world of uncertainty and, at times, unreality, it is well that my father gave his own version of his life. *My Life and an Era* is by no means an effort to have the final word, and it is not even, as John Henry Cardinal Newman would put it, an *apologia pro vita sua* (an explanation for his existence). Rather, it is one last effort on his part to engage in a creative act that was a part of him for most of his life. He would have been more than satisfied if this did not bring one more rejection slip. That it did not is a tribute to the importance of his message and the zeal with which he worked to make it available to succeeding generations. We are the fortunate beneficiaries of his persistence as well as his wisdom.

John Hope Franklin

PREFACE

$\mathcal{I}$ have attempted to write the story of my life and the years it covers, because I believed I could do it without the slanting or the coloring of the facts. And too, I wanted to preserve for my children and posterity the fact that I had the greatest parents that ever lived in any age. My dad in a sense was a hardheaded, rugged individualist in keeping with the times; but also a philanthropist, building and contributing to the building of churches and schools. Although unable to read, he remembered the substance of everything that was ever read to him. He was always broad enough to respect the views of Mother, which was a rare thing in those days, and he encouraged her in whatever she wanted to do or attempted to do. He had one motto that he righteously followed: "Give to good and worthy causes, but never mix charity with business. In business, deal with every man as if he was a rascal."

I have also written this story because I wanted to pay tribute to my wife, who was a part of me for thirty-three years; and because my children knew nothing of what the life of a pioneer was.

The public has read much about the alleged savage Plains Indians and their alleged bloodthirsty chiefs; but never in the history of the Old Indian Territory did one of them ever steal a black man's stock or raid a Negro settlement. It is a sad commentary for the government to record that it had to murder thousands of its wards in the battle of Washita, near Fort Sill. Black Kettle, chief of Cheyennes, tried hard to surrender; but at daybreak on the 27th of November, 1868, the 7th Cavalry, under General Custer, in a surprise attack massacred them. It was commonly known back there how the general hated and disdained all Indians and, later, how that unreasonable hatred and disdain led to his defeat at Little Bighorn and the death of so many other brave and loyal soldiers. The records of the War Department disclose all these facts. There always existed the most friendly relations between the Five Civilized Tribes and the Negro, especially the Creek and Seminole Tribes, the latter dating back to the Second Seminole War.

ACKNOWLEDGMENTS

With this story of my life, and the era it spans, I am placing in cold print, so far as I know it, the part played by Negroes in the building of the Old Indian Territory into the great state of Oklahoma. Hence, this effort, in part, is simply a portrayal of the activities and contributions of a people, not mentioned in the school storybooks or encyclopedias, in the erection of a vibrant and growing commonwealth, of which Negroes, by birth, adoption, and worthwhile contributions and achievements, are integral parts.

For the history and traditions of the Franklin family, prior to my birth, I am indebted to my father; my oldest and youngest uncles, Alexander and Bailey Franklin; and my paternal aunt, Matilda Settles.

The following persons have been very helpful in the collection of materials having to do with people and incidents that took place within the eras connected with my life: Madames Adlissie Moore and Alena Murray, my nieces; Rosa Welch, my maternal first cousin; John Tyler Smith and Frank Smith, nephews; and Anna Sewall, niece of my wife. Also, I am deeply indebted to Elmira Ridley, niece of the oldest attorney in Oklahoma, G. W. Perkin, and to Lubertha Chambers of Guthrie, one of the first Negro woman civic workers in the Indian Territory. I am especially indebted to William Sulcer, who is my senior by many years, a retired schoolteacher in the Oklahoma Territory and, I believe, the best-informed man of his time regarding the early history of this state. He knew personally and had business with every territorial governor and many minor officials, and he knew personally every prominent Negro of the different professions. I am also indebted to Ellen Nora Rentie, now past ninety, who taught school at the old Muskogee Agency as a tribal teacher and who was well acquainted with, and knew well, the tribal officials of that time. I am especially indebted to the *Black Dispatch* and the *Oklahoma Eagle* for materials collected from the files of their newspaper. And for certain documented and authenticated facts I have used, I am especially indebted to *From Slavery to Freedom*, by John Hope Franklin; *A Pictorial History of the Negro in America*, by Langston Hughes and Milton Meltzer; and *The Negro in American Life and Thought: The Nadir, 1877–1901*, by Rayford W. Logan.

This effort is dedicated to the lives and works of two women, both of whom were pioneers in their own right in a raw, new world, although the closing of their respective, active careers is separated by forty-nine years. The former birthed me and the latter preserved me. And, although neither knew the other in this world, I've often wondered if its not within the realm of possibility that they have often met, and become acquainted and learned their relationships to me, as they prayed together in the chapel in the sky for my strength and direction as I stumbled on toward the sunset of my earthly ending, and on toward that common meeting place where all the saints often gather to offer up prayers and supplications for the safe arrival of their countless beloved kith and kin. This the cheering and abiding hope that burns eternally in the breasts of most wayfaring pilgrims as, with legs weary and feet sore, they come to the last lap of the journey.

BUCK COLBERT FRANKLIN

$\mathcal{M}$Y LIFE
AND AN ERA

B. C. Franklin's Oklahoma

ca. early 1900s

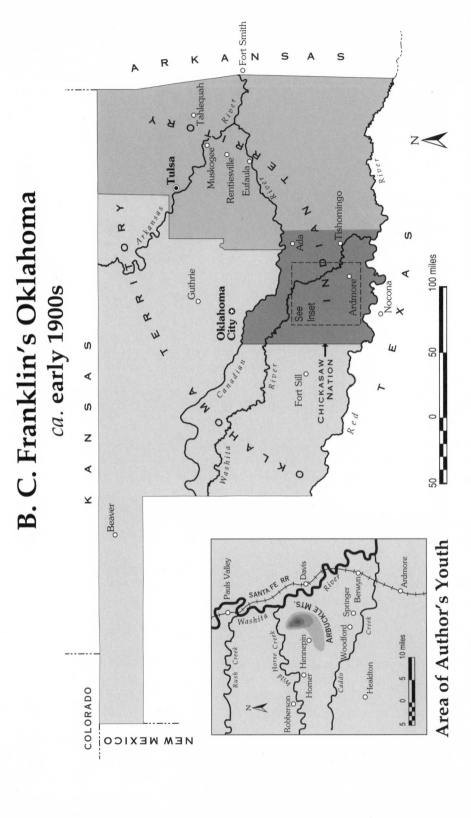

Area of Author's Youth

1

DAYS OF EARLY CHILDHOOD

$\mathcal{I}$ was born on the sixth day of May, 1879, near Homer, a small country village in what was then Pickens County, Chickasaw Nation, Indian Territory.[1] I was the seventh of ten children born to David and Milley Franklin. Dad was born in Tennessee not far from Gallatin, and Mother was born in Mississippi, not far from Biloxi. I was christened "Buck" in honor of my grandfather Buck, who died long before I was born. As a slave, he was the property of a full-blood Chickasaw Indian family, the Birneys, and he must have been above the average slave in intelligence and business, for he purchased himself, his wife, and their ten children long before the Civil War.[2]

My mother was of one-fourth Choctaw Indian blood, the other three-quarters being Negro; but she never knew the meaning of slavery in her early childhood days; for she was born in the home of her Indian kin; she ate,

1. Homer was a village a short distance west of Hennepin, Oklahoma, about twenty miles southwest of Pauls Valley. It had a post office and appears on maps from around the end of the nineteenth century but ceased to exist many years ago. It should not be confused with the present-day Homer near Ada.

2. There is another account of the origins of the Franklins as free blacks. It claims that at the time of the Civil War, David Birney ran away from his owner, joined the Union army, and subsequently gave his name as David Franklin. In 1895, when applying for a disability pension, David Franklin testified that as a slave he had belonged to the Birneys. Then he ran away, "went over to Fort Gibson, [and] there joined the Union and served little over a year." Case of David Birney, No. 662,383, deposition submitted to the Bureau of Pensions, Department of the Interior, in Record Group 158, S.C.894516, National Archives.

slept, played and attended their tribal school and church and spoke their language. She and Dad were married in 1856 near Biloxi and moved to Pauls Valley, in what is now Garvin County, Oklahoma, where their two oldest children, Walter and Andrew, were born. After that, they moved near Homer, in what is now Carter County, Oklahoma, where the rest of their children were born. There were principally two things that caused Dad to move from Pauls Valley. Since he was what is known as a Chickasaw freedman and his wife a Choctaw, and as the lands of the two tribes were then held in common, he could hold, use, and occupy as much of it as he desired, provided he did not attempt to occupy or use any that was occupied or used by any other Indian or freedman of the two tribes. The second reason was that his oldest and youngest brothers, Alexander and Bailey, and a sister, Matilda, had already moved to this settlement.

It is strange how a decision can so often change the whole course of one's life and the destiny of one's children as well as unborn generations.

Had he remained at Pauls Valley, the best he could have ever hoped to be was a janitor or some other menial worker. Whereas, as we shall soon see, the change brought him into the great open spaces, where there were vast uninhabited areas where the virgin grasses grew profusely and luxuriantly. Here, amid these untamed surroundings, where there was plenty of elbow room, Dad's spirit was lifted high above the valleys and low places, upon a tower, as it were, from which he could view distant vistas and horizons unfolding and widening like the rippling waves of a pebble cast into the still waters of the lake. Here, he found breathing easier and the intake of the rarified atmosphere drove the cobwebs from his mind, and there rushed into the vacuum new aspirations and inspirations, seizing and engulfing his entire being and transforming him into a new creature. Before, he had felt limited and circumscribed; but now, for the first time in his life, he had a clearer and broader outlook. He told me about this new birth. He said that after he left Pauls Valley and saw the progress being made by his brothers and sister and listened to them talk about the new life in the new West, about the tremendous possibilities for getting ahead, a new surge came upon him and he believed he could outstrip them.

Since the days of Grandpa Buck, the Franklin family had been a clannish lot whether they lived far from or near each other, and Dad's brothers and sister insisted on helping him get started. They sold him, on credit, workhorses, milch cows, brood sows, and opened an account for him at the Tom Grant general store at Fort Arbuckle. He was able, on his own, to get some credit and other things he needed from the Freeman general store at Pauls Valley, and within two years, he was able to square his accounts with his creditors, including his brothers and sister, by working day and night. This remarkable feat redoubled his confidence in himself. He had become a shrewd trader, and by the end of 1863 he had accumulated many hundred head of livestock and other personal properties. He had under cultivation over two hundred acres of land, under fence almost a section of pasture land with a sizable spread, and one of the best young orchards in the entire Chickasaw Nation. It seemed that everything he had touched turned into money and chattels.

It was in the midst of his almost miraculous rise to success and prosperity that Dad became restless and morose and neglectful, and he grew more so as the days came and went. His sister and younger brother did not understand and became deeply concerned. Mother had guessed the trouble after hearing bits of a conversation between Uncle 'Zander and him, and when he informed her of what was ailing him, she frankly told him she had guessed it.

At the time, the Civil War was at fever heat and casualties were daily mounting on both sides. Uncle 'Zander, who had always had an uncanny influence over Dad and who had seen service in the Second Seminole War, had persuaded him to enter the conflict on the side of freedom. 'Zander had fought by the side of Osceola and painted glowing pictures of his risks and daring, even of the time when he narrowly escaped the massacre at the hands of General Zachary Taylor, later president of the United States. He convinced Dad that he and his brothers and sister would look after his family and property and see that it grew and nothing would be lost or destroyed. They both, like their father, hated slavery and oppression, and Dad became convinced that it was his solemn duty to do his bit for the cause of freedom. Among other things that his older brother had said to him: "Slavery is hell's twin monster, and it's both wicked and immoral."

Most of the Indians and all the freedmen hated Andrew Jackson for the war, although he was dead; they believed he had stirred the hatred between the races, and the Five Civilized Tribes and their former slaves blamed Jackson for their treatment and the wars against them, including their banishment and removal from their old homes to the Territory. Years later, my uncle repeated, I am quite sure, the same things he had said to Dad when he influenced him to enlist. Dad was inducted into the army on the 17th day of March, 1864, and assigned to "B I Indian Home Guards as a private, as a detachment of U.S. volunteers."[3]

During the time Dad spent in the army, Uncle 'Zander and Uncle Bailey and Aunt Matilda, true to their promise, looked after his business with the same fidelity and earnestness as if it were theirs. Uncle 'Zander galloped the six miles from his home to ours daily, supervising the work while Uncle Bailey, whose home was just two miles away, looked after the details. And the business, every phase of it, grew and prospered.

An examination of Dad's war record discloses a wide discrepancy between it and the record as told by him and his family and contemporaries. Some parts of this war record I know are wrong. It says that he was a runaway slave when he enlisted. He was not a slave, as I have pointed out. Uncle 'Zander might have had him say that in the belief that he could enlist easier in "Bleeding Kansas." He was a Chickasaw freedman and never lived in the Choctaw Nation as the record claims. The Burney (the correct spelling of the name is Birney) family that once owned my grandfather Buck came to the Territory under the general removal treaty with the Chickasaws in the early 1830s, and they settled near the Texas northern border, around or in the town of Burneyville, across the Red River from Gainesville, Texas, on the Oklahoma side. None of my family lived in the Territory then. My Uncle Alexander was between 1835 and 1837 engaged in fighting the Second Seminole War. It is over a hundred miles by the Santa Fe railway from Pauls Valley to Burneyville, and it is more than two hundred miles from Burneyville to Topeka, Kansas, where all of Dad's war records were originally kept. The war record places Dad's age at twenty-five when he enlisted in 1864; but he was born in 1820.

So we have government records v. traditions, or folk facts. In this instance, I prefer to believe the latter, for two reasons. First, Dad was unable

3. The 1st Regiment of Indian Home Guards was organized at Leroy, Kansas, on May 22, 1862. It moved into the Indian Territory later that month and saw action at various points in the Territory in the succeeding two years. At the time that David Birney (or Burney), later David Franklin, enlisted, the outfit was in the area near Fort Gibson, where it remained until it was mustered out in May, 1865. Frederick Dyer, *Compendium of the War of the Rebellion* (Des Moines, 1908), 1740.

to read and did not know how or why the records were compiled as they were—one thing is clear, it seems to me: he wanted to enlist and that was possibly the thing he had uppermost in his mind. And second, the bits of information he gave me from time to time about his participation in the struggle indicate that after his enlistment, he went to Tennessee and saw his first engagement near Knoxville and finally joined up with Sherman and marched with the army to the sea.[4] Don't ask me how he did it, I don't know. He told me the color of the soil around Knoxville, and I saw it myself for the first time in 1899. I know I used to read to him about the siege of Atlanta and the march, and he disputed many things the history book contained and said "that happened this way or that," and what he said and the argument he made seemed like common sense to me. I'm not puzzled about how he got to Tennessee; for, in those days, there were many freedmen who made the trip back to their old home and thought nothing about it. They had good horses and thought nothing of such a journey, and it was the most natural thing for him to want to fight on the soil of his birth.

I knew nothing of the discrepancy between his war record and the things he had told me until a few years ago. I went to Pauls Valley to see his old lawyer, O. W. Patchell, but he had died and so had his wife. He had a young son living, but the son knew nothing of the things I wanted to know and could find none of his father's records. I was sure Patchell had assisted Dad's Washington attorney in working up his pension request, and looking about, I found that his oldest kin and relatives, who might have been able to explain this discrepancy, had passed.

———————
———————

By the time I was of sufficient age to pay attention to things, Dad was the owner of two spreads, one at home and the other about six miles northwest of home.[5] He was easily the best known cattleman in the Nation, with the possible exceptions of Cal and Ike Suggs and Jack Brown, and by far the most popular and most highly respected. He was an active paid-up member

4. The Indian Home Guards did not see action outside Kansas and the Indian Territory. *Ibid.*

5. In the West in the late nineteenth century, the term *spread* denoted an amount of land of undetermined size, held by one person.

of the Texas Cattle Raisers Association and attended all of its annual meetings. He was well acquainted with most of the cattlemen in southern Kansas, especially in and around Dodge City, Abilene, and Caldwell, from which points he often shipped cattle before the Santa Fe went into operation through the Chickasaw Nation. He had early commenced the improvement of his livestock—cattle, horses, jackasses, jennets, and hogs in the main—and he therefore raised and sold them to better advantage and for better prices than the average stockman. In the improvement of his livestock, especially horses and cattle, he owed much to his brother 'Zander, who had made a specialty of dealing in fine breeds of horses and cattle before the close of the war, and from whom he got his start of fine breeds.

In the matter of swine, there was an exception, as I recall. Dad had an old, blue brood sow. She was different from the rest of the hogs. She and her offspring had as little to do with the other swine as possible. I don't remember how Dad came by her. The first time I remember having seen her was after the first light snow. Then she came home with her own drove of different sizes, all of them shy of human beings. You see, Old Blue, as she was called, had a way of spending the winter months at home. As soon as spring weather commenced to arrive, she would leave with a boar of her brood for the creek bottoms and woods where she would subsist upon acorns, farrow her young, and return home after the snow had fallen. Dad always kept her offspring of the former season at home. He tried to detain Old Blue, but he was unable to build a fence to hold her. There was an instinct in her that warred against confinement. The wide open spaces beckoned her and she was obedient unto the call of the wild. Not so with her former broods. After the winter had passed and they had feasted upon corn, they were content to remain at home.

There was another peculiar phenomenon at the home spread. Dad had a dun mare named Fannie. She was a pet, a natural-born pacer and as beautiful an animal as I ever saw. And the many foals she delivered were all natural-born pacers and of her color, although their sires were all of different colors.

Looking back across the years, I recall two personal experiences that stand out in my memory as vividly as if they happened yesterday. The first occurred in May, 1884, just a few days after my fifth birthday. It was in the late afternoon when Dad had just ridden in from Fort Arbuckle. He tethered Old Button to the hitching rail and went into the house. I was playing alone in the barnyard, teasing old Tom, our peacock, as he strutted around me with dragging, flaming plumes, in barbaric pride and vanity. As I looked toward the hitching rail and saw Dad's horse hitched to it, a strange and compelling something seized me. I loosed the horse's bridle reins, led him to a stump behind an outhouse, climbed up into the saddle by way of the stirrup, and rode away into the sunset.

As I rode away toward the west, I recalled a broad, expanded prairie, by which I had ridden many times behind Mother as she took me to the Oil Springs schoolhouse. It was called the "Sam Williams Prairie" because he lived upon one edge of it. The prairie was as level as the floor of our house, except that here and there it tilted, and was almost treeless, except on the northeast corner, where there was a grove of oaks. The edge of this prairie extended to the foothills of the Arbuckle Mountains. To the south lay the Oil Spring Flat, carpeted with mosquito grass.

I guided Old Button into the grove of trees to the side as I was approaching, and stopped. In the spring, summer, and fall seasons, this prairie was a gathering and camping place for cattle from many herds. They came late in the evening, when the sun was not so hot, and grazed upon the tall and tender grass and bedded down after their fill. Often the bulls of the different herds challenged and fought each other for the mastery of the herds. Earlier that evening, wild turkeys had flown from the bottoms out near the prairie into the sumac groves to feed upon the red berries. Subsequently, I would see them there in droves that could not be counted. I have watched them as they flew up to return to their roosting places and witnessed how their wings completely hid the sun from view and darkened the earth beneath over an extended space.

Just how long I sat in the saddle or how or when I dismounted, I don't know. The first thing I remember afterward was that I was sprawled upon the ground, canopied by tall blades of grass and a huge hairy face against mine. The face was that of old Dash, my Newfoundland shepherd dog, that had been my almost inseparable companion since birth. Dad had purchased him when he was a pup from a friend in Caldwell, Kansas, when I was a baby. He was so large that I could ride him; but he allowed no one else to do it. He must have seen me leave home and followed me at a distance. Dash was an unusually smart dog. My mother's cousin, Pleasant Shoals, had taken great pains to train him for me from the time he was a mere pup. He could send him around the fence to see if any cattle were in the field, or to Homer to get the mail or to other neighbors in the community to carry messages, and so forth.

I had been afraid lying there on the ground before Dash came, but now being reassured, I soon fell asleep again. Next I heard a voice calling me; first it seemed at a great distance, and then it drew nearer and nearer. Then I felt Dad's breath against my face and he was next lifting me to my feet. He was saying, "Wake up son, my God! I'm so glad we have found you safe and sound. Let's go home. Your mother is up and waiting for you." Rubbing my eyes, I was fully awake now. He went and fetched Old Button grazing nearby and shouted to some other hunters not far away. He placed me on his horse behind him and led Old Button. Someone fired a shot or two, signals to other seekers that I had been found. Near home I saw a light burning in Mother's room window. She kissed and disrobed me without a word; but I could see that look in her eyes, and I knew that there was more to come. She never whipped one of her children when she was angry or under a great strain. She always took her time and lectured to us while she applied the lash.

The other experience occurred in July of the same year. In those days it was the custom of the Baptist churches throughout the Nation to conduct joint revivals, or camp meetings, after crops had been laid by. They would move from settlement to settlement, holding their meetings from ten days to two weeks in each community where there was a church. That meant that they covered an area of sixty miles or more. They went on horseback, buggies, and covered wagons, each with enough to set up light housekeeping, and each resembled a tented village. On this occasion, this moving church was encamped at the Salem Baptist Church upon the same spot where it stands today. (On November 21, 1955, my brother Andrew died of a heart attack in this very church as he was rising from a prayer he had just said.)

Then, the country was wild and untamed. The deer were more numerous then than the rabbit is today, and the wild turkeys and prairie chickens abounded everywhere, and the panther and mountain lion skulked in every forest and creek bottom ready to pounce upon man and beast. Wild Horse Creek was truly "wild," and dangerous to cross. Its waters ran swift, deep, and muddy. The grass grew tall and luscious, and wild grapes and plums and berries of all sorts were plenteous. Only cow trails and dim roads pointed the way, except for the fact that the government road, called the Doadesville–Fort Arbuckle–Fort Sill Trail, ran nearby. Now, State Highway No. 7 and farm-to-market roads belt and thread the environs.

It was late one evening, after different preachers had been preaching all day, and some of the womenfolk were preparing evening meals, with the men butchering a yearling or hog or lamb, while to the east in the bottom bordering on the banks of Wild Horse Creek, desperadoes and murderers with prices on their heads engaged in selling whiskey and gambling. Among them there existed bitter hatred, jealousies, and feuds. Particularly was this true about Dick Glass and his friend Henry Farrow and their enemy Mose Clay.

Dad and Mother took my brothers David and Fisher and myself with them to church that evening and stopped our wagon behind one owned by Jim Williams. I was left in the wagon to look after my brothers, my juniors, while Dad unhitched the team from his wagon and hobbled them on the grass, and Mother retired to the church. Soon after that Mose Clay rode up, dismounted and tethered his horse behind the wagon of his half brother, Jim Williams.

It was after nightfall, but the moon was full and shining as bright as day, and peering through our covered wagon I could see everything that was taking place in front and to my side. Mose took some corn from his brother's wagon and fed his horse in the feed box and disappeared for a short time. A man, whom I did not know, removed Mose's horse from the feed box and placed another horse there. Soon Mose returned to the wagon, and seeing a horse had been substituted for his at the box, inquired with an oath who had done it. The man, whom I was soon to learn was Henry Farrow, said, "I did it, you s.o.b., and if you don't like it help yourself."

As fast as lightning and before the last word had died from the throat of the aggressor, two shots blazed from the hip of Mose and the challenger fell to the ground. But before Farrow's body was prostrate, two or three shots came from the outer edge of the crowd that had gathered to watch the finish of this long-standing, well-known feud, and Mose's body reached the ground almost at the same time as Farrow's. Farrow died instantly, and Mose lingered and died about noon the next day. As young as I was, I hated pistols and revolvers from that day on, and hated murder even more. It was common knowledge that Dick Glass had killed Mose. He was to lose his life before the year was gone as he was returning from Paris, Texas, with a wagonload of whiskey.

———
———

I think the two spreads that Dad owned were busier places the year round than any other two spreads in the Nation, if not the entire Territory. At the home spread there were more than three hundred acres of land in a high state of cultivation, and there was something to be done every day in the year. Dad had a blacksmith shop housed at home, fully equipped with all the tools of the trade. In February of each year, every plowshare was sharpened and made ready for plowing, and all others that needed to be mended were looked after. Dad believed in autumn plowing—deep plowing. He believed that this created a deeper plant bed in which the root hairs of the plants could feed, out of reach of the scorching rays of the sun, and the plant was less likely to be affected by the drought. He also believed that the less rain there was, the more plowing should be done. He never sowed wheat in the fall or early winter, like most farmers did; he sowed his in the early spring when he sowed his oats and millet seeds. He planted his corn, then his other small grain seeds and sorghum cane, and in their proper seasons those crops had to be harvested and grannied, cribbed, or binned, as the case might be. There was the sorghum cane to be stripped, cut, and made into molasses, and wheat to be harvested, threshed, and some of it stored in the weasel-proof bin and the rest taken to the accommodation flour mill and swapped for flour and its by-products, shorts, seconds, and brans. The millet had to be cut and stacked, and the oats had to be harvested, threshed, or stacked.

The fall season was one of the most charming and enjoyable of all. The tree leaves were tinted and brown. When the winds whistled among the tree-tops and their branches, they squirmed and fluttered to the ground. This was hog-killing time, and Dad never killed less than fifty, weighing an average of 250 pounds; then followed the making of sausage and the hickory smoking and curing of meats. Dad used three or more farmhands the year round, but they took the most of their wages in meats, flour, and molasses.

Then there was the quilting bee, when women would come from a distance of twenty-five miles. I well remember one log-rolling and house-raising event. The logs were hewn and dressed, and when the house was put up or built, the logs were "pinted"—*i.e.*, lime with a very small mixture of dirt, not enough to change its whiteness, was daubed between the logs. This kind of house is among the warmest that can be built, and they make beautiful buildings. Our home was a nine-room house of such a construction. The houses were covered with boards riven from different timbers.

When it was too wet to work outdoors, the bins had to be examined for weasels and doctored if any were found. There were peas and beans to be shelled and placed in different containers. I was not considered too young to help the "hands"; nor was I regarded as too small to help cut sprouts from fence corners and in rows of and between growing things. Sometimes a limb of the twig would fly back and whip me in the face. After five years of age, our parents thought we should begin to learn to work. At six years of age, I commenced getting up in the mornings when the others arose. Certainly I was up in time for the morning prayer, which just had to be said. At bedtime, the services included Scripture reading and sometimes a verse or two from an old familiar hymn.

But our home was also the social center at times. Saturday evenings it was a commonplace thing for teachers Shoals and BeShears, who often substituted for Mother, and Dad's pastor, the Reverend Brown Peters, to gather at our home and discuss many subjects. My sister Dolores and other girls of her age and my two older brothers and their friends would gather in the "parlor" and engage in the square dance. Brother Andrew would "call the figures" while a cousin, Joe Franklin, would play the fiddle. I sat in the corner where Dad and his company were and listened to the discussion until Mother made me go to bed.

As a rule, I always preferred the company of grown-ups. I could learn more, and learning is what I craved. This is not to say that I did not believe in fun and sports. On the contrary, I loved to romp and play. I loved to go hunting on the prairie for the eggs of prairie chickens in the springtime. I recall that many times I returned with a pail full of fresh eggs that I had taken from their nests.

While I was a bookworm, loved school, and was always inquiring and seeking information from grown-ups, I was no saint. I loved horses and horseback riding and as I grew older, I became a bronco-buster and an expert with the lariat. I was daring—no swollen stream or creek out of its banks ever stopped me from crossing it. If its currents were very swift, I always put my mount in above the crossing so he could swim diagonally and thus avoid the impact of the current to a great degree, and with my coat and boots tied to the horn of the saddle, I would slide off the rump of my horse, grab him by the tail, and float to the opposite bank with him.

More than once, my brother Matthew and I ran horse races on the Sabbath day, notwithstanding the fact that our parents had always taught us to keep that day, above all others, holy. Many times my brother David and I stole melons from our cousin Sander's patch, although he would have given us all we might want for the mere asking. They just didn't taste as good as stolen melons, so we argued. Then look at the fun we derived from pilfering! Strange, we never stole melons from a nonrelative or a stranger. At night we would sometimes steal apples or other fruits when we had plenty of them in our orchards, so many that they were going to waste.

If we had had laws then like the ones we enacted later, we would have been pronounced delinquents and sent to reform school. We were simply mischievous and never considered that we were committing crimes. We were simply having so much fun. After all, these escapades were only for a season. We soon forgot about them. I became that serious little boy again, preferring the company and companionship of adults instead of boys my size and age. What with a united, clannish family life and the family altar lit and burning twice a day, and everyone in the family with chores to do and tasks to perform all through the day, there was never a chance for the devil to set up his workshop in our home. It is not strange that such a family tie very naturally becomes an anchor, converted into myriads of spiritual symbols that keep living on and on through eternity, revisiting the living, those left behind, in the form of "the angel's presence," inspiring and steering them through their natural lives to that perpetual masthead, not made with hands, "but eternally in the heavens."

That fall term of the school began on the 15th of September with increased enrollment. Pupils came from Upper Salt Creek, Bee Branch, Long Branch, from a community between Zander Creek and Fort Arbuckle. The schoolroom was overcrowded, and it became a physical impossibility for Mother to teach all the pupils. The first evening, Mother told all the children to tell their parents to meet at the schoolhouse the following day. About 90 percent of them came. Although Dad was the chairman of the trustee board, he thought it would be more tactful for another member of the board, Manuel Williams, to call the meeting together and state its purpose. Mr. Williams very briefly stated the facts: that there had been a tremendous increase in the enrollment over the last school year and that the present room was woefully inadequate; that Mrs. Franklin could not possibly take care of all the pupils; that an assistant teacher would have to be employed and another room added to the school so as to accommodate the increase—or the new pupils would have to be sent back home; that it would take money, cash on the barrelhead, to buy lumber, shingles, nails, etc., and hire carpenters to do this extra work; that what money Mrs. Franklin had been paid for teaching was paid by her husband and one or two others; that Mr. Franklin had paid the money that was already invested in the present building, had promised to pay the balance, and that it would not be fair to him to assume any further responsibilities in the education of other parents' children.

He then asked my father how much more was due on the present structure and what was the balance due on Mother's salary. Dad stated the amount due on the school debt and then said, "As to how much, if anything, you owe my wife, you will have to ask her." She arose and said, "You can forget about that if you will add more space to the school and hire an assistant." No money was raised, although Mr. Williams asked for it. My father had had experience with subscription schools, and he knew what to expect. He told the people he would see a carpenter and get an estimate of the cost to make an addition to the school and equip it with seats and so forth, and would let them know at another meeting two days hence.

About a fourth of those present appeared at the following meeting. None promised to assume any obligations, and only six of them agreed to take their wagons to Pauls Valley to haul building materials. Dad finished paying the old debt and obligated himself as well for the material for the new addition. He gave his word. Mortgages and notes as evidences of indebtedness were then unknown. Before Thanksgiving, the room to the school had been added and fully equipped and Pleasant Shoals, Mother's cousin, had been hired to assist her. Mother and a few other good women used Thanksgiving night as an occasion to raise money to pay on the debts of the school and equipment. The remainder of the school term moved smoothly and showed progress and advancement in every grade, although very few of the patrons came forward to assist in payment of the bills.

At the close of the school year in 1886, Mother gave notice that she did not intend to teach any more and that the board would do well to select another teacher and an assistant. The close of this term of school stands out very vividly in my memory. The last week was spent in public examinations of the different classes, in grading the pupils, in promotions and, in some cases, demotions, and in recitations, spelling bees, and outdoor activities such as footraces, wrestling, horseshoe pitching, and the like. On the last day all the patrons brought food, and dinner was served to everybody. The members of the board presented Mother with an appropriate gift, a large red silk handkerchief. This article was very popular and in great demand in that day and time. A woman considered herself very fortunate to possess one. It served as a head gear and shawl.

Late one evening in July, my Uncle Andrew, Mother's brother, came out to visit her. He lived near a little village, Lukfatah, in the Kiamichi Mountains. I heard Mother speak of him often but had never seen him. He was riding a mule, a very beautiful animal about fourteen and one-half hands high. He was at the gate before Mother saw him, and she ran to meet him with all possible speed. My uncle's visit was more than a pleasure trip. He was a member of the C.M.E. church, and with him came Reverend Pinkard, his presiding elder. This was a comparatively new sect, and under Bishop [Isaac] Lane of Jackson, Tennessee, Reverend Pinkard and my uncle had been building churches in the Choctaw Nation and had come into the Chickasaw Nation to try their luck. Most of the freedmen in the Nation who belonged to any church at all were Baptists—my mother was an exception—and I am sure they never had heard of my uncle's church and cared less.

At the supper table that evening Uncle told Dad that he and his elder had come to the Nation to build a church or two and that he wanted Dad to use his influence to assist them.

"You can't expect me to do that, Andrew. I'm not only a Baptist, but a deacon. I have no prejudice against different denominations; but I just can't help you. Let your sister help you. I know her feelings in this matter, and she will be glad to assist you."

"I certainly will," spoke Mother, "but you cannot expect Dave to help us. He might be able to secure the use of his church on off days, but I really doubt this."

After much talk, Dad agreed to try to secure the use of his church for my uncle and the elder. He would invite his pastor over for dinner the following Sunday.

The Reverend Davis, Dad's pastor, was very old, self-opinionated, and as stubborn as a mule. Added to these deficiencies, he was very ignorant. All this added up to at least two strikes against the proposal, if not three. After Sunday services, the family, with Uncle and the elder, returned home. Dad's pastor rode behind the family surrey. At the dinner table, Dad introduced my uncle and his preacher to Rev. Davis and was bold enough to state the mission of the two to the Nation. He could see that his pastor colored under the knowledge of the reason for their visit. He also saw how firm the pastor's jaws became and how his eyes flashed. Not noticing any of this, Rev. Pinkard started into a further explanation of his mission.

Rev. Davis stated without so much as batting an eye that the elder's mission was a waste of time; that the Negroes all over the Nation had never heard of any church other than the Baptist, and he was quite sure they would not believe that there *was* another; and that according to the Bible, there could not be another. As pastor he would never consent to the use of the Salem Baptist Church by some association claiming to be a church.

Rev. Pinkard told him he would like to debate him on the subject; that he would give him twice the time and the right to open and close the debate. Words grew pretty hot, and Davis said, "There is no room for argument in this matter. I would be remiss in my duty and obligation if I did not mash the false head of this false god. The Bible is the only guide as to the true church, and you, Dave," he said, looking straight at Dad, "are responsible for this foolishness. You should resign as a deacon of the church because you do not meet the qualifications of a deacon. Your wife is not in association with you in the church, which shows you do not control your own household."

"You had better stop there," stormed Dad. "I'd hate to invite a man into my home and be forced to make him leave. I could say more, but not now. I did not intend to go so far, but I now warn you that I shall take this matter up with the official board, and if I cannot get this matter adjusted along the lines of self-respect and common decency, I shall appeal to the entire church. Now we will not discuss this matter any further."

Within a few days, Dad called the official board together, including the pastor; but there he was beaten down. There was only one man who stood by him: the Reverend Robert Jackson, a very intelligent young preacher. He worshiped my father. He almost lived with us, and considered our home his home. He called my mother his mother. Dad had helped him in his quest for knowledge—in fact, had sent him to a seminary for one term.

When the church conference was called, Jackson took charge of the meeting. He argued that inasmuch as the pastor was involved, he was disqualified to preside over the meeting, and this argument carried. He saw, however, that the members would never consent to Elder Pinkard preaching in the church on the Sabbath Day, and so he submitted the following proposition as a compromise: that some weekday be selected for the use of the elder and his friends, if any, to attempt to justify the right of his organization to exist according to the Bible; but that under no circumstances would he ever be allowed the use of the church on Sundays.

This proposition was debated, and finally it was adopted. The pastor opposed it but was overruled. The meeting was set for the 25th day of August.

Meanwhile, a strange thing was to happen. The Reverend Pinkard got a permit allowing him to build a church, and before the 25th of August the structure was completed and a well had been sunk. Any number of people believed that Dad was behind the move. They had come to learn the nature of the real David Franklin, how bitterly he hated denominational narrowness and all frivolous things calculated to divide a community; but to the end, he swore he had nothing to do with it.

The 25th of August became the most important day in the settlement when the community learned what was to happen, and as the people talked about it, they worked themselves into a dither. The news spread rapidly throughout adjoining communities across the Nation. The occasion got into a newspaper or two and into the other Nations of the Territory, where it was represented as the "Ides of March" or "Doomsday." It was sheer temerity for this new and strange sect, or for any sect, to challenge the "faith" of Negroes in the Territory. They must crush it so effectively that never again would such audacity raise its head among them.

Once the young Reverend Jackson said to some members of his church, "I am not so sure but that the elder will be able to establish his right to preach and teach his faith." He was immediately charged with blasphemy and an attempt to spread heresy, and was cited to appear at a church conference. He ignored it, but Dad appeared. The pastor charged Dad with being the cause of all the dissension and said, "I'll entertain a motion to expel him." The motion was lost for want of seconding. Then Dad arose and spoke briefly. "I have not discussed this matter with young Jackson. In fact, I have not seen him since we all agreed to allow Elder Pinkard to use the church. To the members, let me say we all are neighbors and have to live together, wait on the sick together, and bury our dead. Our homes and all we have are here. Reverend Davis does not live among us, and this church is not his. It belongs to God and to us His servants, who built it. We must not allow him to destroy our peaceful neighborhood. I am a Baptist and intend to stay in this church unless you vote me out. Even then, I'll still be a Baptist but not a fool. If other people want to belong to some other church, I'll not hate or fall out with them." Then he sat down.

The morning of the 25th came. Elder Pinkard had put his last prayerful touches to his sermon—or lecture, depending upon the viewpoint of the listeners. He had had the use of Mother's reference Bible and a companion biblical treatise. She had ably assisted him, and like all Indian students, she had a pretty fair knowledge of the Scriptures, having spent several years at the Armstrong Academy under missionary teachers who felt it their duty to stress the Bible in preparing the student for civilization and Christian citizenship. She was head and shoulders above the average preacher of that day.

People were coming in droves from every direction, on horseback and in vehicles of every sort. Then came my uncle, Mother, Elder Pinkard, and Dad in the family conveyance. No committee welcomed the elder. Who would make him welcome and introduce him to the audience? He was unperturbed as he got out of the carriage and with his saddlebag made his way to the door of the church.

At the door, he came face to face with a tall, sinewy, bronzed, coarse-haired man with high cheekbones and piercing gray eyes. They embraced each other warmly and proceeded into the church and to the pulpit. This man was Professor Riley, the noted missionary Indian professor, educated in a seminary in Connecticut, who had spent twenty-five years of his life in the classrooms of the great Indian school in the Smoky Mountain area of western North Carolina and who had met Pinkard many different times on the mission field. He had been spending the summer at the Indian school at Tahlequah and, seeing an account of the meeting, had come down to renew his acquaintance with Elder Pinkard and to render such service as might fall to his lot.

Just as they sat down, Reverend Jackson entered the side door and, smiling broadly, ascended the rostrum, grasped Elder Pinkard's hand warmly, and sat down. The elder introduced him to Professor Riley, and after a brief conference between them, Jackson arose, still smiling, and invited the pastor to share the pulpit with them. Rev. Davis didn't budge from his back seat near the door. Still smiling, Rev. Jackson outlined the order of the meeting. He mentioned who Professor Riley was, part Cherokee Indian and freedman, who would have something to say later on. "You know why Elder Pinkard is here. He has asked me to conduct the devotional services and to introduce him, which I am delighted to do."

The crowd overflowed the church. There was no more standing room and dozens of heads were looking through the windows and doors. There were as many or more people out of doors as inside. Deep silence, weighing tons, had prevailed until Rev. Jackson wisecracked appropriately: "Loosen up. It's not as bad as you are imagining. This is still God's church. Paul and Silas had to pray in a stinking and lousy jail, and surely you can sing with me in Salem Baptist Church. Now join with me in singing 'Onward Christian Soldiers.' " The congregation loosened up. When the second song was sung, "Must Jesus Bear the Cross Alone," it was at fever heat. After reading the Scripture lesson, the master of ceremonies introduced the speaker.

After thanking the minister for conducting the devotional services, and the people "for your understanding hearts and cooperation, and Pastor Davis for the magnanimous use of your church," the elder went immediately into a discussion of the subject "Sheep of Many and Different Folds."

The major portion of his address was written. He gave it to Mother, and since that time I have read it many times, and it had much to do with shaping my religious thoughts. The speech was finally lost, or I would quote from it here. At any rate it went over in a big way.

In those days it was the custom for members to serve dinner "on the grounds" after service. A special table was set for the elder and his friends, and each sister vied with the other in serving them. The only lonely and miserable person on the grounds was the pastor. Elder Pinkard invited him to sit at the special table, but he refused. His own people became disgusted and ashamed of him. But they did not fire him. I believe, however, that the result of that event marked the beginning of a very slow and painful process toward the breaking down of the different religious denominations in the Territory.

In the treaties of 1866 between the federal government and the Creek, Seminole, Cherokee, Choctaw, and Chickasaw Indians, later to be known as the "Five Civilized Tribes," the Indian Territory was just about equally divided into the western and eastern Indian Territories. The western half was reserved for the settlement of the various Plains tribes, with certain exceptions; but the eastern half was to belong to the Five Civilized Tribes. Each of these tribes owned slaves before and during the Civil War. In each treaty it was the purpose and intent of the government, with the consent of each tribe, to make each former slave a full citizen, and there had never been any doubt that this had been accomplished with the Cherokee, Creek, and Seminole tribes; but it was widely believed that this had not extended to the Choctaw and Chickasaw tribes. If these tribes denied citizenship to their former slaves, and if it was finally determined by court action that the tribes could not be forced to adopt their former slaves, what was to become of them? What would happen to former slaves who had purchased their freedom? This last question concerned my father. Since my mother was only one-fourth Indian, would she be included in the final enrollment that allotted land in severalty to the tribes?

Insofar as the ultimate rights of the Chickasaw and Choctaw freedmen were concerned, the courts would decide. However, in the matter of proving whether one was Indian by blood and as such entitled to an Indian's rights and privileges, the testimony of those who had known the person all of his life would be brought to bear. Thus, Mother and Dad decided that it would be wise for her to go back to her old home among her friends and collect written evidence to prove that, although only one-fourth Indian, she had always been treated as and considered an Indian. The quicker she did this, the sooner she would be able to secure depositions from the older Indians who knew her in Mississippi at the time of her birth, through childhood, schooldays at Armstrong Academy, especially of her return to Mississippi to marry, and of her return to the Nation and to Pauls Valley.

So within a few days, with her son Andrew, she left for Old Boggy Depot, her first stop, reached after three days on the road. They remained there for two weeks before going on to the academy, where they spent a week. From there they proceeded to Tuskahoma, the Nation's tribal capital. With them went a distant relation, a Chickasaw Indian who was a descendant of Winchester Colbert. He had attended the academy at the same time as Mother and had known her all her life. Her late father, a Choctaw Indian, Tim Colbert, had been related to Josiah Colbert, who made the trip with them and whom she paid handsomely to collect the affidavits of all who had agreed to assist her, and to forward same to her at Homer.

Feeling that she had had a successful trip, and fully satisfied that her business was in good hands, they started for home by way of her brother's home near Lukfatah, where she intended to spend two or three days. But after having a very strange dream, she only remained one night. Her brother could not understand the sudden rush to return home. She could not understand it either, she said, but she feared that something might be wrong.

On the first night's journey, there came a hard rain that blew through the bottom part of the wagon sheet and dampened the bedding, and much of it reached Mother. The following morning she had to put on wet clothes and wear them all that day, and try to sleep on wet bedding the second night. None of these inconveniences slowed them up. They barely took time to eat their hurried lunches, and feed and water the team by the light of the lantern. Daylight found them on the road. Jim and Dolby, the team of brown horses, never tired and appeared anxious to accommodate in the rush back home.

A sneezing spell seized Mother, and in the middle of the evening her temperature rose and she had aches and pains in her limbs and body. It was near sunset, and she ordered Andrew to pull off the dim road and find a suitable place to camp. The wet beddings had been stretched atop the wagon sheet and were now dry. She thought that if she would take a dose of quinine and a tonic made of whisky mixed with sassafras tea, go to sleep between dry beddings, and have a good night's rest, she would feel better the following morning.

Andrew had fed the team and brought in some wood in preparation for the evening meal. Mother was sitting in the only chair, facing west. She was looking hard, as if in expectation, when in the distance she saw a lone rider. She sat quietly, unmoving, staring fixedly at the approaching object. The horse was in a slow gallop and almost at that instant she recognized the animal. It was Old Button, Dad's riding horse. She gasped audibly and strode toward the horseman. Now recognizing the rider, she shouted, "Which of my boys is hurt?"

"No one, Cousin Millie," lied Bob Butler.

"It's no use, Bob. You can't fool me. I saw the incident as plainly as I see you, except that he was on the porch and people were all around him and I couldn't see his face."

He knew that he could not deceive her, and he told her everything.

For several days my oldest sister, Dolores, had been promising to kill and cook a chicken for us to carry to school, and now she stood on the back porch, lantern in hand, with my sister Hattie, my brother Matthew, and myself, on her way to the henhouse. The sun had set. It was between dusk and dark. Away to the west there was a bunch of half-drunk hoodlums returning from the cemetery, where they had gone to bury a neighbor. One of them remarked to the others that he could shoot the lantern from the girl's hand, and before any response was made by the others, his revolver spat fire and lead. At the report of the weapon, my brother Matthew, who was just two years my senior, jumped high upon the porch and whirled and raced through the doors of the house and fell with a thud. He bled profusely, leaving a trail of blood from the back porch through the house to the front porch. His little body switched and he was as still as death.

Providentially, Dad rode up just about the time his son reached the front porch and fell. The cowardly, drunken crowd had fled in all directions. Dad knelt down over his son, placed his ear on his left breast, and felt his pulse. He looked up as if searching for someone to send for help. All the older boys were at the upper spread. He said to me, "Son, you have been to Dr. Roberson once with me; do you think you can find your way?" "Yes, Dad," I answered positively. He told Dolores to put the bridle on Old Snap and fetch him from the barn stall.

"I want you to go at once and bring Dr. Roberson here. If you think you might get lost, stop at your Aunt Matilda's and have her or George go with you, or go on to the ranch and tell whichever of your brothers is there about it and just what I want done, for the doctor must be notified at once." By then the horse was at the hitching pole and, aided by my sister, I was on the gelding and off in a rush, bareback and without even a blanket on the ten-mile jaunt. I made straight for the deep fork crossing on Wild Horse Creek. I sped past my cousin Richmond's house to the crossing and past another cousin's home, Calvin Prince's, and on across a long stretch of stunted jack oak to Salt Creek and across it and up the hill past Aunt Matilda's, never stopping. I came to a fork in the road, the right leading to the ranch and the other, I remembered, to Dr. Roberson's, and without hesitation I took it. Old Snap was plastered with lather, but I went on for two or more miles on a wide treeless prairie. I remembered that across it and by a narrow strip of trees was the Roberson home, office, and barn, all painted white and all enclosed by one white picket fence. The doctor was just entering his office when I rode up. He had only seen me once to my knowledge, but he knew me and inquired anxiously what the trouble was. I told him briefly and said, "My dad wants you at once."

It hardly took him five minutes to get ready. "Father, shouldn't you take the buggy?" asked one of his sons. "No, the buggy cannot go fast enough," he answered as the last cinch was tightened. "We had better be off. Do you think your horse can make it?" "He can go the gait all day," I answered in confidence.

It seemed that within a matter of minutes we were at my home. By the time the doctor reached Matthew's bedside, he had his coat off and his sleeves rolled up very high, while talking to Dad all the time. I shall never forget the first operation. He produced a long red silk handkerchief and ran it all through the bullet wound. It had entered under the pit of the left arm and come straight through and out under the right armpit. Without food, except a cup or two of coffee, the doctor sat by the bedside of his patient all night. At daylight, he washed his face and hands, took a brisk walk, and returned to the bedside until the middle of the afternoon. He gave a sigh of relief and got ready for home, telling Dad that he thought the danger period had passed, but that if Matthew appeared to worsen to notify him at once. In any event, he would return for a checkup the following evening.

Is there such a thing as mental telepathy? What do you think?

On the last leg of the trip, Mother's temperature mounted and she seemed to grow progressively worse. They reached the home of her old family physician, Dr. T. P. Howell. He was aroused out of bed, went to his office, gave her a careful examination, and insisted that she remain there the rest of the night. "I was at your home today, and your son is out of danger. Dave called me there for a conference with Dr. Roberson. The boy is doing well. The doctor did a fine job," he assured Mother. "Let the rest of them go on home, and I'll take you tomorrow."

Dr. Howell came in with Mother in the afternoon of the following day. Walking unsteadily and trying to smile, she went bravely up the steps of the porch, leaning on Dad's arm, and into her son's bedroom. She bent over and kissed him on the forehead, and sat down beside him wearily.

"Mother, your face is as hot as fire," he told her.

"Yes, but I'll be all right," she smiled wanly.

In the weeks that followed, Matthew grew stronger and stronger and was soon on the road to recovery. Mother lingered, and some days she was able to sit up for a while and to walk into the kitchen; for the most part, though, she was confined to her bed. The middle of the fall season had arrived, with a frost that tinted the leaves fluttering and falling to the ground. This was the busiest season of the year at home. It was hog-killing time and there were a thousand other chores to do. But there were no quilting bees for Mother; nor was she able to superintend the rendering of the lard, the making of sausage, hog's-head, chitterlings for present and future use, and dozens of other delicacies. I, though young, knew she was thinking of these things as she looked wistfully out the window at the branches of the shade trees blown by the wind and scattering their leaves upon the sill. She did ask Dad one evening as the family gathered in her room for Bible reading and prayer: "Have the sweet potatoes been banked and the slips separated and stored for spring planting?"

Dr. Howell came more often. He consulted with Dad, and later he returned with Dr. Walker—a younger physician not long out of medical school—and, by previous arrangement, Dr. Roberson. All three went into Mother's room and remained a good while and then conferred in the parlor. Dr. Roberson was the first to leave, and then I, who was always near, heard Dr. Howell tell Dad, "Millie will not recover. She is literally worn out. Teaching school, going from dawn to dusk, and many times far into the night, having babies, eight of whom I myself have delivered, and doing a thousand and one other things, have used up her strength. She knows she will not recover, and don't you feel bad about it. She would not have had it any other way."

I slipped away from my hiding place and went out behind the smokehouse and wept. I never told a soul what I had heard; but all day, every day to the end, I was in her room or lingering at the door. I insisted on waiting upon her, bringing her medicine, water, and her Bible, which she read most of the time.

The first day of December came, and for the first time in several weeks Mother actually seemed to be improving. She ate a good breakfast, and all of us, even I who had overheard Dr. Howell's prediction, thought she was on the road to recovery. She sat propped up in bed. All the children left the room but me. I lingered at the door, and Dad, sitting by her bedside, joked with her and predicted that when spring came she would get out of bed and "be up again as good as new."

"No, Dave. I shall never recover. When I leave this bed, I'll be carried to the 'cooling board.' "

He tried to laugh and take it as a joke, but he failed miserably.

"This is no joke," she said. "I had hoped to live to see all my children grown, especially to see my legal rights established; but God wills otherwise and His will must be done. The best part about the matter of dying is that I'm not afraid to go and will be ready whenever He calls. I have no doubt but that our children will always be industrious and honest. I know they will always have a good example in you. Only one of our children seems to crave an education, and that one is Buck." She saw me standing in the doorway and called me to her bedside. She patted me gently on the head without speaking. She turned her back to both of us and went to sleep. That evening when she awoke she read aloud the Twenty-third Psalm, the Scripture lesson for bedtime devotion.

Christmas Eve came and Mother had worsened. A light powdery snow was falling, driven hither and thither by a stiff north wind, and it was biting cold. Undisturbed by the cruel winds that blew without, Mother was sinking, passing slowly away. Every child was either at her bedside or somewhere in the house. I would not be driven to bed.

The morning dawned cold, gray, and cheerless and the sun rose, casting its unwarmed rays upon a frozen earth blanketed with the snowfall of the previous evening. Two lanterns hung on the wall, and one cast its lone beam full on her face. She stirred, sighed resignedly, and just above a whisper, said something to Dad. Huskily, he told Andrew to summon the rest of the children. The younger children, David, Fisher, and Lydia, the baby, had slept through the night and were still asleep. Now, in a calm, reassuring voice, Mother told us that she was dying; that she had had a full life and was ready to go; that she knew that we would never forget what our parents had tried to teach us; and that we would always be truthful, honest, and industrious. She told Dolores to be a mother to the baby and for all of us to honor and obey Dad. Then her head turned ever so slightly and she fell asleep with a glorious smile upon her face.

The picture of her as she lay there, December 25, 1886, with her long coarse black unplaited hair extending to her waist, looking so young, has remained with me throughout the intervening years. Through evil and good reports, in poverty and plenty, it has remained with me as a symbol of that eternal verity that death is only the beginning of a fuller and more complete life for those who die in the Lord. And there is another memory I carry of that experience. Old Santa Claus had not forgotten to visit us. In every stocking he had deposited appropriate gifts for all the children, whose belief in him was still unshaken. This showed thought for the living as well as for the dead.

Spring came slowly and planting was retarded; but when warm weather did set in, we caught up and worked with increased force until things were well in hand. There was a rush, however, on the spreads to complete the branding of the calves and yearlings before the annual roundups started, so that there would be no mavericks among our cattle. Shortly after the branding had been completed, intermittent rain began falling. Then came the heel flies, botflies, and cattle flies to torment the herd. They chased the cattle into the creeks and watering holes and detained them there the livelong day. A rash of sores appeared among the stock, and in these sores were first larvae and then maggots. Even the boar shoats and pigs, recently castrated, became infested with these crawling parasites. It took dozens of cowhands, gallons and gallons of cresylic ointment, chloroform, and lint cotton by the bale to stamp out the epidemic.

Dad and the three oldest boys, Walter, Andrew, and Thomas, visited different roundups, fifty miles away in one case, a hundred miles distant in another. Dad went to the one farthest away. On such an occasion they might be gone for a week to ten days. Each would take an extra hand, a packhorse, and an independent mount. It sometimes happened that some of the DF (that was Dad's brand) cattle would stray, and if they were found in any of the roundups, they would be "cut" out from the herd and taken back to the DF spread. Or, in not a few instances, they would be sold to any cattleman looking to increase his herd. Dad's brand was registered with the Cattle Raisers' Association and was generally known, so that ranchers often notified him, even before roundups, that some of his cattle had wintered with theirs. Sometimes one or two of them would go further and offer to purchase them, thus saving Dad's time and expense in making the trip. When I grew older, I often made the trip with Dad or one of my older brothers; but mostly with Dad.

There was nothing I personally liked better about the ranching business than these annual roundups. The ranchers and foremen were so nice to Dad. Without exception, they all seemed to genuinely like and respect him. They never tired of assisting him in, for instance, getting his stock separated from the main herd, or in helping him get started, or in getting a buyer for his strays at the best price possible. And long before the Santa Fe ran through the Territory into Texas, when he had to ship his cattle through Dodge City, Caldwell, or Abilene, I heard him say that he never lost a cow in a stampede or by rustlers, while in so many cases cattlemen considered themselves lucky to reach the market with half of their herds. I have wondered since, why this difference? Was it because Dad never swore, or drank with the crowd? Or, possibly, that certain situations called to mind previous experiences that were associated with a certain danger, and automatically set up a protective shield against repeating the experience? Who knows the answer? Only He who made us. When the great philosopher said, "The proper study of man is man," he should have added, "within human limitations."[6]

I recall a mild excitement at our home one evening in late September just as we children were returning from school. I saw many horses at the hitching post and our home surrounded by United States marshals from the federal court at Fort Smith, Arkansas. That was the only court at that time that served the vast Oklahoma and Indian Territories. If one wanted to file a complaint against an outlaw, he had to travel possibly two hundred miles, depending upon where he lived, to Fort Smith to do it. And because of the size of the area, no single warrant would be taken out; the clerk was ordered to hold the warrants until several had accumulated before taking them to the U.S. marshal's office to be served. The marshal would then send out as many as twelve of his deputies to try to run down, arrest, or kill the men against whom the warrants had been issued.

A conservative estimate of 90 percent of the wanted men were murderers, cattle rustlers, and horse thieves (the latter two crimes ranking in penalty with that of murder, as did bank robbery and highway robbery). Some of them had prices on their heads, and the standard instruction was to bring them in "dead or alive." Such was the order against Cornelius Walker, for whom these

6. The quotation is from Alexander Pope's *Essay on Man*, Epistle II: "Know then thyself, presume not God to scan; / The proper study of mankind is man."

deputy marshals were searching that evening at our home. Somebody had mistakenly informed the marshal that Walker was related to us and might be found at our house. John Swain, one of the deputies, had disputed this. He knew my dad too well, he said, to believe that he would shelter a criminal, even if he were a relative. But Jim Williams, who was in authority, overruled Swain. Walter and Andrew were going to resist unlawful search, but Dad stopped them, saying, "No harm will come from the search," and he opened the doors and told the officers to help themselves. Williams was the only one who accepted the invitation to search, remarking as he moved toward the door, "Cornelius and I will eat breakfast in hell in the morning."

At that very moment, Walker was at the home of my dad's brother, Russell Franklin. Whoever had informed the officers had his facts wrong. Cornelius was a near relative of Aunt Reecie, Uncle Russell's wife. Swain and Bass Reeves, a Negro deputy, apologized to Dad for the embarrassment, but he told them to "forget it."[7]

It was the custom of the marshal's office to send his men out with a chuckwagon, a cook, and plenty of provisions, including plenty of blankets, sheets, and pillows. At daybreak, we learned that they had flushed out Cornelius Walker at my Uncle Russell's. Jim Williams, moving toward the door, called out to Cornelius to come out or he would break the door down. At the threshold he called out again, hesitated a brief moment, kicked the door ajar, and started in with drawn gun; but as he stepped across the threshold, the outlaw's carbine belched and the leaden bullet flew at the officer's head, blowing the top of it away and spattering the deputy's brain all over the floor. The women of the house were in panic, and the outlaw quit the house, negotiating the distance between it and a nearby tree, but Swain's revolver cut him down at the tree's roots. That was the last of Walker—and the last of Jim Williams, a brave but foolish man.

School went on, but not quite as smoothly as when Mother taught. The two teachers were Pleasant Shoals as principal and his half brother Batt BeShears, and they did not always get along. Shoals was a good administrator, but BeShears was younger, fickle, not always truthful, overambitious, and

7. Bass Reeves was a highly respected African American deputy United States marshal until his death in 1910. See Arthur T. Burton, *Black, Red, and Deadly: Black and Indian Gunfighters of the Indian Territory, 1870–1907* (Austin, Tex., 1991).

thought he knew more than his half brother. He told Dad that Mother thought more of him than she did his brother, that he was smarter than his brother, and that she wanted him to be head of the school and not Pleasant. "Stop there," Dad told him. "I'll hear no more of your lies. You know I know better. You will teach under Pleasant or go back to Bailey's." Dad's brother Bailey owned and operated a cotton gin, and Batt was the general manager.

A killing frost came early and sudden, so sudden that Dad had to call up extra help to plow, dig up, and gather in the sweet potatoes in one day to keep them from becoming frostbitten. Within a few days, the leaves and vines and shrubbery were brown and the trees became more and more barren as the leaves began to fall. Signs of an early and hard winter began to appear. Old Tom spent a good deal of his time flying to the tall steeple on the barn, and squalling. He would sit perched there for a long time, a sure sign of a hard winter. The feathers on the fowls had grown thicker and ruffled, the bark on the north side of the trees was thick, and there was more hair on the livestock. The blackbirds stayed nearer the millet stacks and the prairie chickens roosted in the nearby trees, making their guttural sounds just before daybreak. Father Boochita, an old Indian friend of Dad's, came down from Pauls Valley and warned him of the approaching hard winter. He said he saw signs in the bark of the trees and the feathers on the birds and the hair on the livestock—and in his old aching bones!

On the evening before Thanksgiving, between sundown and darkness, a sharp cold blast bore down upon the Indian country from the north. It felt like fans of icicles with needle points sticking into one's bare face. Then came sheets of rain mixed with sleet that bit and tore at the already tender skin. It had grown pitch dark, and Dad, lantern in hand, was first under the long shed and then in the barn to calm the cows and the horses, who were neighing with fright. When he returned to the house, his slicker was frozen as stiff as a board. It was pleasant to be tucked in bed snugly beside my sister Dolores. I soon fell asleep soundly in our hewn-log, sealed and plastered house, undisturbed by what was going on without.

The bitter cold weather must have abated somewhat, because next morning there was a new fall of snow, adding at least five feet to what was already there. With daylight, the weather turned colder, so that by noon the new snow had become an integral part of the old and one's footsteps made a crunching sound. For a solid week, the weather made a habit of sending new snow every night; then followed a week of hard frosts. The whole earth was white and glazed and so slick that neither the feet of man nor the hoofs of beasts were secure. At night, under the full moon and with the icicles hanging from every bough, one could imagine oneself in dreamland where white pearls hung suspended in the heavens.

Wildlife had already begun to suffer. At the upper ranch a whole covey of quails, with frozen feet and legs, fluttered over the ice- and snow-covered earth, unable to fly. Unable to secure food, and unable to get water because of the frozen creeks and ponds, they had become so weak that they just could not survive. Many jackrabbits were lying dead upon the snow, and droves of wild turkeys and prairie chickens perished. The timber wolves, in packs, attacked not only the calves and yearlings, but grown cattle as well. The mountain lion, always preferring horse meat to cattle meat, killed many colts for food.

Long Branch ran south into Salt Creek. It skirted the ranch houses about three hundred yards to the north. Along this branch, on both the east and west sides, we had built what we called a pasture or feedlot, because we cut and placed therein stacks of hay one after the other, more than a mile long. In the winter, especially such as the one we were having, the gates of this feed pasture were opened and the cattle would enter and eat the hay. These rows of stacks of hay also served in a measure as breaks against the blasts of the wintry winds.

At home, the livestock did not suffer as much for food or water. Both Eight Mile and Massey Creeks were deeper and wider than Long Branch Creek, and it was not necessary to cut as much ice to get down to the water as in Long Branch Creek. Then, in addition to the numerous stacks of hay, there were many stacks of straw from the oats and wheat that had been threshed, and from these the cattle ate their fill. Every fall, Dad bought a thousand bushels of cottonseed from Uncle Bailey and hauled and stored it at home to feed hundreds of head of steers and cows for an early spring market. In the feed pasture, the hundreds of troughs were kept filled with these seeds, which the fattening herd ate through the day. For roughage, hay, millet, and canestalks were stacked in "ricks" from which the stock fed.

It was not difficult for the prairie chickens to find their way around the millet stacks and into the barnyard, where plenty of millet seeds and thousands of grains of corn lay scattered over the lot, left there by the livestock and the employees. There were several stacks of bundled oats in one part of the lot to which the prairie chickens and quails found entrance.

As the winter lasted and the wildlife grew more hungry, the prairie chickens began to come to the barnyard and lots in droves. They ate among the domestic fowl as we threw shelled corn upon the frozen snow. Even the quails would dart from behind the crib or outhouse and timidly grab up the grains of corn. We watered them by pouring hot water into the iced troughs upon the ground, and it seemed that they knew to drink before the water turned into ice. In those severe cold winter days, my brother Matthew and I, well clothed and "shod," as the term was then used, remained out of doors almost all day, and with old Dash we ran down and caught jackrabbits. The cottontails always remained in the hollow logs or trees, or so close to them that they would escape to safety before we or the dogs could get them. Sometimes we succeeded in twisting them out of their hiding places. Dad kept loads of homemade salt that he had purchased away up in the northwest corner of the Territory. It came in blocks and we had fun transferring it to the feeding troughs or throwing it on the ground in the lot for the livestock to lick.

One evening my dad's brother Alexander came for me. I was his pet. He had no minor children and lived about six miles from our home and about a mile off the Fort Arbuckle road up Zander Creek, near the foothills of the mountains. He was mean and stingy, I thought, but his wife was sweet. It took us a long time to make the trip because the ground was so slick, and had the horses not been shod, we might not have made it. That night one of his grandsons, Lonnie Douglas, came to spend the night with me. Lonnie was older than I, but Uncle made me read to him until bedtime.

The next morning down behind the lot, there was a mountain lion in Uncle's bear trap. He had stepped both of his front feet and legs into the trap. He was a mean-looking, vicious animal and we had fun poking poles into his mouth and watching him fasten his powerful jaws on them. Uncle shot the brute and we took his carcass and dragged it along the south pasture fence that ran parallel to the course of the mountain as a warning to other mountain lions and bobcats that infested the region and preyed upon pigs, yearlings, and colts. They were terrors to Uncle's livestock, and it was a toss-up whether they or the timber wolves were the more devastating.

The dull, bitter-cold days of the winter dragged wearily on and the sun shone intermittently. Its ray was so feeble that there was, at first, no evidence of melting snow or thawing ice. We returned to school on foot: it was too dangerous to ride, so Dad thought. It took an hour to walk three miles; but we had fun going and returning, and enjoyed every minute of it.

Finally the sun became bold and shone more warmly and brightly, and the snow and ice and frosts began to thaw. Great icicles that had clung to the boughs of the trees loosened their hold and fell, breaking the tree limbs and making it extremely hazardous for any rider passing under them at the time of their descent. Then the ice in the creeks and on the ponds began to break up in large ponderous chunks and float down toward the Washita and Red Rivers. The snow and ice were gone, and grass and vegetation began to make their appearance. Buds overanxious to get on with their task of evolution burst into bloom that sent forth their fragrance to the delight of those who passed.

The spring season was here and growing things and busybodies were pursuing the patterns of their lives. The bees had come forth from a hundred hives in search of their first nectar, and the farmers and ranchers were busy at their common tasks of the season. There was just one task that did not need to be done this spring. The winter had been so severe and so hard upon the rabbits that they had not attempted to chew upon the fruit trees, and it was unnecessary to wrap or treat the trees just above the ground, which had always been an arduous task, considering the vastness of the orchard.

———

Dad and I had been pals longer than I could remember. I think it was because I had always preferred the company of my elders. I was always asking them questions, and in my father's case, I was now thrown into contact with him daily. After school and after the evening chores were done, it was my task to read him the news, especially about the market; what Congress was saying or doing with regard to Indians' rights; about the final enrollments of the Five Civilized Tribes and the allotment of their lands in severalty; and any news of wars. After supper, I would read to him until long after bedtime from his favorite papers, the Saint Louis *Globe Democrat*, the Memphis *Commercial Appeal*, and the Dallas *News*.

From time to time I would come across articles telling about Judge Isaac C. Parker, the district federal judge at Fort Smith, the trial of outlaws in his court, their convictions, his sentencing of them to die by "hanging by the

neck until dead," and I longed to visit his court and witness the whole procedure.[8] I hated outlaws with a bitter, burning hatred. The judge was called
"the hanging judge" throughout the Nation, and I then wanted to see an
outlaw "hanged by the neck until dead." I thought every outlaw was, indeed,
guilty! The fact that some of them might be innocent of murder never entered my mind. Now, I don't even believe in capital punishment, except for
the rape of a girl or woman of previous chaste, good character.

That chance to visit Fort Smith and see the judge in action came a few
years later. The man on trial was one of a gang indicted for an alleged bank
robbery and murder. His attorney was Ben Craven, the best-known criminal
lawyer at that time in the Southwest. My belief that all outlaws were guilty
was somewhat shaken after Craven's argument, although the jury's verdict
was that he was guilty. Now, I had seen many United States marshals, and
they and their duties had a strange fascination for me, and I would have liked
to be one when I grew up; but there was just one fly in the ointment of my
ambition: I hated pistols and revolvers, and could never see how I could ever
be enticed to buckle on one. It was a question with me which was the greater
evil, the outlaw or the revolver. If there were no pistols, possibly there would
be no outlaws. That is the way I reasoned then.

The spring, summer, and fall of the year 1888 were no different from the
seasons of the previous two years, except that Dad and a few of the other patrons had completed some substantial improvements on the school when the
fall term opened. New blackboards and crayon had been substituted for slate
and pencil, and school seats with desks attached had taken the place of the
backless, three-legged, hewn-log benches. Also, out-of-doors "girls" and
"boys" toilets had been built, and they and the schoolhouse had been painted
and a large schoolbell installed. Home seekers had come into the settlement
and located upon tracts of land under permits from the citizens and, most of
them having children, caused quite an increase in pupil enrollment. The
school again became inadequate both in space and teaching force, and another room had to be added. But another teacher could not be readily found,
and the two current teachers had to carry on for the time being.

The new patrons coming into the settlement from old states contributed
much to the school and community. They readily contributed their fair share

8. For an account of Judge Parker's career, see *ibid.*, 5–7, 75–77.

to the overhead expenses in the operation of a subscription school, much to the relief of Dad, who had had to bear from 75 to 95 percent of the expenses. While two teachers were unable to do a complete job of teaching the children, due to large classes, they did an average job. By the end of the term all the patrons appeared to be satisfied. The leader of these new immigrants was a man by the name of Gus Austin. He was a most remarkable man. He easily adjusted to his new environment, in every situation. He was not only the acknowledged leader of these new settlers but soon became a leader of the community. Industrious and a good farmer, he soon became a success at cattle raising. It seemed that everything he touched turned into money. Had he not passed too soon, he would no doubt have become a very rich man.

When Christmas came, it marked the end of the second year of the passing of Mother. At the breakfast table, Dad had me read the second chapter of Matthew before he offered prayer and said grace. There had been no daily Bible reading, nor at night since Mother's death. It seemed that the family just couldn't get organized for it, and Dad referred to that in his prayer that morning, asking God to understand the situation and to forgive him for anything amiss. I thought about such a strange prayer and could not understand it; nor have I since. I think he had in mind that he just could not fill Mother's place in the family organization. When he had finished, he looked around at us so wistfully and hopelessly. At that moment I'm sure he felt alone, although surrounded by all his children except the oldest.

He had wanted to marry and had discussed the matter with the oldest of us. We all knew the woman, a widow about his age. She was a good Christian woman, loved to work in the church and with children, but had never had any of her own. We had been so clannish all our lives that we rebelled and told him no! He was a man of many parts. In some things, he was a real he-man, bold, brave, and daring, but never ruthless; in other things, he was tender, soft, and easy. When it came to his immediate family, he was also clannish and loved us to distraction. The latter part won out. On this matter of a second marriage, such a unanimity of opposition existed among us that he never afterward brought up the subject. That was and is my personal belief. But it is not right for one's personal belief to interfere with another's desires, especially in such a grave matter as marriage, the first sacrament of a certain church.

Winter was over and spring came on apace, with its same duties and chores at home and at the ranch. I had grown fast, would soon be a strapping lad of ten, and Dad promised that he would take me down to Nocona, Texas, and fit me with an entire cowboy outfit. I'd never had one—had been using the old saddle that my brother Tom had used but now had outgrown. After my tenth birthday Dad took me to Nocona to keep his promise. Below Ardmore we met Si Love, whom Dad knew slightly. He lived to the east in an exclusive Negro country village and "ran" the first freedmen community in the entire Territory.

It was well that we met him, for we had left the road of our objective four miles back. After he had redirected us, and in the course of his conversation, Dad learned from him that, as freedmen, he, his son Aaron, and their families had issued joint permits to Bill Douglas, whom we came to know as a real man and friend for many years, to use and occupy grazing lands just north and east of Dad's upper ranch. Dad also learned that the little railroad town through which he had passed many times, on the north bank of the Red River, called "Burneyville," was founded by the Birney family, the Chickasaw Indians who had once owned his father back in Tennessee. Dad told me about this as we proceeded on toward the little town, which we reached near sunset.

As we rode down the hot dusty road that the inhabitants called "Main Street," we could catch glimpses of a few scattered, unpainted houses through the trees and over tall sunflowers. I scented the smell of Jimson weeds, and my mind flashed back to the time when Mother used to prepare a concoction of this revolting stuff to "clean us out" just before giving us blood tonic, which she brewed with a mixture of sassafras roots and bark and high-powered whiskey that Dad would bring back from Gainesville on his annual trips there. Farther down the road appeared a two-story building on the left with a sign thereon, "Hotel." On the opposite side of the road was a general store in which was located the post office. In front of the store was a hitching rail to which were tied many horses that bore the appearance of cow ponies or ranch horses.

Dad and I dismounted, leashed our horses, and went over to the blacksmith shop next door. Being told that a family of Burneys (Birneys) lived on another street, we proceeded to look for the place. Through the gathering dusk we could see two elderly people sitting in an unfenced, littered yard, and all around were flea-bitten dogs and cats.

"Do the Burneys live here?" asked Dad in a loud voice.

"Yes," answered the male of the couple.

We advanced and sat down without being invited to do so. We could see the pair were full-blood Indians, and Dad asked, "Was this town named for you or your people?"

"Yes," the man grunted.

Further exchange of talk brought out the fact that their names were spelled "Birney," that they were full-blood Chickasaw Indians and were from Tennessee. Back down the road, the aged Indian explained, someone misspelled the name as Burney.

The Indian remembered that his parents once owned a slave named Buck Franklin. He had been told that, and also that the slave had run away. Dad told him he had been misinformed—that the man Buck was his father and had purchased his freedom and his family's from his former master. The two talked very friendly until they began talking about the late war. The Indian said, "I think the government made a mistake giving the slaves their freedom." The moon had just risen and I could see by its light that Dad was angry, very angry, and he answered heatedly, "I think the biggest mistake was made by your people in buying slaves from the white man. Your people were not in fact free; were merely wards of the government. Your people had no citizenship, no self-direction." Then Dad actually bragged about his own possessions and independence, which was unlike him. I had never seen him do that, nor ever saw it again. Then he went on to tell the Indian that he, Dad, had spent the last two years of the war in the Union army and that his oldest brother, Alexander, had fought with Osceola, side by side with him, in the Second Seminole War, on the side of freedom and the liberation of that tribe.

Instead of remaining in Burneyville the rest of the night, Dad and I returned to the livery stable, resaddled our mounts, and rode across the river and into Gainesville,[9] where there would be better accommodations and where he was known almost as well as in Pauls Valley. After stabling our horses and giving directions for their care, Dad and I put up at the home of one of his old friends for the rest of the night. It was about ten in the morning before we arose and had our breakfast. It was afternoon before we started

9. Gainesville is at least twenty-five miles from Burneyville by modern road. Nocona was thirty-four miles west of Gainesville.

on the last lap for Nocona. We rode there without stopping. We again slept late, arose and found something to eat, and then went in search of my cowboy outfit.

Nocona was then a small town, but it was cosmopolitan in spirit. It was a saddle-manufacturing town, and cowboys and ranchers gathered there from the Indian Territory and every cattle-raising state and territory in the great Southwest. Down the street Dad ran into a rancher with whom he had become acquainted a year or two previously at the Cattle Raisers' Association in Fort Worth. They talked for a while, I don't remember what about, for my mind was on my cowboy outfit. Then I followed them to a very large building. There were many men sitting and loitering around there. I soon learned it was a sort of headquarters where stockmen and ranchers usually met while in the little town. There were several men who knew Dad and many whom he did not know, one of whom was Bill Douglas, who had leased the grazing acreage near Dad's upper ranch from Si Love and his family.

Two of Bill's older sons, Johnnie and Willie, were with him, and as they were the only boys present, we soon became acquainted—and fast friends. When they learned what had brought us to the little town, we told our fathers that we would go ahead to the saddlery. The proprietor knew the Douglas boys, and he was well acquainted with my dad. When I told him what I wanted, he began to show me saddles that would be suitable for a boy my age and size, and when Dad arrived, the merchant showed him what he had picked out for me, and after observing them slightly, Dad asked me if that was what I wanted. I said, "Yes sir." He said, "What about your bridle, saddle blanket and roll, and your spurs, quirt, boots, and lasso?" Together we began to select those items. "You know, a cowboy needs these things," he said, beaming down upon me. The proprietor delivered the outfit to the livery stable where our horses were and picked up the old outfit. The Douglases left that evening, but Dad and I stayed overnight.

From the time we reached Nocona, the talk of the town was about "No Man's Land," the spot that for time beyond the memory of man had been a hideout and rendezvous for thieves, outlaws, and men with prices on their heads. This badland had become a part of the Territory. A county seat had been established after the "run" on April 22, and sheriffs, marshals, and other peace officers were now for the first time daily entering the heretofore forbidden area. It was rumored that these lawmen were determined to clean the place up. It had been a forbidden strip, 34 miles wide by 165 miles long, since before both Texas and Kansas had either refused or neglected to include it within their borders when their governments were set up and admitted to the Union. In 1887 the squatters had called it the Territory of Cimarron and tried to have it admitted to the Union but failed. Today it is known as the Oklahoma Panhandle, composed of the counties of Texas, Cimarron, and Beaver.

Dad itched to see the area now and just what it looked like. So after coming to Nocona, he decided to give it a brief once-over before returning home. He had always had an inquisitive mind, especially about the old Indian Territory, wanting to watch and keep up with its every evolution. This strip was not entirely unknown to him. Different United States marshals had told him about it, and once after the Civil War, before I was born, he had come face to face with some of its outlaws while on his way to Dodge City with a bunch of steers for market. They were determined to rustle his herd until the leader remembered that Dad had fed him and another of his companions at his home. They also knew Dad's cattle brand and respected it.

Dad was telling me about this experience as we rode on toward Beaver that afternoon. "In all their lawlessness, their cattle rustling, their robbery, and violations of the law in every field, these bad men have always respected my person and property."

"Why, Dad?" I asked him. "Why the difference?"

"I'm afraid I can't answer that. I've made it a rule of my life to attend to my own business, to do good as far as I know toward all. I've never wronged a living soul, as far as I can remember; yet I believe that all the bad know that I would never side with them. Nevertheless, they all, without a single exception, did make a difference when it came to me. Yet, in the overall, that doesn't seem to be the whole answer. I've thought of another rule, or rules, of my life, the Golden Rule, and its by-products; observance of and dedication to the family altar. I've never considered or gone into a new venture, or started into the business of a new day without first consulting or talking with God about it and asking Him to take over."

"You mean you have made Him a silent partner in everything you have done?" I asked.

"Not my silent partner, but my senior partner," he answered simply, as if looking back and remembering many things.

We crossed Red River on the Chisholm Trail and rode north on it to the little village of Ryan, where we left it and headed northwest over a dim, seldom-traveled road. The sun had gotten hot and the air was humid and sultry. We came to a clear sparkling branch of the river, where there was plenty of shade on both sides. We dismounted to rest our horses and let them drink. Upstream, the branch was indented, and there water had accumulated belly deep to our horses. We let them drink there—not much, for the water was cold and Dad feared, it being so hot, they might take the cramps.

We soon learned the cause of the cold temperature of the water: the stream was fed by numerous springs oozing from the bank. There were strange wildflowers, the names of which we did not know, that gave off sweet scents. Among them, hundreds of bees were busy gathering nectar. There were so many that Dad knew their hives must be near. He investigated and discovered two hollow trees containing beehives. We were in the act of riding on when two men approached us from different directions with drawn revolvers. They were U.S. marshals John Swain and Bob Fortune. They recognized Dad and immediately lowered their guns. Swain told Dad they had been trailing a gang of robbers who had the day before robbed the little bank at Beaver. He said there were many of them all the way to the badlands and that they were determined to clean out the place.

Farther on we came to another creek, on both sides of which were many trees and thick underbrush. My mount, Old Coaly, snorted, reared straight up on his hind feet, and refused to go on. Dad was puzzled at this caper of my horse, but I was not. He had done the same thing before at the Buck Horn crossing on Wild Horse as I was returning home late one evening from the upper ranch. The scare then had been the presence of a panther in the vicinity, and I now told Dad about it. He immediately dismounted, drawing his gun from the scabbard—and at that point we heard a low throaty groan off in the trees. "You stay here," Dad ordered. Triggering a cartridge into the barrel of his carbine, he stealthily reconnoitered in a half circle and disappeared into the woods.

I sat on my horse trembling from head to foot. I was scared to death, not for Dad, who knew the nature of every ferocious wild beast and who had slept among them many times at night with his lantern hanging over his head. I was scared for myself, left alone and out of Dad's sight. He seemed to have been gone for ages before I heard on the deep stillness a sharp rifle shot, and then, after what seemed to be an endless period of waiting, Dad emerged from the underbrush. I have never felt, before or since, such utter fear and loneliness, such helplessness. I don't believe I could have survived another minute.

Dad led his horse back to where the dead animal lay, while I rode behind. "That's strange," he was saying.

"What's strange?" I asked.

"The way that beast acted, as if she wanted to make friends. The way she looked down at me when I aimed my gun and fired. I want to look at her more closely."

We had by then reached the place where the beast lay still. She was a big long animal. Dad stooped down and commenced to examine her head and neck as if he was very sure of finding something, and I heard him say, more to himself than to me, "That's what I thought."

"Thought what, Dad?" I asked.

"That she belonged to some circus," he replied, as he lifted the animal's head, parted the long shaggy hair on her neck, and displayed a metal collar. After much work, Dad pried the collar loose and I read a single word on it, "Cora." We kept this souvenir until Dad's death, and then it disappeared or got misplaced.

Again back on the dim road, we traveled toward Beaver. Before us stretched a long, almost even, and endless prairie. Here and there it tilted and indented ever so little. We rode on leisurely. The heat and humidity had somewhat abated. A gentle breeze was blowing across the plains, swaying the tall virgin grass on the roadside. Down the dim road ran some birds, two long-tailed, ring-necked ones and many striped little ones, about the size of quails. "What are they?" I asked Dad. I had never before seen that kind. "They are pheasants, a covey of them," he answered. "In western Kansas, they are as plentiful as prairie chickens are around our home. I'm told that they belong to the partridge, grouse, and quail family. I'm also told that the house cat, the lion, the tiger, and leopard are of the same family. I don't know. When you get more education, you will know and you can tell me if it is true." He was always talking to me as if I was a man. He was a man who could remember anything that had been told or read to him, and I think I believed that anything he told me was true.

Farther down the road, we met a wrangler and inquired the distance to Beaver. He told us, then said, "You can't make it there before dark. About a mile from here, if you'll look to your right, you will see a house and barn. That's where Uncle Josh and his woman live. If you go there and tell them I sent you, they will put you up. We call them the 'good Samaritans.' "

"What's your name?" Dad asked him.

"Dave Long," he answered.

"It won't be hard for me to remember a part of your name," Dad assured him.

"Is anybody here?" Dad shouted as we rode up to Josh's house. From behind the house appeared an elderly man, with a frank, open face—a face disarming and so pleasant that one felt immediately at ease. "We are going to Beaver, and Dave Long told us that you would put me and my son up for the night," Dad told him. He invited us to dismount. There was a sort of lean-to behind the house that served as a store. His wife was in there, and Josh introduced Dad to her. She offered to cook for us, but we declined and bought canned goods from the keeper of the little grocery store for our lunch. Josh had a fine melon patch and we bought one for our dessert. I leashed Old Coaly to the end of a long rope in the midst of tall tender grass so that he could eat his fill during the night. Dad hobbled Old Button. Josh told us that no rustlers or thieves ever bothered anything around his place, and we believed him. Isolated as he was, Josh was no outlaw. On the contrary, he hated lawlessness and was glad that law enforcement had finally come to the Territory.

We rode into Beaver about noon the next day.[10] Our first stop was the general store. People were still excited about the robbery. Many peace officers were in town trying to pick up clues and leads, among whom was Heck Thomas, the smoothest and shrewdest United States marshal of them all. He took Dad behind the blacksmith shop, where they remained for more than half an hour. Dad never told me what they talked about and I never asked him. We spent the rest of the day and night in Beaver and left the next morning for home.

It was interesting to watch the comings and goings of the people in the little town against the imposing presence of peace officers, a thing none of

10. Here and occasionally elsewhere in his narrative, the author greatly compresses the time required for a journey. The distance from Nocona, Texas, to Beaver, Oklahoma, is more than two hundred miles by today's roads. It must have taken at least five days for David Franklin and his son to make this trip, and about the same amount of time to return home from Beaver.

them had ever been used to. Some of them were lighthearted and gay, as if rejoicing that these men would at long last bring law and order to an area too long neglected. They could attend church on the morrow, which would be the Sabbath, without fear and in comparative peace. Some looked sullen and resentful, so Dad said, and one could guess that they were not in sympathy with the minions of the law. I'm sure those venerable peace officers were alert to this challenge and that nothing escaped their watchful eyes.

On our way, just before entering the town, we passed dozens of dugouts and sod houses with not more than one or two milch cows, a team of horses or mules munching the grass nearby, and a few farming implements and an old wagon in the lot near a rickety crib. Here were squatters who would soon homestead upon their holdings, paying the government not more than one dollar and a quarter per acre. Through rough and dangerous years, living in the midst of desperate men with prices on their heads, they had no doubt dreamed of the time when social order and stable government would come. They had dreamed and prayed for the time now at hand. Now they were a part of that group of decent citizens, heretofore without a country, rejoicing in the good fortune that had at last come.

Dad ordered the horses to be fed early in the morning so that we could get an early start for home. When we left, I did not know that there had been a long, fierce battle between outlaws and peace officers. Dad knew but had told me nothing about it. Nearing Beaver Creek crossing, I saw a man with both arms dangling, stumbling across the road and disappearing into the underbrush. I told Dad what I had seen. He drew his carbine from the scabbard, triggered a bullet into its barrel, and rested it across his saddle in front of him. "You get behind me, son." It was a stern order, which I didn't question.

Near the crossing, a man with pleading eyes and useless arms dangling at his sides said to Dad, "Please take me away; if not, kill me out of my misery."

"I'll do neither," said Dad, as his face hardened, "I wouldn't take you away, nor am I going to kill you. I have no authority, nor the right to do either. I suppose you are a part of that bunch that had that running battle back in Beaver in which women and children were killed."

"Yes, but we didn't intend to harm or hurt the women or children. We thought we were fighting those marshals who have never let up hounding us. It was either them or us."

"I'm going to take you to Fort Sill," Dad told the trembling outlaw.

"You can't do that. I know you, and we have never harmed you, none of us. My men and I could have robbed you of your cattle on your way to Dodge City. Remember."

"But that has nothing to do with my duty now. I'd take my brother and turn him over to the authorities if he was guilty of the things you and your bunch are guilty of." Dad put him behind me on my horse and changed our course toward Fort Sill. The man was bloody from his waist to his feet. In fact, he had lost so much blood that he was almost as weak as water. I was worried about my new saddle and blanket. How would I ever get the blood-stain out of them? Lucky for me, five miles farther on, or possibly less, we met a contingent of the 10th Cavalry of the United States Army, and Dad turned the man over to them after making a full report of what he knew.

Near daylight the next day, we reached home, undressed, and tumbled, almost fell, into bed completely exhausted. Neither of us woke up that entire day, and the girls, sensing our tired condition, didn't try to wake us. I woke before Dad, and seeing what time it was, I aroused him at once. We rose in time for supper, and all the boys being present from the ranch, except Walter, sat down together at the table. Dad, I think to the surprise of all of us, asked sister Dolores to read the Twenty-third Psalm. He prayed a very long prayer (it looked like he was trying to make up for those he had already missed) and sat down. Then he said grace and looked around at all of us with happiness and contentment written all over his face. It seemed as if all of us were full of joy and happiness. I think we all must have been thinking the same thing—that it was as it used to be in Mother's time, just one big, united, happy family, afraid of nothing.

After supper, amid laughter, and after the dishes and other evening chores were done, we all retired to the veranda and talked, bathing in the silvery rays of a new moon until midnight. Dad told of all the experiences through which we had passed. He inquired about the business in general. Abruptly, Tom said, "Dad, you recall Old Blue did not bring in her brood last winter as she has done for the last ten years. She has always worked herself and brood nearer and nearer home this late in the year."

"You have seen nothing of her?" Dad inquired of all the boys.

"No, I haven't," said Matthew, "and what's worse, I saw a bunch of wild blue shoats and a young blue sow and a boar about her age."

We all knew that that bunch were offspring of Old Blue, her children and grandchildren, and that she was dead. Later on, Andrew came across a wild bunch of blue hogs fifteen miles from Rock Creek, about ten miles or so from home and sixteen or more from the place where Matthew saw the other bunch. Old Blue had become famous through many communities in her lifetime, especially for the way she had lived and raised her litters, including her habit of leaving and returning with her broods.

The years stretched, and all of the southern part of the Nation became crowded with wild, fierce blue hogs. They were fleet-footed and dangerous, and Dad sent out word for everybody to treat them as common enemies, to be killed on sight. They grew more in length and height than in girth, and the boars' tusks grew so long and sharp that they extruded and hung from their mouths. The saying was that they could rip a dog from head to hip with one slash, and that they learned to travel in droves and could successfully defend themselves against a pack of timber wolves; and that the coyote never came near them. People organized hunting parties in the effort to exterminate these brutes that had become more dangerous to human beings than the panther and mountain lion. But they were not completely exterminated until after I had gone off to the academy in 1894.

2

LIFE ON THE RANCH

*I*n 1890 there came a change in my mode of living. I spent the nights at the northwest spread, except weekends, when I would be home. During the week, I commuted daily between the upper ranch and school, which, after all, were not more than six miles apart. I could and did gallop the distance in no time without tiring my horse. When the rains came, a different picture presented itself. I had two streams to cross, Salt and Wild Horse Creeks, both of which lurked with danger when their waters overflowed their banks. At such times, I always pulled my boots and top shirt off so that there would be nothing to interfere with my swimming if it became necessary—and it often did.

The Salt Creek crossing was not nearly as dangerous as the Wild Horse crossing. The bed of the former was narrow and deep and seldom overflowed. The banks on either side were well marked, even above the waters that reached the highest possible stage. If the currents were swift, one could point his horse upstream and swim diagonally across. One could see a log or other barriers floating downstream from quite a distance and could beat them across.

The Wild Horse crossing, called the "Buck Horn crossing," was different. The bed was deep, and on the east side the bank was steep; on the west side, the bank was more shallow. It easily overflowed out into Oil Spring Flat, which spread out west for a quarter of a mile. As a matter of fact, in flood times, it was impossible to locate the west bank of the crossing. Hence, many times I could not return to the ranch by that route and would have to return

44

by way of the "deep crossing" five miles downstream. There the banks were steep and contained the water.

Once I had a narrow escape. It was after sunset, near dusk. Rain had been falling all day and the sky was dark and watery. I was returning to the ranch from school and the banks of the creek at the deep crossing were full. I cared nothing about that. I had crossed there many times under similar conditions. Old Coaly swam shallow, but on such occasions, it was my custom to guide the horse with the reins or slap him on the neck to indicate the course I wanted him to swim. When past midstream, I would slide out of the saddle, down the rump of my horse, catch him by the tail and float with him to the opposite bank.

On this occasion, the unexpected happened. Near the opposite bank, Old Coaly lurched and swam forward with such rapidity that I missed his tail. Peering to the side. I could discern in the fast-growing darkness a log bearing down on me, borne on surging, rolling waves. Instantly I dived, and the log floated on downstream over my body. I came up about the middle of the ford on the opposite side of the creek directly behind my horse. I climbed into the saddle and started for the ranch. Had I not been at home in the water, the outcome might have been disastrous. But I had been swimming since I was five years old, on my stomach, my side, and my back, and had learned to tread water.

I never knew why Dad shifted me, instead of my brother Matthew, who was two years my senior, to the upper ranch with my brother Tom, and I never asked him. In fact, none of us ever questioned his management. Brother Andrew now spent all of his time at home overseeing the farm and looking after the livestock there. It often happened that Tom was away from the ranch all night and my only companion was old Dash. I was never too brave to keep from getting scared.

I had a cousin, Serena, who lived two miles east of the ranch on the Minton Trail with her husband and several children, and more than once, through fear, I stayed with them overnight—with my dog. At that particular time, when Tom was away, I had no other protection. I was temporarily afraid of guns. The year before, I had killed a wild turkey with an old muzzle-loading shotgun and it had kicked me unconscious. I had always hated revolvers and pistols as evil things. Up to then, I had never had a carbine or Winchester in my hands. Once, Dad, knowing that Tom would be away from the ranch at a roundup, came to spend the night with me. I was not there. The door was locked and he could not get in the house. He spent the night there, sleeping out of doors, waiting for me.

Before sunrise the following morning, I returned. I told him truthfully that I spent the night at my cousin's because I was scared. He disliked very much for his children to be afraid of anything. "Your brother's Winchester is there in the house; that's all the protection you need, and old Dash."

"I've never had that gun in my hands," I confessed.

"Well, it's time you learned to handle and use it if necessary," he said, not altogether pleased by his discovery.

"I didn't know what you'd say about my trying to shoot it," I said.

"Only revolvers and pistols I've refused to allow my children to own or use," he said.

After I had cooked our breakfast, he spent the rest of the day teaching me how to use his carbine and Tom's Winchester. He remained with me until Tom returned. Deer were plentiful and he killed one, and we spent the better part of the day preparing some of it for drying on the top of the house. I still feared using Tom's gun when Dad left. Within two weeks' time, Dad had his carpenter add two more rooms to the ranch house with lumber brought in from Pauls Valley. Then he filled them with furniture. I knew he would be visiting me often in the future. He bought a new carbine for me and taught me how to shoot. In time, I became an expert, for an eleven-year-old, and wasn't afraid anymore. I did, however, take the shakes when I tried to kill my first deer; but that soon left me.

I well remember the first deer I did kill. He was a young buck, horns not yet pronged. A boy of eleven was not able to lift the deer and place it on the saddle, so I fastened my lariat around the deer's horns, tied the other end of the rope to my saddle horn, got astride my horse, and dragged my game to the nearest tree. I unloosed the rope from the saddle horn, threw the end over a tree limb, pulled the other end back around my saddle horn, tightening it so as to draw the deer off the ground, rode under the deer and allowed it to fall into my saddle. Riding behind it, I reached the ranch with my kill.

In the summer of 1890, Dad had mown, stacked, and baled more prairie hay than ever before. On such occasions, he used two mowers, two rakes, three balers, and enough men to tend to the baling and stacking, the entire crew amounting to two dozen or more men. That fall and early winter he had men build a huge pond, covering ten or more acres, to catch the spring and early summer rains. The dam was high and the pond deep, and the expanse of water resembled a lake. Some of the water of Long Branch was diverted to its basin, along with water from a few springs in the higher reaches. Within the next few years, this lake was to become a sort of resort for fishing, outings, and sporting events. Of course, Dad kept it enclosed against all who might want to enter without his permission. He opened it to his own personal stock and use whenever necessary.

Once I had a chance to play detective. It happened in this way. A fellow by the name of Minton had established a general store about a mile east of my cousin Serena's home. The nearest trading point from the ranch and the settlement had been Fort Arbuckle, or Pauls Valley. The Minton store, being near and convenient, became a trading point for an extended area. As a result, that merchant did a land office business, a fact that did not go unnoticed. On my way to Pauls Valley early one morning, I went by way of the Minton establishment just in time to see the place being robbed. I waited until after the men had robbed the store before riding up and dismounting, just as the robbers were mounting. They had pulled the masks from their faces and paid no attention to me, a mere boy. I got a good look at them, their faces, clothes, and horses. The storekeeper stood in abject despair, hopelessly wringing his hands and lamenting that he had been robbed of more than two thousand dollars. He asked me if I had seen the men, three of them. I answered dishonestly, "No."

I knew many routes to Pauls Valley, and so instead of going around the wagon road, I decided to take a trail through White Bead Hill and come into the road just before crossing Rush Springs. I came upon the robbers just as they dismounted and disappeared into a ramshackle, unpainted house with a lean-to, about two miles beyond White Bead Hill and a mile from the road to the crossing. I looked innocently in the other direction. Out of sight, I went directly to attorney O. W. Patchell's office and told him about the robbery and the men. He immediately found a deputy U.S. marshal and had me retell my story. Patchell promised me that if they arrested the men and recovered the money, I would not ever be known as the informer. The lawyer knew the place, and I didn't even have to show it to him and the deputy. Patchell, who was our family lawyer, afterward told Dad that the men were surprised, arrested, and the money recovered. Neither the deputy nor

Patchell ever mentioned me to the dozen or more other men who helped to make the arrest. Patchell took no part in the arrest. He simply pointed out the house to the officers. Dad told me I had done the right thing, although it was a dangerous thing to do. Looking back, I do not believe I could have done otherwise, for I hated such men most bitterly.

———

Since the 22nd day of April, 1889, the people had ceased talking about Pauls Valley, Muskogee, Ardmore, and Gainesville, Texas. The conversation now was about Guthrie, Oklahoma City, Kingfisher, and other towns that had sprung up or were coming into existence in the western part of what had been the Indian Territory. What was the reason for this sudden change?

Prior to the year 1866, the area today known as the state of Oklahoma, excepting what was then No Man's Land and Greer County, was the Indian Territory. In that year the United States government made treaties with the Creek, Cherokee, Seminole, Chickasaw, and Choctaw nations, in which the tribes ceded to the government the western part, roughly, of the Territory. The government needed this area on which to settle certain other Indians and to create reservations for certain Plains tribes. In 1870 a general survey was made, pursuant to the treaties of 1866, of the Chickasaw Nation and the old Indian Territory, except for No Man's Land. The starting place of the survey was about a mile south of old Fort Arbuckle. (This point happened to be about nine miles due west and about two hundred yards south of my birthplace.)

These treaties placed the above named tribes, known as the Five Civilized Tribes, in the eastern half of the old Indian Territory, the western half to be known as the Oklahoma Territory. The Five Civilized Tribes had their own separate governments, with capitals located at Okmulgee, Tahlequah, Wewoka, Tishomingo, and Tuskahoma. Federal courts had been established, limiting the jurisdictions of the tribal courts of these nations in certain cases, while the western half, or the Oklahoma Territory, was under the exclusive jurisdiction of the federal courts. On the 23rd day of March, 1889, President Benjamin Harrison issued his proclamation describing certain lands by boundaries that were to be opened for settlement; and in pursuance of the proclamation, Oklahoma Territory experienced its first "run" at high noon on April 22, 1889, for "free homesteads."

Out of the area created by the "run," certain counties were designated in the bill by numbers, and the citizens of each area gave them names: Logan County, with Guthrie as the county seat; Oklahoma County, with Oklahoma City as the county seat; Cleveland County, with Norman as the county seat; Canadian County, with El Reno as the county seat; Kingfisher County, with Kingfisher as the county seat; Payne County, with Stillwater as the county seat; and Beaver County, with Beaver as the county seat. Originally, Beaver County covered the whole of No Man's Land; later it was divided into Cimarron, Texas, and Beaver Counties. Today this area is commonly referred to as the Oklahoma Panhandle.

The Organic Act of the Congress in 1890 made possible the organization of the Oklahoma Territory, the creation of a full territorial government, the appointment of a governor, the election of delegates to Congress, and so forth. It also enabled the appointment of a U.S. attorney, the creation of a supreme court, and the appointment of justices. The first legislature moved with speed and efficiency. County laws and organizations were perfected and educational facilities were provided.

I had never been so close to a live local government before, and like everybody around me, I wanted to see it in operation. I wanted to see why the people around me had stopped talking about the Indian Territory and were spending all their time talking about the Oklahoma Territory. I did not know then that the same Organic Act had done much also to eventually change the complexion, habits, and laws of the Indian Territory. In fact, it had gone a long distance in the preparation of the Indian Territory for final statehood, either singly or in combination with the Oklahoma Territory.

My desire to visit Guthrie became all-consuming.[1] I wanted to see the newly formed territorial government in action, and I especially wanted to see the part being played by Negroes in education, business, social organizations, religious activities, fraternal organizations, in politics and other professions, and Negro activities generally. In fact, I wanted to see what they were doing to help develop this new and virgin field. I had read again and again, until I could envision it, about the first "run" of people of all races on April 22, 1889. I could see hundreds and hundreds on horseback, in wagons, buggies, surreys, even in oxcarts and on foot, making the race for homesteads. Now,

1. Guthrie was the territorial and then the state capital until 1910.

when I read that there would be a second "run" in September, 1891, at Shawnee, my desire to see this one sharpened beyond all proportion. Dad had to take me to see this one, and that was all there was to it.

"I'll take you to Guthrie and let you see and learn what you can about the new people and the new government. We will then move on to Shawnee and witness this second 'run,'" he told me. I was jubilant beyond control. We spent two full days at Guthrie before moving on to Shawnee.[2]

At the very start, there was a strong, separate school system in Guthrie. Queene Lee and Lalla Shaw taught at the Mayflower, the first school built, and Dr. Granger and Mrs. Judith Carter Horton were the high-school teachers. Later on, Mrs. Horton organized the Excelsior Club and Mrs. H. P. Jacobson organized and became the first president of the Territorial Colored Women's Club, to be succeeded by Mrs. Horton. During the administration of S. J. Faver as county commissioner, a separate high school was built and named for him.

One of the most unique and strongest characters in the first days of Guthrie was Judge G. N. Perkins.[3] He was born a slave in Tennessee, fought in the Civil War, and was honorably discharged. After the war, he moved to Arkansas, founded the town of Woodson, and later moved on to Little Rock. He attended night school for four months and was admitted to the Arkansas bar in 1880. He served in Little Rock as justice of the peace and as police judge. He came to Guthrie in 1891, and after looking over the situation and seeing that his race needed a constant mouthpiece, he bought a printing press and other equipment and established a weekly newspaper in 1892, which he named the *Oklahoma Guide*. Through this medium he influenced many Negroes from the Deep South to move to Oklahoma, which he called "God's Country."

He carried on a never-ceasing battle against racial prejudice and intolerance; but in all his battles, he was fair and square and had the respect—and often the support—of all the races. For many years he served on the city council. In the operation of his paper, he was ably assisted by his niece, Elvira S. Ridle. As justice of the peace, he meted out exact justice to all who came

2. The author provides no further information about the visit to Shawnee.
3. An outline of the career of George N. Perkins is given in *Who's Who of the Colored Race, 1915* (Chicago, 1915), 214.

before his court, and colored and white constables worked out of his court. He presided over and tried cases involving subject matters within the jurisdiction of his court without regard to racial origin or class.

Within the decade that followed, Negroes moved fast politically, educationally, in business, and in other professions generally. W. H. Smith, whose sister I was to marry many years hence, became a wholesale cotton buyer and one of the leading merchants. Later he moved to Wagoner, where he engaged in general mercantile business, covering a large area in trade. It was there that T. J. Elliott learned the fine points of the mercantile business while working for Smith. After his apprenticeship he moved to Muskogee, where he built and operated one of the city's largest dry goods businesses, which he conducted successfully until his death. J. A. Key, another successful Negro merchant of the period, finally moved his business, following a boom, to Okmulgee, where he established a bigger and better store. At Luther, J. M. Armstrong conducted one of the largest general stores in the town.

Over at Perry, in the Oklahoma Strip that opened in 1893, Clem Taliaferro established a general merchandise store, which he operated successfully until his death many years later. He was a graduate of Roger Williams University and a very able and progressive man. He, R. Emmett Stewart of Guthrie, and a man named Curin, of Dover, were among the first Masons of the Territory and the first to merit the 32nd degree of that fraternity. Stewart was elected to two successive terms as county clerk of Logan County, and he was followed in that office by two other outstanding Negroes, Johnson and Morton. Within the decade, Dr. Granger became the first principal of the Negro high school at Guthrie, and Mrs. Horton his able assistant. She served as assistant principal of the city school under Perry and afterward as principal. Within the decade, Morton was elected as representative to the territorial legislature, and Reed and Faver were elected county commissioners of Logan County.

During this period, only Negroes served as county jailers, in the persons of Jordan, Noble, and Emerson, followed by the appointment of E. B. McCabe as assistant territorial auditor. Within the same decade, aside from Judge Perkins, the following Negro attorneys lived in and practiced law in Guthrie and Logan County: W. I. Wallace, E. I. Saddler, R. Emmett Stewart, G. W. P. Brown, W. H. Twine, J. A. Anderson, and G. W. Hutchin. Guthrie and Logan County became the mecca for some of the most cultured, best-educated, and progressive Negroes in the United States.

In the first few months of the official life of this new government, the religious life of the people was by no means neglected. In the year of the first "run," 1889, the First Baptist Church was built and pastored by the Reverend H. P. Wigley, an exceptionally able man, such as was needed in raw pioneering country, able not only to interest and lead the people, but also to exert a tremendous influence over them and, through them, upon all the people of the community. At Kingfisher, another First Baptist Church was erected in 1890, served by the Reverend Dan Wilson. At Oklahoma City, the first public school for Negroes was opened with J. D. Randolph as principal, and at Kingfisher with M. J. Johnson as principal, a man of unusual ability who afterward became assistant president of the first Negro state college, Langston Agricultural and Mechanical University.

In June, 1889, one Martin Young came from Gallatin, Tennessee, to Oklahoma County. He was a farmer. He purchased a farm in Choctaw Township in what is now a part of the Green Pasture community. The following year came William Sulcer, also from Gallatin and educated in the public school there and at Roger Williams University, since closed. Sulcer was a teacher by training and profession. Soon after his arrival, he married one of Young's daughters in the Calvary Baptist Church, the first church wedding to be performed in Oklahoma City between colored people. In 1892 he secured a position as teacher in Choctaw Township, where he taught three terms. Sulcer went directly from Choctaw Township to Edmond, where he taught for several years. At this time, there were three territorial colleges for the whites and not one for the colored people. The white state schools were the University of Oklahoma at Norman (where at that time no Negroes were permitted to live); the State Agricultural and Industrial College at Stillwater; and the Central State College at Edmond. This condition rankled Sulcer, and he thought out a scheme to challenge the situation. He accordingly had Mrs. Cynthia Ware, a cultured and highly educated colored woman, file a written application for a teaching position on the faculty of Central State.

The white citizens, sensing a test in the courts of this discrimination, called an election to decide whether the schools should remain separate. Being in the majority, the white citizens won. The schools would remain separate, and of course Mrs. Ware did not get the job. The result, however, did not satisfy either side. Sulcer was considering other means of securing justice, and the other side was convinced that such discrimination would not stand up in a territory where the federal government had the final say. So certain influential parties in the legislature came to Sulcer and promised him that they would see to it that his people got a state college, if he would wait a while.

Sulcer was the first and oldest Negro Democrat in the Territory, and the leading lawmakers were Democrats. He thought he could get better results for his people if he worked alone, which he did. He agreed to the offer and filed, or addressed, a petition to the legislature for a Negro state college. The speaker of the house was a Democrat, and the president pro tem of the senate was also a Democrat. Other influential Negroes joined in and helped lobby the bill to create Langston, which opened its doors in 1897. This is, perhaps, the first time that the true story has been told about how and why Langston was created. There was a sharp conflict as to where the school would be located. Choctaw Township offered ten acres for the site, but Langston offered forty acres and got the school. It is to Sulcer's everlasting credit that he was offered a position in the school a dozen times but always refused.

Langston would have had a more glorious future, and a more useful one, had future politicians been as unselfish as Sulcer. The school had many great presidents, but it has been from time to time disrupted and injured by politicians of both races. I speak of its first president, Dr. Inman E. Page, one of the greatest educators and administrators that ever graced the office of president of any college or university. He remained president until 1915. Finally, this great man, a graduate of Brown University and other leading eastern colleges and universities, was forced out by two-bit Negro politicians, aided and abetted by strong, powerful, and corrupt white politicians. Dr. Page had two girls, the older being Mrs. Zelia Breaux, a great musician, who was head of the Music Department of the separate public-school system in Oklahoma City for more than thirty years; and the other, Mrs. Mary Pyrtle, whose husband, Nolan Pyrtle, was later a professor at Central State University, Wilberforce, Ohio, and was a schoolmate of mine at Dawes Academy.[4]

4. The founding of Langston University is discussed in Jimmie Lewis Franklin, *Journey Toward Hope: A History of Blacks in Oklahoma* (Norman, Okla., 1982), 28–29.

In the early 1890s the Reverend John W. Dungee, the greatest Baptist preacher of all, came with his family from Minnesota in a covered wagon. He was a contemporary of Frederick Douglass and had been closely associated with the Underground Railroad, that great humane organization that did such effective work in helping hundreds of slaves find their way to freedom in the North. He established and was pastor of the Tabernacle Baptist Church in Oklahoma City. In faith and by training and discipline he was fully prepared for the hardships and rigors of a pioneer life. He had been a pastor on the frontiers of Ohio and Minnesota and had experienced the dangers that existed immediately before and after the Civil War. Amid it all, he yearned for and was a slave to education. His thirst for knowledge was never quenched. He brought with him to the new territory a vast collection of books, and opened up the finest library to be found anyplace in the great, untamed Southwest. It was at this fountain of knowledge that he and his children drank continuously, and this great greed for knowledge and wisdom found its partial fulfillment in his children, it was said.

From what I have reliably learned about this great man of God, I'm prepared to say that one of his children, the only one I have known over the years, Roscoe, is an exact copy of his father. Roscoe Dungee founded a newspaper, the *Black Dispatch*, years ago in Oklahoma City. Through all the intervening years he has used its columns to advocate freedom through education for all the children of the human race in Oklahoma and everywhere throughout the world. Not only has he used the columns of his paper in his fight against racial discrimination, but he has traveled all over the state to speak against it. And the strangest thing about his fight for equal justice under the law has been the fact that he has been invited to deliver his message in all the state colleges, and was received gladly while many timid souls of his own race trembled in fear.

While all the members of his race kept silent, Dungee with pen and tongue continued a ceaseless onslaught against the dividing walls of racial prejudice of every kind. He spearheaded the fights through the courts in *Sipuel* v. *University of Oklahoma*, 332 U.S. 631, and *McLaurin* v. *Oklahoma State Regents*, 339 U.S. 637, to name two. He prepared the hearts and minds of the people of Oklahoma for the reception of the U.S. Supreme Court decision on the 17th day of May, 1954. His father fought to liberate the race from physical slavery. He has fought to free the human race from mental and spiritual thralldom, the most subtle and devastating of all forms of slavery. It is to be hoped that some future historian will perpetuate the things that this great American has done for the good of every citizen in the state of Oklahoma.[5]

The upper and lower houses of the legislature were in session, and I wanted to see these two bodies in action. I wanted also to see Governor Steele.[6] I had never seen a live governor—or a dead one. Jordan, the county jailer, was with us showing us around. "Come with me," he said, "I'll take you to the governor."

I was all eyes and ears when we entered His Excellency's office. Jordan introduced Dad and me, and the chief executive received us graciously. He chatted with me more than with Dad. That made me feel important and Dad very proud. He asked what grade I was in school, my age, and what I wanted to be. I answered him truthfully. But then he asked me, jokingly, whether I'd be a Republican or Democrat when I grew up, and I hemmed and hawed. Jordan said, "Republican, of course."

I hesitated and asked, looking first at the governor and then at Jordan, what was a Republican.

Jordan said, "Everybody around here is a Republican. All Negroes are Republican. That party freed us."

I was not convinced. A stubborn streak rose up in me, and I said proudly, "My people were never slaves." Then I asked, "What was Thomas Jefferson?"

The governor said, "The party to which he then belonged was called Republican; but he and his party were, in fact, Democrats. They belonged to the slaveholding class."

"But my Uncle 'Zander said he was a great and good man, and freed his own slaves before the Civil War; that, in fact, he never believed in slavery."

5. The highlights of Roscoe Dungee's career are provided in *Dictionary of American Negro Autobiography* (New York, 1982), 203–204, and in Franklin, *Journey Toward Hope*, 54–57.

6. George Washington Steele, a four-term member of the House of Representatives from Indiana, was appointed the first territorial governor of Oklahoma by President Benjamin Harrison. He served from May 15, 1890, till the end of 1891. He subsequently was again elected to the House, where he served four more terms.

Jordan was agitated, confused, and taken aback. He must have felt uneasy, having introduced us to the governor. He looked down at me scornfully and at Dad sharply. "Do you allow your children to be taught such heresy?" he asked Dad, who replied, "Frankly, I did not know his mind was on such matters. 'Zander is my oldest brother, and before he came to the Territory, he was in Virginia much and associated with some of Mr. Jefferson's former slaves and had a chance to pick up things about Mr. Jefferson that are not found in books. I'm trying to educate my children so they will be able to investigate and think for themselves."

By this time, the governor was highly enjoying the episode, and to relieve Jordan's discomfort he said pleasantly, "The boy already has an investigating mind, and if he keeps it up, he may some day start your people upon a new, untried era." When tension had subsided, we moved on to look upon the legislative bodies in action. I enjoyed the debates, sallies, and arguments, even if I could understand but a very few things taking place.

I had had a lot of fun and some experience, but it was debatable just how much I had learned. However, I was ready to go home. I'd have much to tell my brothers and sisters. Dad had always given me every educational advantage, and none of my brothers and sisters were ever jealous. In fact, they enjoyed hearing me "pop off" and got a great kick out of hearing me tell about the trip. Once Dad left the room, I hurriedly threw in something that never happened. Somehow, I didn't feel ashamed of that lie for some years. It was a big lie, too. I told them how the governor had bragged on me and invited Dad and me to stay for lunch. However, at school when the teacher, Miss Muelnix, who was then boarding at my home, asked me to tell the schoolchildren about my experience at chapel services (she was a New England missionary and never omitted these morning services), I left this lie out of my little speech. It must have, after all, been something foreign and never became a part of me. Miss Muelnix was different in another respect from my former teachers. If I or any of the other children were absent and missed classes, she would conduct written examinations covering the subject missed. I always liked this, because I made it a rule to do my homework at the end of each day. If I was going to be away from home, or at the ranch overnight, I carried my books in my saddlebag that Dad had bought at my request for that purpose.

It was about this time that I came to know well Bill Douglas and his entire family. He had established his ranch a few miles north of Dad's upper ranch on permits of the Love families. As I now recall, he had seven boys and two girls, and Ludie and Bee were boys about my size. Johnnie, the oldest, and the stuttering one, left home and went to Old Mexico and was never heard from again. "Uncle Bill," as we called the older Douglas, looked very much as if he was part Mexican. He had ranched for a number of years in southern Texas, near the Rio Grande, and may have had relatives in Mexico. It was not the custom in those days to pry into a man's background. I was sure, however, that the family had nothing to hide. Uncle Bill was every inch a cattleman. He could drive a bunch of cattle alone, all the way across the Territory, without losing a single one. The Franklin and Douglas families became inseparable and were indispensable one to the other in their trade.

It was in my thirteenth year that I became widely known as an all-around cowboy. It was argued that I was the best bronco buster, horse wrangler, rifle shot, and calf roper in the Territory. Give me time, and I could overcome any unbroken or unridden horse. Dad strictly forbade my taking on bulls, steers, or any grown-up cattle. My test was to come on the Fourth of July at the upper ranch. A full day's program had been carefully prepared for the occasion. The huge lake had been stocked with all kinds and sizes of fishes, seined and dumped into it since it had been built, and it contained thousands of them. The womenfolk from far-flung and nearby communities had been fishing and cooking since early dawn, and people came from great distances to witness the prowess of contestants or to participate. I was cool and confident. The contests in shooting, riding, and roping were to take place in that order. After the contests there was to be a large fish fry—and eating. The Declaration of Independence would be read, and attorney O. W. Patchell would deliver a patriotic speech.

Three contestants entered, besides myself. I experienced no difficulty in winning all the contests, except the shooting—in that, I tied with a cowboy named Foster, a hand from Bill Douglas' ranch. The rest of the program was carried out as planned. I read the Declaration, when no one else would, or could, and Patchell delivered what I thought was a great speech. He mentioned things I had never before heard of, and which I doubted until they were confirmed both by my teacher and my own research. Later that evening I demonstrated my swimming expertise. There was nothing I could not do in the water, diving and treading being my specialties.

There was a bright full moon, and many of the young and old people enjoyed the old-time but ever-popular square dance. I have remembered that day of sport and fun through the years as vividly as if it were but yesterday. Still, I've always entertained one regret. I didn't believe anyone could beat, or even tie, me in marksmanship. It hurt my pride. Yet Dad and all the rest thought I had performed miracles.

The cosmopolitan papers were now full of news about the opening of another vast area in the Oklahoma Territory to people seeking homesteads. There was to be another "run" in September, opening up the Cherokee Strip, under the proclamation of President Cleveland. I wanted to go to it very much but was afraid to ask Dad. I knew he would be absent from the Territory at that time and would not be able to accompany me if I went. However, I made it my business to read to him everything that appeared in the papers about the event. Finally, he saw that I wanted to see this thing, and so he said to me one day, as he was visiting me and my brother Tom at the upper ranch, "You want go to to that opening very badly, don't you?"

"Yes, Dad," I confessed.

"I'd like to see you go, but you know I can't go with you, and I don't know who could. If you can find some trusty person who can make the trip with you, I'll let you go."

I grinned and said, "I'll look around."

A week later, I returned. "Bee and Ludie can go with me."

"It's too far for you boys to go alone," Dad said. "But if Mr. Douglas can spare Willie, I'll consent."

In a few days, I returned and reported, "He can't spare Willie." Dad thought for a long time and finally said, "I've taken you with me many times, and you should know how to act and get by." And then he thought again for a longer time and said, "We'll talk again the next day or two." After two days, he came to me and said, "I think I can trust you and the two boys." And then he added, as an afterthought, "By no means must Foster go. I don't trust him."

"Is it because he tied me in shooting that you don't like him?" I asked.

"Nothing of the sort," he answered earnestly. "He has a shady record, he is wanted in Old Mexico for killing a Mexican. But don't mention this to a living soul."

Foster did want to go, but I told Bee I didn't want him along. He asked me why. I lied, "He is a man, and to take him along will spoil our fun and, too, it'll prove that we could go by ourselves and didn't have to have an over-seer." Foster didn't leave with us. He looked at me with hate in his eyes.

With a packhorse each, we left two days ahead of time. The trip was un-fruitful, a complete flop, so far as the main events were concerned. To begin with, we got lost and traveled over vast areas, across great rangelands where thousands of cattle grazed. Some ranchers, or cowhands, misdirected us, maybe intentionally. We slept out two nights and heard wolves howl all night. I was unarmed and frightened. Dad wouldn't allow me to take my carbine on the trip. The Douglas boys were unarmed too. We wandered into Perry late in the day, and we didn't see a single run. But the town was full of people, the largest crowd on the main street in front of a large two-story building.

We saw a colored man leave the building, headed in our direction. We went to meet him, and he introduced himself as Clem Taliaferro. He was the owner of a large general store. "Where are you boys from?" he asked.

"We are from the Indian Territory, a few miles south of Pauls Valley," I answered. Then I introduced us.

"I've heard of David Franklin. Are you related to him," he asked me.

"I'm his son."

"What are you boys doing away out here?"

I told him.

He said, "You are a day late. The run was yesterday."

"What are all these people doing in town," I asked him.

"Perry is one of the land office towns in the Strip," he answered. "I think it's called the 'Cherokee Outlet' in the papers; but out here it's called 'the Strip,' the 'Cherokee Strip.'"

We sat in his store and talked, while his clerks were busy serving the many customers who came in. He was from Tennessee. He told us he was a graduate of Roger Williams University, located in Nashville, and asked me if I had heard of the school. I told him yes, that I had a teacher, Pleasant Shoals, who once attended the school. He was doubly interested. I told him that Shoals and my dad wanted me to attend the school after I had finished at Dawes Academy. I of course didn't know then that this man had come from that part of Tennessee where my future wife and her family lived, and that he had known them all his life.

Although I had made a mess of the trip, I wanted to get as much infor-mation about the Territory and the people as possible. There were still many things about the Territory that I hadn't learned when Dad and I were out there. I spoke of the number of Negro lawyers in Guthrie. He told me that there was one in Kingfisher, whose name was Lewis, that lawyer Lowery lived and practiced in Oklahoma City, attorney E. T. Barbour at El Reno, and that there was a new one at Chickasaw. Most of them were Masonic brothers of his, and they were all, more or less, members and officers of the St. John Masonic Grand Lodge.

When we arrived home, I was crestfallen. I had nothing to talk about. I confessed to Dad when he returned home two or three days later that our trip was a complete flop. He patted me on the head, very fatherly, and said in a careless way, "Forget it."

"How can I, Dad? I feel so ashamed."

"You did better than I could have done at your age."

I knew better. I knew he was trying to console me. Uncle 'Zander had told me of Dad's exploits before the war—how he used to ride at night, out of Tennessee into Virginia and back home without being apprehended by white riders. But I was glad to drop the subject and if possible to forget it.

The year 1893 would be the last full year I would spend on the ranch, for in the fall of 1894 I would enter Dawes Academy. It seems like a good place in my story to tell what I know of the part Negroes played in creating the state of Oklahoma.

———

From about 1868 up to and including the year 1893, what part had the Negro played in the taming of and laying the foundation of stable government for what was to be the state of Oklahoma? For obvious reasons, this question cannot be completely answered; and even in attempting a partial answer, there must necessarily be some repetition in recapitulation.

On March 3, 1825, Congress authorized the extension of the famous Santa Fe Trail, which had its beginning at Kansas City and its end at Santa Fe, New Mexico. At Dodge City, this road forked into a northern and southern passage. The southern fork veered west across the Oklahoma Panhandle (No Man's Land), south of the mountains at Raton. Moving from the east to the west, a vast amount of human and freight traffic—long wagon trains filled with pioneer passengers seeking homes in the west, and long trains of caravans loaded with commodities—invariably took this southern route out of Dodge City. In the beginning, the Plains tribes and the white desperadoes took turns in killing these pioneers and taking their property. Often an entire wagon train would be massacred and all the property confiscated.

At Fort Sill, the Negro 9th and 10th Cavalries and the 24th and 25th Infantries had been stationed after the Civil War by the government for the purpose of putting an end to this lawlessness and widespread depredation. These expert cavalrymen soon became known throughout the West as the greatest Indian and desperado fighters who ever wore firearms in Oklahoma. They became so efficient and effective that it was said that no pioneers would enter the Territory from Dodge City unless they were met there by the cavalrymen and escorted all the way through the Territory. At the beginning of the campaign, it took all four of the Negro units to put down the raids; but toward the end, only the cavalrymen were used. The cavalrymen became a terror to all forms of lawlessness throughout the Oklahoma Territory wherever the federal government was involved.[7]

On the east side of the territory, known as the Indian Territory, there were around fifty Negro U.S. marshals, the most prominent of whom were Bass Reeves, Billy Colbert, Zeke Miller, Bob Fortune, and Neeley Factor.[8] There was absolutely no color line then. These men were chosen upon their merit. The government wanted only to know whether her peace officers could ride hard, were quick on the draw, and could shoot straight. If they could do these things, had guts, were close-mouthed, and were not afraid of dying, that was enough. There were no jokes in their lives and no place for them. Chester of "Gunsmoke" fame did not depict any part of the lives of these great peace officers.

In 1875, President Grant appointed a then-unknown lawyer, Isaac C. Parker, as judge for Western Arkansas and Eastern Indian Territory Districts. From that time to 1896, he was described throughout the United States as the "hanging judge" and was the flaming and unmoved nemesis of all the bad men in his jurisdiction. The great Negro marshals of that period worked out

7. For an account of the role of African American troops in attempts to establish law and order in the Territory, see William H. Leckie, *The Buffalo Soldiers* (Norman, Okla., 1967).

8. These and other African American deputy marshals are discussed in Arthur T. Burton, *Black, Red, and Deadly: Black and Indian Gunfighters of the Indian Territory, 1870–1907* (Austin, Tex., 1991).

of his court, and it was said that he leaned heavily on them to furnish grist for his mill. The heavy work at keeping the peace did not abate for the cavalrymen and infantrymen on the west side until April 22, 1889. The work of the U.S. marshals continued beyond the death of Judge Parker in 1896. In fact, a few of them rode the peace trail until November 16, 1907.

I never came in direct contact with the soldier boys except on the way back from Beaver, and when a small contingent, ten of them, stopped over at our home one night, with a dozen of the worst criminals, on their way to deliver them to the federal court at Fort Smith. The prisoners were being transported in a wagon. Each was handcuffed and each chained to the other. They were fed one at a time. Steel bracelets were locked around their legs when they were being fed. They alone occupied and slept in the wagon when night came. The soldiers withdrew in different directions and slept on the ground. I asked Dad why. He said it was to be prepared against surprise attack from possible absent members of the gang. The soldiers never talked. All around them was as quiet as a graveyard.

I often saw United States marshals, especially Bass Reeves, whose home was at Muskogee, and Bill Colbert, who lived at Atoka. In fact, he knew many of my mother's people who lived in the old Choctaw Nation, all the way from Atoka to Lukfatah, where my uncle lived. Bill Colbert himself was a half-breed, Choctaw and Negro.

I also recall the red-haired, red-mustached Dutchman, John Swain, and the tall, slim Jim Williams, whom Cornelius Walker killed. And I remember another white marshal, named Meshawn. All these officers at times traveled together, ate together, slept together, and fought together, side by side, and if one of them was killed by some outlaw, the others would bury him if it was in the summertime, when the body could not be preserved. These men had but one business, and that was to get their man, to establish law and order in an outlaw country; and they went about this single task in deadly earnest. It is strange how racial and religious prejudices and bigotry and intolerance are almost unknown in the rough and raw frontiers. These same traits spread and grow and expand unrealistically in communities, highly developed, where there is a church on every corner, a steeple and church bell in every tower that tolls remembrance of every Sabbath morn. Is real Christianity bankrupt?

Before 1904, W. H. Smith, the former cotton buyer at Guthrie, had moved to Wagoner and established one of the largest, most complete mercantile establishments in the entire Territory and had built a large trade area. As a result, he became generally known. His business grew and expanded. J. A. Key's business at Okmulgee was among the largest general stores in the town, and his trade territory eclipsed that of any other like business in the town. I've already referred to the much-alive and thrifty business of Clem Taliaferro at Perry. There was the big general store of J. T. Armstrong at Luther, able to compete successfully with any other store in the community.

Incidentally, Luther boasted a well-known Negro lawyer, Sam Hilton, who also maintained an office in Oklahoma City. In the years ahead, Sam Hilton would accumulate much livestock and many acres of farmland. He became the first and only Negro lawyer for a white bank in the Territory, or the state of Oklahoma.

I have not referred to Jim Rouce of Hitchcock, the owner of hundreds of acres of rich farm- and rangeland, and the largest wheat grower in the Territory. He was a substantial businessman and citizen, an acknowledged leader in his mixed community, and known throughout the state in politics, business, and Masonic circles. He was an outstanding leader in the promotion of educational opportunities for the youth of all races. He passed about a year before this is being written, and among his surviving children is his son, J. A., Jr., principal of the Ralph Bunche school in Tulsa, the largest in the system.

I find that a lot of people become confused in trying to understand what originally constituted the Indian Territory. Originally, the Indian Territory covered the entire area of the state of Oklahoma, except for No Man's Land and Greer County. In the Organic Act of the Congress of 1890, it was provided that the western part of the Indian Territory would be designated the Oklahoma Territory, including No Man's Land, and the act authorized the institution of a lawsuit against the state of Texas to recover Greer County, which would be added to the Oklahoma Territory. The act legally made the remainder of the area, roughly one half, the Indian Territory. This half was inhabited by the Cherokee, Creek, Seminole, Chickasaw, and Choctaw Nations. In course of time, they were to be known officially as the Five Civilized Tribes, in view of their past histories and in contradistinction to the Plains tribes and other American Indians, some of whom lived as primitive nomads. The parent stock of the Creek, Seminole, Choctaw, and Chickasaw tribes was Muskhogean.

It seems that originally, in the dim past, there was no Seminole tribe. They were a part of the Creek tribe; but when they pulled out from their common tribe, they became known as the Seminoles. In the language of the Creek, *seminole*, liberally translated, means a splinter, twig, or branch—an offshoot of the Creek tribe. To this day there is no substantial difference between the languages of the two tribes.

The Cherokee tribe is of the Iroquoian stock. The time they left their ancestral abode is lost in antiquity. History does not record with certainty when any of these tribes migrated into any of the southern and southeastern states. It appears certain that they were well established there in the early part of the sixteenth century, owning livestock and living in improved homes.

While it appears that these Indians came, generally speaking, from the same cultural group, the Cherokee tribe, in some members more noticeably than in others, were restricted in thought and action by certain ethnic traits, probably inherent in their common ancestry and which had been developed and practiced by it. The great leaders among their forebears had always shown initiative, originality, and other qualities of superb leadership, which finally came to fruition in the organization of the "Five Nations," which operated against the Dutch and other early fur traders as the Confederacy of Iroquois Tribes. I never met Chief John Ross, who was the chief of the Cherokees for upward of forty years, nor the great Sequoyah; but I did have the honor of counting among my best friends persons of Cherokee descent, such as the late United States senator Robert L. Owen; the late congressman W. W. Hastings; the late judge O. H. P. Brewer; the late Will Rogers; and especially Andy Payne, clerk of the supreme court and court of criminal appeals of Oklahoma. From the senator and the congressman and from Judge Brewer, when he was postmaster at Muskogee, I learned much about the tribe's history from the few times I met with them.

If one is to get a clear understanding of the eastern half of the old Indian Territory, it is well to remember that it made up the homes of the Five Civilized Tribes. When Andrew Jackson became president of the United States, he made it his policy to remove those tribes from their old homes: in Georgia, where the Cherokees lived; Florida, where the Seminoles lived; Alabama, where the Creeks lived; Mississippi, where the Choctaws lived; and Tennessee and parts of other states, where the Chickasaws lived. They were then settled in the eastern half of the Indian Territory. Under prior treaties and acts of Congress, the boundary lines of each Nation had been fixed. Each Nation had its own constitution, laws, courts, and officials. It elected its own governor, or principal chief, judges, and other court officials; and lawmakers were elected to the upper and lower houses of the legislatures. In civil and criminal matters, the tribal courts had exclusive jurisdiction in the respective Nations, in matters concerning both freedmen and Indians.

Jails were seldom used. If an Indian was convicted and sentenced to be shot for killing another Indian, he was invariably released until the day and hour of his execution, with instructions to return at the time appointed for the carrying out of the sentence. I heard my Dad tell of such a sentence being meted out to an Indian who lived near him. Between the trial and the date set for the execution of his neighbor, Dad said, he saw the condemned man every day. He visited our home and acted as if nothing unusual was pending. Stoically, he came and went. He was married, with two children, and each day he tried to make some money to leave to his family after he was gone. About four days prior to the execution, the defendant came to bid Dad goodbye, his wife accompanying him thus far. Walking, he said it would take him about three days to reach Tishomingo, the capital of the Chickasaw Nation and the place of execution. Dad asked him if he was going to walk all the way. He answered in the affirmative, and nonchalantly said goodbye as he ambled away down the road, leaving his wife dry-eyed behind.

The Organic Act of the Congress not only created the Territory of Oklahoma, making it possible for the opening of that rich and diversified area to homesteaders. It also took the first long and effective step toward curbing the jurisdiction of the tribal courts, preparatory to eventual statehood. It created federal court districts with Ardmore, Muskogee, and South McAlester as court towns for the new Indian Territory, in addition to the courts to be held at Chickasha and Purcell. The treaties of 1866, with the Cherokee, Creek, Seminole, Choctaw, and Chickasaw Nations giving their consent, provided for rights of way for railroads through these nations. As a result, the Missouri, Kansas, and Texas Railway Company extended its line by 1871 from the north through Muskogee into Denison, Texas, and the southern branch of the Union Pacific Railway Company extended its road from the Kansas line south through the Indian Territory into Fort Smith, Arkansas.

By 1882, the M. K. & T. had extended its line through Tulsa. With these railroads, and with the Santa Fe already running from St. Louis through Oklahoma City, through Ardmore, and on into Texas, and with towns springing up, noncitizens pouring into the Territory from every direction, and land increasing in value by the hour, every chance for the lands of these Nations to remain in the hands of the Indians "as long as grass grows and water runs" disappeared forever.

3

DAWES ACADEMY

*I*t was now late in September, 1894, and within seven days, I
would enter Dawes Academy as a student in my first boarding school away
from home. I do not know even now who was the more excited, Dad or myself. There was some sadness in the family. My oldest sister, Dolores, had just
died, leaving my sister Hattie, then about eighteen, as the woman of the
house. She and Dad had arranged a going-away party for me as if I were to
enter Yale, Harvard, or Princeton. I had made my last trip to the upper ranch
and as I thought of that, a lump came into my throat. Of course, I could not
look into the future, and it was well that I could not. My brothers Walter,
Andrew, and Tom had married and were beginning families of their own.
The children at home had narrowed down to Hattie, Matthew, myself,
David, Fisher, and Lydia. But Dad was jubilant, more so than I. I was the first
of his children to want to go off to school.

No doubt he was recalling Mother's prediction. I'm sure he did not think
more of me than he did of his other children; but we had become pals and
grew closer together over the years. We seemed to like the same things and
sought the same answers. When together, which was as often as possible, we
talked as two grown-ups. During my two years at the ranch, a little church,
called Little Flock Baptist, had been built a short distance from the ranch toward Long Branch, and I had been going to Sunday school there every Sabbath instead of making the trip down to Dad's church; and I had come to
love the Sunday school lessons. In fact, the pastor had given me a class to
teach.

Finally, the reception for me turned out more like a picnic, and my many friends came, colored, Indians, and whites, and all had a great time. Dad was so proud that he made a little speech, and in his excitement, called on me to say something. I was stunned, and lost for words, but I finally blurted out, "I thank you, Dad, for everything. I hope I will always please you and pray God that you will live long." Miss Muelnix made a nice, pointed talk. I remember a word or two she said, to the effect that it was going to take education to get through in the future and that she hoped and prayed that more young people would take advantage of attending the academy. It was the first time I learned that she knew Miss Dawes personally.

Dad drove me to the academy in his surrey, through the Arbuckle Mountains, instead of going around through Homer, Pooleville, Milo, Woodford, and Glenn, which would have taken more than a day. Too, he wanted to teach me a new and more direct route from the academy to our home. We made the distance before nightfall, although we had stopped at Robert Cobb's for lunch, called "dinner" then.

The academy sat in a grove of trees on a hillside, overlooking the Santa Fe Railroad approximately two hundred yards to the east. Across the track on a hill, half hidden by a fine orchard, one could see the country home of Ephriam James, and down the tracks was the town of Berwyn (now Gene Autry), three miles away. School would open its fall term the next morning, and Dad remained overnight for the opening. He did not stay at the academy, however, but at the home of an old friend, Charles Cohee. There were three spacious buildings on the campus, besides the boys and girls dormitories; the main building consisted of the dining hall and kitchen, with rooms upstairs for the teachers, except for Miss Dawes and two teachers, who lived in the girls dormitory. There was a laundry building, and a manual training building with many large classrooms. There were about a hundred boarding students and more than two hundred day students. Then, there were only lamps and lanterns to furnish light for the school. Every building on the grounds was a frame structure, each painted white, clean and well kept. The room assigned me had two other occupants, M. F. Jones, who afterward became a prominent physician in Oklahoma, and Henry Colbert, a distant relative of mine on my mother's side.

That first night, as I heard the footsteps of teachers moving up and down the hall, I realized for the first time in my life that there would be a difference in my surroundings from those I had been used to. All my life I had been used to the great open spaces, where distance meant nothing, where I could ride and roam at will to my heart's content. Now I must conform to certain restrictions and I would, of necessity, be regimented and contained. I knew nothing about the phrase "Don't fence me in," but I'm afraid the meaning of that song just about expressed my feelings on that first night at the academy and, indeed, many nights thereafter.

Dad appeared the next morning at the opening session of the school in company with Ephriam James, Albert Johnson, Binton James, his old friend Charles Cohee, Rev. G. W. Hall (the pastor of a local church), and Rev. Dave Whitaker, whom I came to know quite well during the next two years through his son, Dave, Jr. Of course, there were hundreds more at the opening. The school was surrounded by almost solid Negro communities, thinly dotted with Indian families. Here and there lived one or two white tenants.

The opening of the school was impressive, yet very simple and forthright. The principal, Miss Mary Dawes, presided. She was a New Englander. Her family had been one of the very first to settle in Massachusetts, each generation had been prominent in education, government, and business, and each was a strict, unyielding, uncompromising abolitionist. Up to the founding of the academy, she had given most of her adult life to assisting the Indian and Negro, encouraging them in self-help. She was the sister of Henry L. Dawes, who was appointed by the federal government as one of the three commissioners to prepare the Indian Territory for statehood. The commission was named the "Dawes Commission" in honor of Mr. Dawes, who was made its first chairman. (I shall have more to say about this commission later.) Miss Dawes was a good administrator and teacher, and so were the other members of her faculty, who were all women. I became adjusted to my environment gradually, and for the two years of school, I applied myself as much as I was able.

Miss Dawes and her teachers were deeply religious. The Bible had a fixed and definite place in the school's curriculum, and devotional exercises were conducted every morning, from Monday through Friday, before class assignment. Sunday afternoons or at night, some local preacher was invited to preach a sermon. I was to learn later that all schools established in the South for the education of Negroes following the Civil War placed the major emphasis on religious training. It was the common belief of the benefactors that the hope of the race depended upon well-trained religious leaders.[1]

Having been taught from my very earliest childhood to kneel at the family altar and to love church and Sunday school, I endured this setup at the academy for a time; but then it began to bore me. I had to do something to relieve the growing tension. I talked the matter over with Elwood Cobb, a day student who lived about three miles down the south side of the Arbuckle Mountains from the school. He was the son of Robert Cobb, at whose home we had dinner on our way to the academy. He suggested that I could easily drive or ride home during the weekends.

I wrote Dad, carefully concealing the facts, and told him what was on my mind. He came down to the Cobb residence one Thursday evening, leading Old Coaly, and the next morning he went on to the academy. After talking with me, he went to the principal's office. She sent for me, and with my heart in my throat, I knocked on her door. She told me to enter. Dad was in her office. She told me what he had told her and asked me to explain why I wanted to spend the weekends at home. With a straight face, I told her that there were many things I could do at home and assured her that I would keep up with my classes.

"I have no doubt of that," she said, "but it's the custom for boarding students to remain on the grounds during the term, except in cases of some sort of emergency." After considerable discussion, she finally said, "I can only allow such an arrangement during the spring and early fall seasons. In other words, when the weather permits. In the winter months, you will have to remain on the campus, except for the holidays."

This was in early April, 1895, and the weather was warm. So that evening I returned home with Dad. On our way something happened that I thought would upset my plan to spend the weekends at home. Before reaching the top of one mountain range, we heard a cow bawl, as in deep agony. Ascending to the top of the mountain and looking down into a valley, we saw a half dozen timber wolves and two large mountain lions. Between the lions and the wolves, we saw a heifer trying to rise from the ground. She could only

---

1. See Robert C. Morris, *Reading, 'Riting, and Reconstruction: The Education of Freedmen in the South, 1861–1870* (Chicago, 1981).

lift her front legs; her hind legs and hips were useless. The wolf pack were standing, fangs bared and snarling, facing the approaching lions. Dad did not have his rifle and was helpless to do anything for the poor, scared, moaning animal, sad eyes appealing for help. The nearest house was possibly six miles away and so we passed on. Old Coaly snorted and reared and became almost unmanageable, making a wide arc around what he thought was the place of danger. I asked Dad why that animal was alone—off to herself. He explained that evidently the wolves had separated her from the herd and chased her, cutting and slashing at her hind legs, just above the hoofs, until they were severed at the muscles and ligaments and she could not carry her rear end. He had known wolf packs to kill large, wild bulls in the same way. He was silent the rest of the trip home. I did not disturb him; I could always tell what he was thinking. He was thinking about not allowing me to come home for the weekends.

We had supper and I read all the latest news to him. It must have been near midnight before I had finished, and then I said to him: "Dad, I know why you have been so quiet. You think it might not be safe for me to come home weekends."

"Yes," he answered. "I don't think it's safe for you to make the trip. I would be more satisfied—less disturbed—if you stayed at the academy until this term of school closed, at least. What do you think?"

That was just like him, to ask my advice in matters where I was directly concerned. I weighed my words before answering. "I don't think I'll be in any danger. The close of school is a little more than a month away. I can carry my carbine and leave it at Mr. Cobb's, and pick it up at weekends when I return home. The school will never know about that."

His face brightened. He said, "I never thought of that."

Old Coaly, who like most of Dad's horses was part thoroughbred and part mustang, could lope the distance between home and the academy without letup. In the spring and fall seasons, I could get home from the academy on Friday evenings. On my return I'd leave home Sunday evenings and stop overnight at the Cobbs', and ride to the academy next morning with Elwood. Miss Dawes's middle name was "Strictness," but she never asked me to explain why I did not spend the Sabbath at the school. I believe one reason she did not follow up on this was because I tried to make myself indispensable to her and the school. I always had top lessons and was around her office when there was anything to be done. She made me the postman, and I went daily for the school mail in her buggy. I cared for the horse and washed the rig and never allowed her to pay me for anything I did for her. I became an honor student and was allowed to make trips into Berwyn, and once as far as Ardmore, about thirteen miles away.

In going to Berwyn on such occasions, I would go down to the tracks and board a heavily loaded freight train that was puffing and straining uphill. I had a mishap on the night I was returning from Ardmore. I got off at Berwyn for a minute as the train was switching onto a sideline to permit a southbound through train to pass. After the train had passed, my train, that would have let me off just opposite the academy, did not switch back and come up to the depot; it proceeded north, was switched onto the main line, and left me standing at the station.

I could have walked on to the academy but decided to catch a freight train that was pulling out. I boarded it, intending to get off at the top of the incline, near the academy, as I had done many times before; but I waited until the freight had passed the point and started down. I therefore misjudged the rate of speed at which it was moving, and as I leaped off, I became unbalanced, tripped, and fell hard upon rocks. My right leg was bruised and lacerated. I lay upon the ground in agony for quite a while. Finally, with much exertion, I arose and limped off toward the academy, about two hundred and fifty yards away.

I remained in bed the next morning, still stiff and in much misery. As I did not go to Miss Dawes's office as was my custom, and failed to appear at the breakfast table, she immediately surmised that something had happened. Without fuss, she was very solicitous and administered first-aid with her own hands, which gave immediate, temporary relief. With a visit from the doctor and his treatment of my pulled muscles and strained and torn ligaments, I was able to return to classes and my duties within two days.

School closed, ending my first year at the academy. I was very happy with the progress I had made. Among the student body at the school, I had made friends, aside from Jones and Colbert, with the Pyrtle brothers, Nolan and Emmett, and David Whitaker, Jr. After going through the academy, Nolan and Whitaker continued their education, Whitaker entering the ministry and Nolan the education field. He taught at Wilberforce until Ohio withdrew its aid to the school and created Central State University, to which he transferred.

And there was, of course, my best friend, Elwood Cobb, with whom I was to continue to associate for many years to come at Roger Williams University.

———

From the treaties of 1866 with the Five Tribes, the federal government had been driving through more treaties and acts of Congress to prepare the Indian Territory, and on March 3, 1893, Congress placed a rider on the Indian Appropriation Bill, creating what was to be known as the Dawes Commission, the purposes of which were to secure the consent of the Indians of the Territory to the allotment of their lands in severalty and, that accomplished, to prepare a final roll of the Indians and freedmen entitled to an allotment. The next step was the appraisal of these lands by the government. There were, roughly, 4,420,000 acres in the Cherokee Nation, 4,800,000 in the Chickasaw Nation, 7,000,000 in the Choctaw Nation, 4,000,000 in the Creek Nation, and 400,000 in the Seminole Nation, to be appraised. Each bona fide allottee of the different tribes was entitled to a certain number of acres, figured upon the scale of the price of the average value. Hence the number of acres each allottee would get depended upon the value of the allotment and the number of allottees entitled to share in the allotment. The prices were fixed by the commission.

In the treaties of 1866 between these Nations and the government, the Cherokee, Creek, and Seminole Nations consented to and did adopt their former slaves, making them full citizens. Hence these freedmen not only shared equally with their former masters in the allotted land, but also had full and equal political rights. In *U.S. v. Choctaw & Chickasaw Nations*, 193 U.S. 115, decided in 1900, the Supreme Court held that the Choctaw freedman was entitled to forty acres of the average allotable lands of that tribe. That decision eliminated Dad on two scores. His father had purchased the freedom of his family long before the close of the Civil War, and even if that had not happened, Dad would still get nothing, as the Chickasaws' freedmen were not entitled to any of the common lands of that tribe.[2]

Dad had seen this decision coming for quite some time and had encouraged his good friend Charles Cohee to employ counsel to try to head it off.

———

2. It will be recalled that this account differs from the one that David Burney declared in 1895, when he asserted that he was a runaway slave. See chap. 1, note 2.

Cohee formed a Chickasaw Freedmens Association and hired attorneys Joseph P. Mullin of Ardmore and R. V. Belt to represent them. The effort came to naught. The record shows that they did nothing. When the final enrollment was under way, Dad made two trips to the Old Boggy Depot community and to Tuskahoma to see what had been done by Colbert to complete and file the necessary proof that Mother was entitled to be placed upon the Choctaw Indian Roll. He was unable to find one shred of anything Colbert, who was now deceased, had done. This all meant that Mother's children might possibly be enrolled as Choctaw freedmen and secure forty acres of the average allotted lands. Had she survived, there is no doubt but that her children would have been placed upon the Indian Roll. Stevenson's wife and Eddie Abram's wife, being of less than half Indian blood, had been placed upon the full-blood roll of that tribe. Since the commission was a quasi-judicial body, its finding as to the quantum of blood was conclusive.

There was one outstanding fact that made it almost impossible for an allottee with any Negro blood to get on the Indian Roll, and that was prejudice. Chairman Dawes, who died shortly after the creation of the commission, was absolutely without racial bias and considered every applicant upon individual merit.[3]

This turn of fortune did not discourage Dad in the least. He carefully mapped out a long-range scheme. He knew that most of the unrestricted allottees would be anxious to sell their land just as soon as it became taxable. And, when he could no longer hold land in common, he intended to have his vast holdings increased by allottees who would be ready to sell as soon as they had to pay taxes on their land. He carefully discussed his plans with me during my vacation. "There is no dishonesty in this; they will sell to someone, and I'm sure I'll pay them more than anyone else would," he assured me. "It will be some time yet before the Territory will be ready for statehood," he continued. "The freedmen and most of the Indians do not want it. The commission will have to make more treaties with the Indians, more acts of Congress, more legislation, before the goal is reached. It will be a repetition of the authorities' procedures in Georgia, Alabama, and the other states where these Indians came from."

---

3. Dawes did not die until February 5, 1903, ten years after the commission bearing his name was created.

As he predicted, the commission spent five fruitless years trying to get the Indians to agree to legislation looking to the winding up of their tribal governments in preparing the Territory for statehood. Then followed the Force Act of June 10, 1896, the Atoka Agreement of April 23, 1897, and the Curtis Act of June 28, 1898. It will be recalled that Charles Curtis, a Kaw Kansas Indian, was also a U.S. senator from that state, and finally vice-president. The Crazy Snake Rebellion—in which many freedmen participated—and the Cherokee full-blood rebellions served to delay and complicate matters.

My vacation of 1895 was uneventful. I pretty much did the work I had done previously. Strangely, it at times appeared monotonous, and what I had done in former years with enjoyment and pleasure, I now found to be from force of habit and because I knew it had to be done. At times I found myself missing Miss Dawes and the academy and the new acquaintances I had made. There appeared to be opening up before me a strange new vista. Now and then my old surroundings bored me and became unpalatable. Dad was the first to sense my changing moods and to interpret them. He assured me that my reactions were natural. He said, "This is due to a change in scenes, surroundings, and new associates. Always remember that you must always be ready—and able—to adjust to new situations. Your mother used to say that the gist and real worth and true usefulness of education consist of adaptability; that is, being able to know and work with people." Wise old Dad. I never have since forgotten his advice and counsel.

In the fall, I returned to the academy for what was to be my last year there. I was determined to study and work harder than ever before, to renew old acquaintances and make new friends, to look, listen, and learn. Miss Dawes was my best and true friend. I saw much of her every day, as she taught first-year Latin and algebra, both of which I came to love. She often said to her class, "Greek and Latin are the foundations of English, more true of Greek than of Latin." I still went home weekends during the warm weather, always retrieving my carbine at the Cobb residence where I left it on my return to school. Now, but not often, I returned to the academy Sundays for chapel services that were conducted in the evening.

Miss Dawes often talked with me and thought I should preach or make the ministry my profession. She said that the Negro people, especially in the

Territory, needed trained leadership of their own race. I told her I had no desire or calling for the ministry. I told her that I thought my people needed prepared, dedicated lawyers to protect them from the crooks in her and my race, and leaders who would train my people in thrift, honesty, responsibility, and clean living. I did not discredit Christianity; but I had seen all about me so much robbing by the crooks from the poor and ignorant that it appeared to me that the first thing I should learn to do was to save them from the sharks and evildoers. I told her also that while I agreed with her that the ministry should be trained, that sacred profession first depended upon being called, and I had never had a whisper from the Heavenly Father telling me that I had any talent for the ministry. I was old fashioned enough to believe in a "call" to preach and teach His word. She never again attempted to tell me what I should do or be. I think she knew that whatever I did, I would never disgrace the school.

The remainder of my school year was pleasant, and I never worked so hard—before or since—to acquit myself with honor and respect. Some nights while the entire school was slumbering, I would shade my lamp so that I would not be detected and pore over my lessons until far past midnight. I had persuaded Miss Dawes to give me a single room, and after dinner (called "supper" then) I locked myself in my room to study and admitted no one except Miss Dawes or some other member of the faculty. Of course, I had to pay double for the room, which was the custom, but I have never regretted it.

It was strange, but in all of my weekend trips home during the rest of the school year, I never saw a wolf, coyote, or lion; but I never lowered my guard. As I now recall, the term ended about the middle of May. I knew that that would be my last term at the academy. That fall would see me in Roger Williams University with my good friend Elwood Cobb. We had been planning and talking about it for some time. Here and there, for quite some time back, I had been learning about the school. My old professor and relative, Pleasant Shoals, had told me about it, and then there was an old Roger Williams graduate, Thurston, who taught, I believe, at Gainesville, Texas. He too had told me about the college. Miss Dawes knew of the school too. She had learned about it through the American Baptist Home Mission Board, which founded and supported the institution, along with other Negro schools. I never asked her whether the academy was under the jurisdiction of this board. It could have been, but again it may have been a privately owned and operated school.

I was extremely happy in the summer of 1896, although I worked harder than ever before. My future roommate Elwood would come up and spend some weekends with me, but I was not able to return many of his visits. He had a sister, Victoria, just about the age of my sister Hattie, who would come with him sometimes and spend time at my home.

Dad was not too happy. He saw what I was unable to see: what would happen when the tribes and freedmen of the Five Nations ceased to hold their lands in common. Only the allotments of the full-blood Indians would be restricted from alienation; and in time that would not be the case. The allotments of all the freedmen and the rest of the Indians would be unrestricted, which meant they could sell and dispose of all their allotments at any time after they had received their allotment deeds from their respective governors, or principal chiefs, as the case might be. Roughly, the Cherokee freedmen would be allotted, in the aggregate, in excess of 2,000,000 acres; the Creek freedmen in excess of 1,500,000 acres, and the Seminole freedmen in excess of 180,000 acres. Added to these figures, the Choctaw freedmen would be allotted severally 40 acres of the average allotable lands, which would amount to approximately 200,000 acres. After the Chickasaw freedmen had lost their suit against the Chickasaw Nation, the federal government felt morally bound to allot them 40 acres of the average allotable lands and reimburse the tribe for the costs of such allotments. This meant that the freedmen of the Five Civilized Tribes would receive, in the aggregate, approximately 4,000,000 acres.

The total number of these freedmen was approximately 46,000, of whom not more than 1 percent had any education. They did not know the value of the dollar; everything had always been free to them. Except among the Seminoles, none of them had ever been permitted to attend tribal schools. Separate schools for the Cherokee and Creek freedmen were just about nonexistent. If the Choctaw and Chickasaw freedmen had any schools, they were merely subscription makeshifts, here and there, and far between, and possibly the teacher was poorly prepared for teaching. These people had just come out of slavery, not the harsh and brutal kind of the white master, but one of idleness and indolence. They had been born and bred in, and were the product of, a free, careless life. They were totally unprepared for the change that was just around the corner.

That was what Dad saw, and what I could not see at that time. That was what saddened him. He saw these people being ushered, without ceremony, without benefit of clergy, into an age of harsh materialism, of rugged individualism, that they could never understand until it was too late to salvage anything from their inheritance. They would be thrust into a society of pioneers, not necessarily mean or despicable, but who believed in the doctrine of the survival of the fittest. The result has shown that these people had no chance in the inevitable contest.

It is true that in 1899 the United States government established a school system for the Indian Territory and appointed John D. Benedict as general superintendent, but it was like closing the gate after the horse had escaped. The benefits of this effort did not trickle down to the Negro, except in spots, until about 1903. I was one of the first Negroes to teach under this system, about which I shall have more to say in a proper place in this narrative.

Although worried, Dad never lost sight of getting me ready for the fall term at Roger Williams. As the days passed, all my brothers and sisters became more and more interested. Brother Tom took a special interest in me. He encouraged me by giving me things he thought I'd need, such as ties and handkerchiefs. He had a suit made for me. I was to learn that it was most unsuitable for wear at the college, and my large red handkerchief I never took out of my valise (Dad didn't think to buy a trunk for his son).

As the first month of autumn drew near, there was a double rush at home and on the north ranch to get everything ready for winter. Extra hands were hired to gather and store enough roughage and feedstuff generally, and to make or repair shelter for man and beast as protection against the hardest weather. Mid-September approached, the appointed time for my departure for Nashville and college. I lived in feverish anticipation. The nearer I came to the deadline, the more impossible it seemed to contain myself. My heart appeared to skip a beat. I'd never been out of the Territories before, except on the trip with Dad to Nocona, Texas, to buy my cowboy outfit. I had no way of knowing what lay ahead. Surely a brand new world, things I could not envision and experiences I could not anticipate. There was one great thing the academy had done for me, and that was to begin to teach me how little I knew, what a small gnat I was! I was a very small babe toddling around in circles without direction. And when I realized that I was about to embark upon a strange new universe, fear arose in me for a brief moment; but when

I reflected that I was not the first, and certainly would not be the last, to venture forth, my misgivings subsided and vanished, and there entered the will and determination to dare and explore and understand the myriads of things beyond the curtain of my present knowledge.

My mood changed, my boyish face lit up, and there was a sparkle in my eyes. Dad, who had been watching me intently, interrupted to ask me what I was thinking about. Not able to explain in words that would be understandable, I simply answered, "Nothing." He continued to look at me intently for some time before he turned away and commenced talking about other things. But from the time we became pals, when I was a very small boy, until his death, I have always thought he could tell what I was thinking.

The entire family went with me to the station at Pauls Valley to board the northbound Santa Fe. Dad watched me as I purchased my ticket, a very long one. I could not understand why it should be so lengthy. He explained it would become shorter as I proceeded on my trip. Lots of people, mostly white, came down to the station near train time, as was the custom in small towns, to see the train arrive. Dad was so proud that he introduced many of them to me and told them where I was going. The rest of the family beamed upon me as if I was something special.

4

ROGER WILLIAMS UNIVERSITY

*F*inally my train arrived, but Elwood was not on it. He was to come up on the same train from Ardmore. I was surprised, disappointed, and discouraged. I hid my feelings and pretended that I was not bothered. Dad said, just as I was getting on the train, "The boy missed his train, I'm sure. You will see him in Nashville." My sisters Hattie and Lydia kissed me good-bye, Dad and the boys shook my hand, and I was off into the big blue yonder. I traveled like a veteran and reached Nashville without incident.

I didn't know it, but Dad had the local agent wire the college the time of the train's arrival, and when I got there, Tim Perry met me and inquired if I was Buck Franklin from the Indian country. I was pleasantly surprised, and he told me of the agent's wire. We chatted as we went through the gate and waited at the baggage office for my valises. The large powerful mule hitched to the dray was named Pete. On our way to the college, I learned that Pete was as old as the college; that he had hauled trunks, valises, and all kinds of luggage of students from the depot for more than twenty years, and that he was known and loved by all the graduates of the institution and remembered by every student who had matriculated there.

A few years after I had been at the college, an incident occurred that proved the esteem in which this once powerful and faithful animal was held by the student body. Pete had grown so old that every bone was full of rheumatism, and when he stood still or lay down for any length of time, his body would be racked with pain. At such times, from every building and from great distances up and down Hillsboro Pike, he could be heard grunting and moaning.

President Peter Buell Guernsey ordered that Pete be put out of his misery, which was the merciful thing to do. The entire student body protested vigorously, dared the president, and tacked resolutions all over the buildings and in other conspicuous places condemning the act as un-Christian and savage. Almost the entire student body went on strike and refused to attend classes. The girls were more obstinate and resolute than the boys. The news of the uprising spread into the city, and reporters came out to cover the situation and for interviews. From faraway places where former Rogerites lived or worked came letters and telegrams condemning the intended act of the president. Finally, reason returned to the college. Two students who had kept their heads and a few members of the faculty succeeded in calling the students together in the chapel, and after much discussion, normalcy was restored. During the night, dear old Pete was taken from campus and disposed of. None of us ever knew where he was taken or what instrument was used to dispatch him.

I had, indeed, entered into a new world. The school was located upon a beautiful site (now Peabody College) of twelve or more acres, between Ward-Belmont College for white girls and the great Vanderbilt University. In front of the institution ran Hillsboro Pike from the city into the Compton settlement and past the home of Colonel Stokes, a great lawyer of much wealth. On the opposite side of the college was the Granny White Pike, running parallel with the Hillsboro Pike, past the city reservoir. Between it and the college was a quarter mile of almost open space called "the Commons." At that time just a very few houses dotted the space. When I returned to Nashville in 1946, on the occasion of the inauguration of Dr. Charles S. Johnson as president of Fisk University, there was no Commons. Instead, there were streets and alleys and businesses, tall brick buildings, and beautiful homes. Hillsboro Pike had been changed to an avenue or street, the name of which I do not remember.

As far as I had gone in my studies, I had a good educational foundation, but my ignorance of cultured and educated people, of their thoughts and attitudes toward people and life in its broad human aspects, was abysmal. I had sense enough to know that my attitude must be one of respectful reticence until I was able to absorb and understand, in part at least, this brand new society into which I had been thrust. My first year at the college was therefore one of reserve or aloofness. In the meantime, I kept my eyes, ears, and especially my mind open. Nothing escaped my notice, and I had never studied so hard and applied myself so diligently as I did this first year at the college. I found myself being richly rewarded. I mastered all the subjects to which I had been assigned. My teachers respected and praised me for my work, and I found my classmates beginning to honor me and from time to time consult me about something in the lessons.

Elwood came on to college one week after my arrival, and he was assigned to my room; so we were a great help to each other. I bought a standard school Webster's dictionary and lay awake at night poring over Hill's rhetoric and McMaster's history with the dictionary before me. I was astounded at how my vocabulary increased. In my examination at the end of the calendar year 1896, I made top grades, and I was surprised and pleased beyond words. My confidence in myself, in my ability to master my subjects, was stimulating and reassuring.

In my different classes at the beginning of the new calendar year, my teachers told my classmates that my high marks were a challenge to them. Then, no teacher taught just one subject. The school was not financially able to take advantage of such luxury. The oldest teacher, in age and point of service, except for Dr. Alfred Owen, was J. W. Johnson. He taught all the mathematics classes and one or two other subjects; Miss Mozella Denslow (for whom my oldest child is named) taught the languages, except Greek; Dr. Owen taught Greek and the Bible, which was a *must* subject in the school; Miss Dixie Erma Williams taught English, including rhetoric and the classics; and John Hope was the science teacher. He had gone to Chicago during the Christmas season and returned with a wife, Lugenia Burns. Through the remainder of his life, he affectionately called her "Genia." He became my best and closest friend. I spent as much of his—and my—time as possible in his presence, and came to know and love Mrs. Hope quite as much as I did him. They lived on the campus and often I'd go to their home after school hours for talks and inspiration.[1]

1. For extensive discussions of the life of John Hope, see Ridgley Torrence, *The Story of John Hope* (New York, 1948), and a forthcoming biography to be published by the University of Georgia Press, Leroy Davis, *A Clashing of the Soul: John Hope and the Dilemma of African American Leadership and Black Higher Education in the Early Twentieth Century*. Hope's wife is treated in Jacqueline Anne Rouse, *Lugenia Burns Hope: Black Southern Reformer* (Athens, Ga., 1989).

At the end of the 1898 school year, Hope left the college to accept a position on the faculty of Atlanta Baptist College, now Morehouse College, where I was to follow him later. His place was filled by William Henry Harrison, a graduate of Roger Williams. He became one of my best friends. While teaching at the university, he attended the Law School of Walden, in Nashville. After he graduated, he resigned his teaching job at the college and came west to practice his new profession, settling first in Tulsa, and then permanently in Oklahoma City. He and Mrs. Harrison had two children, Wilhelmina, who was born at the college, and Alfred Owen, named for Dr. Owen of the faculty. Harrison was perhaps one of the greatest orators Roger Williams ever produced, and also the best known and most beloved lay member of the Baptist church. He became a brilliant and fearless trial lawyer and fought racial prejudice wherever he encountered it. He brought one of the first cases involving the Separate Coach (Jim Crow) Law in Oklahoma: *McCabe* v. *A.T. & S.F.R. Co.*, 235 U.S. 151. The plaintiff had been assistant auditor of the Territory of Oklahoma.

I spent a part of the summer of 1897 at the university, assisting the carpenters in the repair work on the buildings on the campus, going to the city post office for the mail, doing other odd jobs around the school, and working for Colonel Stokes, driving him to and from his office in the city. More than once I accompanied him on trips into the country, where he had been summoned by an old couple to draw up a will or to arbitrate some dispute between neighbors. Using foolscap paper, he prepared and drafted the will in longhand. The days of the wide use of the typewriter had not then arrived.

It was the custom in those days for the professions of lawyer, doctor, and minister to be handed down to succeeding generations. A preacher rarely gave up the pastorate of a church, and it was understood that his son, following the same profession, would take his place after his death. Colonel Stokes always took me into the room where he was preparing a will. He would have the maid hand me the lamp or lantern, and I'd hold it so that he could see while writing with his quill. I was curious to know why he took me into the room where he was preparing a will, and so I asked him as we were returning to his estate. He answered quietly, in a matter-of-fact tone, "The experience will be helpful when you become a lawyer."

"Is that possible?" I asked him.

"Certainly, why not?" he asked me. Before I could answer, he answered himself: "It will not be tomorrow, or the next day, measured by the years; but it will be before you die, or your children at the fartherest."

That summer was a profitable one for me. It opened up rich and diversified avenues for experience and learning about things that are not obtainable from books. One of my classmates was Lula Boyd, the youngest of three children of Rev. R. H. Boyd, the founder and operator of the Baptist Publishing House.[2] He was a man of great influence and power. Originally from Texas, he and three other prominent ministers, Rev. Allen R. Griggs, I. Toliver, and E. W. D. Isaacs, although not natives of Nashville, just about ruled the city as far as colored Baptists were concerned. Allen R. Griggs, Jr., and I were classmates.

Lula and I were like sister and brother, and I often stayed in the Boyd home. Her father liked me, and I was accepted as a member of the family. The elder Boyd was like that. He was a father to many young students; but he accepted no divided allegiance. There was no middle ground or neutrality. One was for him or against him. Through Lula—and him—I was able to come into contact with the best social and intellectual colored life in the city. Allen R., Jr., had known Rev. Isaacs and Toliver all his life, and through him I became acquainted with them and their friends and associates.

So during all my college days at Roger Williams, my worthwhile friendships multiplied. Lula became more and more like a sister, and I called her father "Dad," as she did. Her first love was Eugene Allen, a student at the college. After his graduation, he took dentistry at Meharry Medical College in Nashville. On completing his studies, he settled in Philadelphia and practiced there until his death a few years ago. It has always been strange to me why Lula and he did not marry. She finally married a Fiskite, Pete Landers.

Eugene and I played many a football game against Fisk. I recall especially the last one. I—the "black Indian" as the schools called me—was playing center. Gene, as we called Eugene, was playing fullback, Clarence Cabell was playing right half, and his brother Delos was playing left end. The schools had no stadiums then, nor were forward passes known. There was no science in the game. We only had two plays, bi-formation and tri-formation. They

2. For additional information on Richard Henry Boyd, see *Dictionary of American Negro Biography* (New York, 1982), 56–57.

were bone-cracking plays, especially the last one. On this particular occasion, we were running through and all over the Fisk team, when a Fisk partisan deliberately walked on the gridiron, over to where Clarence was standing, and struck his bare head with his gold-headed cane. Clarence fell as if axed. The blood gushed onto the ground. Of course, that ended the game. The presidents of the two schools got together and prevented prosecution for the unprovoked assault.[3]

I was glad to see the end of vacation, although I had had a good time. I was no longer an unknown, timid, backwoods youngster from the Indian Territory. At every social activity Lula had attended, I had been there as her guest and Eugene's (he worked on the Vanderbilt campus that vacation). We all attended the same church and Sunday school. All my friends and associates were members of the Baptist church, but in that I did not join them. This did not make any difference with them, not even Rev. Boyd. I suspect all of them thought I'd "come round" in time. I did everything in church that they did, except pray. I sang with them and was an active member of the Sunday school and in their club work and debating society. The big thing with me was to be known, and in this, at the commencement of the fall term, I had succeeded.

Strange, in my eighteenth year, I didn't care for girls. I thought I had plenty of time for that—until I met Miss Mollie Lee Parker, from the little rural village of Ged, ten miles out from Brownsville, Haywood County, Tennessee. She became my college sweetheart and was to become my wife.

A lot of other boys and girls entered school during this autumn term, and together with the return of the old students, the enrollment was considerably enlarged. We would have the same teachers, except for Mr. Walden, a graduate of Colgate, who was added to the faculty. I don't think any of us knew at the beginning of the term, not even the faculty, that this would be the last term for John Hope at the college.

I was entering upon another new era, a new, enlarging life. Although I was comparatively new at the school, the college spirit had seized and enveloped me. My popularity had grown by leaps and bounds, thanks to Lula,

3. During the author's early days in Tulsa, there was a photograph in his home of the Roger Williams University football team with him in the center of the picture, holding the ball. Unfortunately, the photograph disappeared many years ago.

the Compton girls, Eugene, and others. I had learned to be a good mixer. I had remembered Dad's lecture to me on education as being the ability to adjust oneself to situations, conditions, and societies. I think I had made good use of it.

At the close of the school year 1898, there came a hurried call to the president from an official of the L. & N. Railway Co. for three students to go to Key West, Florida, to serve as porters in the return of the 31st Michigan Regiment to their home state. The president called me into his office and asked me if I would like to make the trip. I was surprised at his asking one so young and a new arrival at the college, out of all the older men of experience on the campus. I did look much older than my years and had earned the reputation of being even-tempered and steady in my ways and habits. He must have known that I knew absolutely nothing about railroading, nothing about the duties of a porter.

While I was contemplating what my answer would be, many thoughts, puzzling ones, ran through my mind. My first thought was a very natural one: that he had asked the older students to go and they had refused because they had other jobs. It was the common custom then for the students, not only of Roger Williams, but of Fisk, Walden, and Meharry, to return to jobs every summer in Chicago or Milwaukee or Detroit or Cincinnati and work until the fall term of school. That may have been the reason. I didn't ask. Finally, I asked the president whether he had selected the other two. "No, you can choose them," he answered. So, after all, I may have been his choice, above all the rest of the student body, to make the trip. If that were so, I did not see then and cannot see to this day how he could have reached such a conclusion.

I finally told him that I'd make the trip and do the best I could. My first problem was to find some student who knew something about railroading, especially about the duties of a porter. I told the president to contact the official who had called him and tell him we would report the next day but one. Theophilus Bond, one of my closest friends, wanted to go "for the trip." He confessed that he knew a little, but not much, about the duties of a railroad porter. He had some advantages that I did not have. He was brought up on his father's farm, near Madison, Arkansas, not far from Forrest City. The elder Bond owned perhaps two thousand acres of rich farmland and planted half of it in cotton. He operated his own cotton gin and shipped hundreds of bales annually. So "Theo" was brought up around trains and railroads and depots. He knew several porters, and to a limited extent spoke their language. I selected him and another farmboy from western Tennessee, Clarence Bond, no kin to Theo. He had known Mollie Lee, my girlfriend, all his life. In fact, she had told me about Clarence and that he had some experience in portering. Both boys were my seniors by from two to three years.

There was one thing weighing very heavily on my mind. I had not heard from Dad for upwards of two weeks. He normally wrote every week. Before leaving for college, I had arranged for Margaret Hurd, a relative, to write his letters to me. She lived just across Massey Creek between Homer and my home, not more than a half mile away. Before leaving the college, I told Dr. Owen, who always spent his vacation on campus, that I intended to find a job in Chicago after the railroad job, and that as soon as I got settled in the Windy City, I'd send him my address so that he could have my mail forwarded to me.

At the appointed time, we showed up at the station, met the official, and received instructions on how to find the conductor in charge of the train that would take us to Key West. We found the train on a sideline, and the conductor was standing by it. After learning who we were, he ordered us to board, to dust and sweep out all the coaches, and not to leave the train without special permission from him. He explained that the train might leave at any time; that he himself did not know when that would be and would not know until possibly a quarter of an hour before leaving time; that all passenger and through freight trains going in opposite directions had the right of way over our train; that we would "dead-head" all the way to our destination; and that he had to get clearance at every station before proceeding to the next. I had entered another world about which I knew nothing, and wondered how many more new worlds I would encounter in this old world before I reached the end of my pilgrimage here.

Before we finished cleaning out the coaches, it was past one o'clock and we were very hungry. We had eaten a very light breakfast in the early morning. We conferred, raised a jackpot, and Theo went out to find food. He soon returned with a large basket bulging with fine fresh food. "Where did you get it," Clarence and I chorused. "At the station kitchen," he replied. I was at first surprised; but it soon dawned on me what had happened. Theophilus and his brother, Waverly, were as white as any Caucasian, and later, when their father, Scott Bond, visited the college, I could see why. The station officials must have thought Theo was a member of their race. Clarence and I would have been chased, if not booted, out of that kitchen. The brothers never referred to their color. One would think they hated it. The girls they went with were black or brown. In any case, our eating problem had been solved, for we did not know how long it would take us to dead-head down to Florida.

It was nearly night before the conductor got the go-ahead, and it took us until the next morning to reach Chattanooga. I was tired and a little crestfallen. I had been off and on the train a hundred times, it seemed, before morning. Now, to complicate matters and to make the remainder of the journey more hazardous and uncertain, the conductor became ill, so ill that at Chattanooga he had to leave the train.

Proceeding south, we didn't encounter any trouble until we reached Thomasville, Georgia, and we need not have then if I had used my head. I was acting in place of the disabled conductor, and must have wanted to know how it felt to be a conductor in charge of a whole train. So when the engineer pulled on to a sidetrack there, I went into the station and asked the agent if the train could make it to the next stop and sidetrack so as to get out of the way for northbound traffic.

"Where is your conductor, nigar?" he snorted.

"He got sick at Chattanooga," I replied.

"I don't give a white man's instructions to a damn nigar," he exploded. "Send the engineer or brakeman here."

"The brakeman is colored," I volunteered.

"Well, get to hell out of here and send the engineer or I'll kick you out of here," he threatened.

The engineer came, got the orders, and we proceeded. Afterward, I sent Theo for instructions and we had no further trouble.

On our return trip, I got back at that agent in a very satisfactory way. I'd told the soldiers of my experience before reaching Thomasville, and they told me to let them know when we reached the town. As agreed, I did let them know. When the train pulled onto a sidetrack, I got off, followed by more than half of the regiment, and went directly to the station for orders or information about schedules of trains traveling in the opposite direction. When I propounded practically the same questions that I asked on the trip south and he looked up to see that I was the same upstart, he almost lunged through the window, reaching out to grab at my throat. The blood almost drained from his face as one of the soldiers standing immediately behind me grabbed his outstretched hand, twisted it with an oath, and told the agent to answer my civil questions. The agent's face was ashen and he trembled with fear. Stammering, he answered all of my questions, some of them very foolish ones, I now think. Those soldiers, with all their pent-up energy, would have done anything to that agent with the least encouragement from me.

In time, we discharged the last contingent at Jackson, Michigan. It was a long, delayed, wearisome trip. We were itching all over and didn't know why until we retired to our rooms. We were covered with cooties. The sight scared me. We burned all of our clothes, took hot baths, and slept naked that night. The next morning we sent a servant to a dry goods store to purchase some makeshift clothes to wear on the street. Then we went out and bought new suits, got haircuts, returned to the hotel, bathed again, and put on our suits.

The following morning we left for Chicago. We came into the city at the old Polk Street depot. We had heard about Mother Gray from the students at the college, and so we took a cab and went directly to her apartment, 2436 South Dearborn Street. This was the place where most of the students stopped every summer when they went north to find work. She was a mother to all of them. It was said that she knew more college students than any other person in Chicago. I recall that the first thing I did after we secured rooms was to write Dad, giving him my new address, and to Dr. Owen, asking him to forward all my mail to my new address.

We retired early that night, and the next morning Clarence and I started looking for work (Theo had decided to go home). Mother Gray told us where to look: "Go to Koohlsaat's Restaurant over at 2346 Michigan Boulevard and make application for a dinner job. I'm sure you can get one. That will sustain you until you can get a better one."

Judge Koohlsaat had a chain of restaurants all over the city. I knew nothing about cafe work but had confidence that I could catch on before I was discharged. We got there early and went to the chief waiter. I told him the truth, that I was a college boy, knew nothing about waiting tables, but was willing to learn and was not afraid of work. He was used to college students and was sympathetic. He first put me to washing dishes, and a few days later he transferred me to the employees' room, where Clarence waited on him and the other top employees. The job was a cinch. It paid seven dollars a week, which was not bad for washing dishes for one meal a day, at the noon hour. I was resourceful. I went in about ten every morning and piddled around until noon. In that way I could eat my breakfast there and, before leaving at four, have my supper as well, hence getting all my meals free. Clarence and I paid $2.50 for our room. We washed and ironed our own clothes. Working Sundays (that was our heaviest day), we did not go to Sunday school or to church except on very rare occasions.

One morning, I went to work early and ran across a streak of good luck. Just off 24th on State Street was a very large secondhand furniture store. Standing in front of the store was a Jewish lady, who beckoned me. She wanted to know if I had any experience in polishing stoves. I lied beautifully and told her I had followed the business as a trade. She invited me into the store and told me to look over the stock and tell her what would be my price for doing the job. After counting the stoves and pretending to do some figuring, I finally told her I would do the job for fifty dollars, provided she would furnish the material. She almost went up into the air and, gesticulating, said it was entirely too much. With an air of superiority, I told her: "Not one cent less. I'll admit you might get an inexperienced jobber, who will botch it; but I've offered you the best price." She fumed but finally agreed to the price and asked when I could start. I told her the following morning.

I rushed through the dinner meal that day, ate a hurried supper, and rushed back to my room. I confided to Mother Gray that I knew absolutely nothing about polishing stoves. In fact, I'd never seen polish or brush. Good old Mother Gray. That wasn't the first time a college student had carried his troubles to her. From long years of experience there was very little she did not know. In confiding in her, I was desperate. That fifty bucks loomed large in my mind. She answered, with a twinkle in her alert brown eyes, "I know just the man to save you. He lives in the next block. I'll send for him."

The man came. I told him about the job, the sizes and number of stoves. I was careful not to tell him that I knew nothing about polishing stoves, but I did tell him the contract price, and about my other job and the amount of time I'd be able to give the second one. He agreed to work through to the finish for twenty-five dollars, half of the contract price.

About seven-thirty the next morning, my assistant and I were on the job. I was all eyes. I had two people to fool now, the proprietress and my helper.

I proceeded to move the stoves and told him to arrange the materials and get them ready. Mother Gray had given me some pointers on the preparation of the polish, about the use of the brushes and clean wet and dry rags or cloths, so as to polish the stoves evenly—that is, apply the same amount of polish all over the stove, after any rust was removed from the surface. We worked through until eleven o'clock, and I announced to the lady that I'd leave my helper in charge, that I had another job, and that I'd return about midafternoon. When she objected, I told her that I thought she wanted the work done quickly, and that was why I had employed the helper; that there was nothing in my contract that prevented me from doing this. She then consented, and I rushed off to my other job.

When I returned, there was not much left to be done. We would finish the next morning before it was time for me to go on to the restaurant. I felt elated—I was a contractor. I was certain that neither suspected that I did not know the job. I had made no mistakes that would reveal my ignorance. When we finished, the job appeared to be a first-class one. The lady hated to pay me the full amount, and she tried to find some excuse. She even asked if I was of age. To cut short the argument, I told her I'd be twenty-two my next birthday.

Later on in the summer, I had some experiences quite the opposite to the one just related. I was not making as much money as I thought I should, and took to watching the "wanted" columns of all the papers. I saw an ad one morning where "a waiter of experience" was wanted to serve dinner meals in a private dining room. It stated that he must be neat and intelligent, no references necessary. The place was on Michigan. I told my employer about the opening, that I was going to apply, and if I was successful, I would not return. He wished me luck and told me if I was unsuccessful and wanted to come back, I could do so and he would find a place for me.

I put on my best clothes and went to apply for the job. It was in a beautiful two-story brick building. There were wide swinging doors at every entrance. The dining room was spacious and beautiful, like a dream. Off the dining room was the kitchen, separated by swinging doors. A curtain separated the dining room from the employer's office. I was admitted to the office through a side entrance. I gave my name and stated I had come in answer to the ad. The lady looked me over dubiously, told me what the job paid, and said if I wanted it she would take me on. I accepted, and she had a helper show me where to go and what to do to get ready for work.

It was noon, guests and diners were arriving, and some were already seated at tables waiting to be served. Meals were served family style. All one had to do was to carry food from the kitchen into the dining room and put it on the table. There were two other waiters, old and experienced. They glided with grace and charm out of the kitchen through the swinging doors, using their shoulders, with their trays resting in the palms of their hands. I followed the second waiter, and just as I cleared one door, the other one swung inward against me and my tray, pushing me into the dining room with such force and violence that the tray went in one direction and I in another, spilling the food over the greater part of the dining room and on guests and tables. I fell at last prostrate upon the floor.

As I was rising, I saw the red and chagrined face of my employer. She apologized profusely to her guests and diners, yanked me by the tail of my coat into her office, and shouted, "You clumsy ———." I think she said "clown." I asked her if she didn't think she owed me my dinner, and she answered, "No, emphatically no," biting her lips in anger.

I refused to return to the other restaurant. I've all my life trained myself never to retrace my steps, never to go backward. I returned to my room earlier than usual, and Mother Gray met me with concern on her face. "What's the matter," she asked.

"Nothing at all, Mother," I answered. "I'm going to change jobs. I'm going to wait table at the Hyde Park Hotel. One of my mother's cousins, Alexander Hughes Shoals, is headwaiter there and he wants me there with him." My answer was half truthful. Shoals *was* my mother's cousin and had been headwaiter there ever since his freshman year at Roger Williams. The owner held that job open for him every summer. He had two more years of college, and then he would study medicine at Meharry. (He would move to Watonga, Oklahoma, after graduation and practice there until his death.) He had never, however, asked me to work at the hotel. He did not even know I was in Chicago.

I did not tell Mother Gray about my temporary setback. That is the way I looked at it, merely temporary. Nor did I mention it to Clarence when he came in from work. Meanwhile, I went to my room to think. I knew A. H., as I called Shoals, would take me on. I had to debate the matter in my mind. I wanted to be independent, to make it on my own. I thought about going home for the rest of my vacation. I was disturbed about Dad, as I had not yet heard from him. But the season was more than half gone.

With my door closed, I lay on the bed looking at the ceiling for a long time in contemplation. I didn't have enough money to go home. I had a very decent bank account in Nashville, but I practiced the habit of forgetting about it, and had no intention of disturbing it. Too, Dad had sent me spending money regularly, as well as school expenses. After thinking hard for a while, I decided not to go home unless Dad didn't write me. I was beginning to think something was wrong at home. I finally decided that if I heard from Dad, I would go to the Hyde Park Hotel and work with A. H. I became calm, and in some strange way the thought of the debacle at the private rooming house, with me sprawled upon that nice, clean floor, and the guests spattered with food, gave rise to a hearty, healthy laugh. If my pride had been hurt, the shame had left me. I recalled Dad saying, "Never take yourself too seriously." Good old Dad, always wise as an owl. Some of the many things he said to me from time to time have followed me, giving me sanity, when needed, in an emergency.

When Clarence came in that evening, later than usual, Mother Gray and I were sitting on the front porch talking quietly. Mother had noticed the apparent change in me between the time I returned in the early afternoon in a mood of despondency, to one of gaiety as I joined her on the porch. She must have felt so relieved that she did not mention it to Clarence, who was quite sure I was more merry and lighthearted than in all the months he had known me. I myself could not account for the strange metamorphosis in me.

I remember clearly the gist of our conversation when Clarence arrived. We were talking about health, sickness, medicines, doctors, and nurses. Among other things, I asked Mother Gray if she had ever been sick. "Once," she answered. "Two years ago. I was very sick and didn't think I would make it. But I had the best doctor in the city, if not in the entire state, and he made me well; and since then I have felt better than I had ever before." She said her physician was Daniel H. Williams, and when I asked her whether he was white or colored, she grunted impatiently, evidently surprised that I did not know the man. "He is a great physician and surgeon, the first I know anything about to operate successfully on the human heart. All the other doctors in the city rely on him for medical advice." I was startled. Then, she proceeded to tell me about this "great man," as she constantly referred to him: that he had lived in Chicago for a long time, that he was a graduate of Northwestern in Evanston; about President Cleveland placing him over the

Freedmen's Hospital in Washington; and about his Provident Hospital there in Chicago.

"Do you see that hospital just across the street?" she asked me. I answered in the affirmative. "Well, it is a part of Northwestern University, and the doctor used to be a part of it until he opened his own office and became so busy elsewhere. Now he rarely comes there, except when he is called in for consultation. And when he does, he invariably runs across the street to see me," she concluded proudly. Later that summer, I had the rare privilege of meeting the doctor at Mother's. He was a very positive yet simple and unassuming man. He clipped his words as if he were stingy with them.[4]

The mailman came early the next morning, bringing three letters for me from Dad, the first time in weeks. Two of them were from Nashville; they had been forwarded from the college. The other was from Homer, my home post office. Near noon, just before I was preparing to leave for the South Side, a fat registered letter arrived. I read the first letters slowly, enjoying every word. They all contained advice, encouragement, and inspiration. I could read between the lines a longing to see me, but not a word was spelled out to that effect. On the contrary, Dad told me to study hard, work hard, and apply myself diligently, but not to forget to play and have good clean happy fun. The registered letter contained only a few words. Money was in it, a goodly amount. He said that he figured I did not need the money, but that it would not hurt to have it, just in case; that he knew I'd put it away in the bank. He was right, of course. Two days later, I sent it to Nashville, with my bankbook.

Now I felt strong, resolute, and determined, ready for and equal to any eventuality. Dad's strong hand had reached a long distance across plains, prairies, forests, farms, and rivers, to touch me with new life and steady reassurance. Maybe that was why on the previous evening lying on my bed I had experienced that calm. I sometimes believe that the pilgrim does, unaware, have an angel's presence guiding him along paths where he fears no evil, although he is enclosed by worldly forces that would devour him, were it not for this Presence. And so, by midevening, I was at the Hyde Park Hotel with A. H., ready to go to work.

---

4. For more on Williams, see Helen Buckler, *Dr. Dan: Pioneer in American Surgery* (Boston, 1954).

A. H. put me in the Masters' dining room to "break me in." He knew I was as green as a gourd at waiting tables in a big hotel dining room. Here, I could wait upon the officers and executives until I caught on. But I had been there not more than three days when there came in for dinner a mighty rush of guests and patrons. This was unexpected. Alex was caught shorthanded, and in his excitement he called me into the main dining room to take orders. He directed me to a table where sat five distinguished people, among them a man older than the others, who looked very much like college people. Timidly and with many misgivings, I approached the table. I started with the elderly gentleman. I attempted to take his full order and the others' at the same time. I noticed that he looked up at me inquiringly, but he said nothing. Into the kitchen I went, rather awkwardly I'm sure, to give my orders to the cooks (there were two of them). As I entered, about six waiters had preceded me. There they stood, twirling their trays dexterously above their heads, cracking jokes, and carrying on a running conversation. I became so excited that I almost forgot my own name. I did not remember a single order. I went to the door and looked for my cousin but didn't see him.

There was nothing for me to do but go back to the table. I approached it with humility, apologized to the senior member of the company, and told him I'd have to take their orders again. He looked fatherly, but the others were snickering. He glanced at them reprovingly and proceeded to give me his order again. Then he said to me in a fatherly voice, "Take one order at a time." With his kindly help, I finally got through. Before leaving, the elderly gentleman tarried at the table and beckoned me. I approached, somewhat reassured. He put a bill in my hand and said as he was leaving, "I want you to serve me every time I eat here." He said it with such conviction that I was sure he meant it.

He returned three times before the summer vacation was over. On the very next trip to the hotel, he said, "I'm Dr. William Rainey Harper, president of the University of Chicago, and you are a student, I know. I've been around them all my adult life." I told him I was a student and gave the name of the school I was attending; I added that I was from the Indian Territory. That fact seemed to intrigue him, and he asked me a few more questions, especially about the Indians.

Dr. Harper returned twice more, and each time I had to serve him and those who came with him. He carried on an incessant conversation. He talked about his hobbies, the ancient languages. He said, "If you ever hope to become proficient in them, visit the places of their beginning and study them there at the feet of the native scholars. You get more than the dead tongues, and imbibe their spirits."

My cousin Alex didn't know who the man was that took up so much of my time, until the manager told him. Neither the proprietor nor Alex guessed that I knew who the scholarly gentleman was. So when Alex asked me if I knew him, and I told him, he was greatly surprised. Then I told him, "Dr. Harper missed an important engagement when I served him and his company that first time, but he said he blamed you and not me."

I've related somewhat in detail my meeting with Dr. Harper because my contacts with the great and near great through the years have contributed immeasurably to what Booker T. Washington called "My Larger Education." My associations, however slight, tended to produce in me understanding far beyond that provided by books and texts. And as long as this is the experience of man in general, then the two schools of thought that raise the question, "Which is of more value in education, heredity or environment," will debate it to the end of time.

Personally, I think one complements the other; that in the broadest, most fundamental sense, education is relative. Its avenues leading to the portals of knowledge are sometimes very dim and indistinct. Is knowledge spiritual, with things physical a by-product? Is it subjective and its by-products objective? Or does it have roots in the subconscious mind to bud and flower into the conscious mind, wide awake and alert? Which, if either, comes first? If the invisible man is the father of it all, then the paths spawning, nurturing, and feeding man's knowledge may be invisible. These questions contain the riddle of life. I wonder if Shakespeare had some such thought in mind when he exclaimed, "One touch of nature makes the whole world kin." Or Solomon when he observed, "There is nothing new under the sun." Who can answer these questions but the First Great Cause, Himself?

Before the end of the vacation and time to return to college, my wages, tips, and little odd jobs on the side netted me a sizable roll. I was anxious to make a good showing financially so that I could report, especially to Dad, how well I had done in what was at first a strange new field of endeavor.

I buckled down to my studies and tackled my subjects with a new zeal. About all of the old students had returned or were soon to arrive. There were a few new faces. Mollie was the first person I saw, at breakfast the morning after my arrival, and I waved to her a cheery greeting. Her response showed that she had welcomed my letters during the summer.

My subjects were heavier than the last term. I had had my beginner in Latin and White's beginner in Greek, the alphabets. Now it was Caesar's *Commentaries* and Xenophon's *Anabasis*, Wentworth's algebra, science, rhetoric, the ever-present Bible, etc. Then, there was football training. We would play three out-of-town games.

There were two distinct unsolicited honors that came to me that fall. I was placed on the editorial staff of our college paper, the *Rogerana*, to write under the title "Among the Colleges," and was elected president of the Young Men's Christian Association set up by the national secretary, W. A. Hunton. Under my administration the organization grew to include nearly all of the male students on the campus. I contacted nearly all the pastors of the city and sent them Sunday-school teachers from the organization.

The whole term of school was pleasant and I enjoyed every minute of it, although I worked harder than I had ever worked before on my lessons, in my practice on the football team, and in all my extra activities, including the social functions I attended both at college and in the city. As commencement neared, there were confronting me two major changes: John Hope would sever his connection with the school to accept a similar position at Atlanta Baptist College; and I would not return to Chicago.

Just before the close of school, there came a call to the president from the owner of the Fountain Springs Hotel at Waukesha, Wisconsin, asking him to send ten college students to work as waiters and bellboys during the summer vacation. A certain upperclassman was in the office of the president when the call came in and readily understood the message. He volunteered to get a bunch together and take them up there. With commencement exercises and a thousand and one other pressing duties to face, the president, although he knew this student was unstable and fickle, didn't give it much thought, and readily assented.

I was the first student this upperclassman told about the job. He painted a rosy picture of the trip and about the prospective job. He said it was a virgin field, business was the very best, and that there was more money to be made there than at the Plankington Hotel in Milwaukee. I told him I had a job for the vacation months, but that his seemed the more lucrative, and if I could see Alex and square things with him, I'd accept the offer. Alex and this upperclassman were classmates.

"——— is fickle and unreliable and will take advantage of his best friends," Alex told me. "You will not get along with him; but you must have your own experience. If he lets you out, your job will be ready for you," he concluded.

As Alex predicted, his classmate started out crooked. He told us the owner was paying so much, and to save time he had made arrangements for the proprietor to pay our money to him, and he would give it to us. The owner, knowing we were all college students from the same school, thought nothing about it. I had been forewarned and knew at once what was being done. When ——— doled out to us the amount he said we were getting, I immediately went to the proprietor and asked him what salary we were getting. He told me it was three dollars more than ——— had paid us. When we faced our straw boss, he at first pretended anger. But when we began to read the riot act to him, he cooled off and forked out the difference. All of us quit the job without notice. We made no complaint to the hotelkeeper, but he evidently knew why we had quit.

I worked on in Waukesha, at a restaurant, until the following Monday. There were only three colored families at that time in the little town of upward of 8,000. I read in the papers about the meeting of the national body of the Elks the following day in Milwaukee, and I decided to make it. Luck was with me. The three days and nights I worked there waiting tables and serving mixed drinks at the big banquet, I made, in salary and tips (mostly tips), better than three hundred dollars. I never before served an organization or gathering where its members were as liberal or as free with their money.

I returned to Chicago by boat, leisurely steaming by Racine. I got a berth, slept most of the night, and disembarked rested and fresh. I went straight to Mother's, engaged a room, picked up a letter from Dad (I had in a previous letter instructed him to send my mail there), and went downtown to send my money, the most of it, to my bank in Nashville. True to my convictions, I did not contact Alex for a job, but worked here and there for the remainder of the summer at odd jobs, many different kinds, and returned to college a few days before the beginning of the fall term.

Mollie did not return to the college. Her father, Harry Parker, had taken sick and died on December 8, 1899, leaving her to look after the farm and livestock and the younger children, Lucy, Lena, Edmond, and Alberta. It was the end of college for her. The next year she entered Lucy in the college and continued looking after the home and the younger children, teaching at a rural school at Ged.

I enjoyed the first half of that school year. My work was heavier and more extensive, but pleasant and very agreeable, especially my literary effort writing "Among the Colleges." There was fun in that, doing research work, reading so many periodicals, catalogs, and so forth. Then letters from home and Dad began to fall off, getting more irregular. I couldn't account for it. I'd write him and Margaret, the cousin who did all of his correspondence. I was sure she got my letters addressed directly to her and those I wrote Dad. The scant mail I did receive from her was short—too short—and guarded. She evaded my inquiries, not like her at all.

I started to think of going home as the weeks dragged on. Elwood was my only consolation, and I turned to him. He treated the matter lightly, saying "You know how busy he must be—you are away, and the older boys having married off." I wanted to believe, and that satisfied me, for a while; but not for long. I missed Dad's always-sane advice and words of inspiration and consolation. I knew I was going home after the final exams, without waiting for commencement.

On the day of the last examination, I got a terse note from my brother Tom. It simply said, "Papa is not doing so good. I'd come home, if I were you, for a while." I knew too well that Dad was more ill than my brother's note indicated. I had had a clear and definite premonition of my old pal's indisposition, and had been trying to do my college work and steel myself, at the same time, for what I considered the approaching inevitability. I considered that although his mien and manner had always been those of the soldier, he was no longer a young man: he would be eighty years of age the next month (June 10, 1900). Though the years had been few since he bade me goodbye as I boarded the train at Pauls Valley, I had wished and prayed many times that I could remember him always as he appeared then, walking straight and proud, with his head erect. Alas, that vision was forever to be denied me.

I started feverishly to pack my belongings, and gave Elwood money to proceed to the station immediately and purchase a through ticket to Davis, Indian Territory. I encountered every conceivable delay en route and spent almost three days and nights before I reached my destination. At Davis, I had the presence of mind to go first to Dr. Walker's office. Fortunately, he was just about to leave for my home. We made the distance to Hennepin, fifteen miles, in an hour. With his permission, I asked Dr. Morton to accompany us the remaining mile and a half to my home. Dr. Walker told me he had been treating Dad for almost a year, since the doctor returned from the hospital at Fort Worth. He said Dad had had the best of care, including specialists from Kansas City, Missouri, for consultation; that Dad had dropsy, now chronic. He had had several "taps"—that is, water drawn from his body—but the disease could not be arrested. The water was now near his heart, and it was only a question of time before the end.

Knowing Dad as I did, I understood clearly the reason for the irregularity of his letters to me. He knew he couldn't live and had made up his mind not to disturb me, as he afterwards put it, in my pursuit of an education. He had Margaret "buffaloed" into not notifying me about his condition.

The sun had set when we reached home, and I entered the sickroom to find a profusion of wildflowers banked all around and up on the dresser, giving off sweet odors. The lamps and lantern had just been lighted, and it was very warm. My sister Hattie was seated by Dad's bed, fanning him gently. My baby sister Lydia came in with a bucket of cool water from the well. Dad looked up at me without surprise and forced a sickly smile through his bloated countenance as he reached with his hand to shake mine. "I knew you were coming," he said in a matter-of-fact way. I steeled myself and fought back a tear as my sister arose from the chair and handed me the fan. As I sat down I said, rather hoarsely, "Yes, Dad, you knew I was coming home."

I made brave conversation for a short time and then arose, saying, "The doctors want to go to work." Fisher and Lydia had already gone out of doors, and my sister Hattie and I followed, to be joined later by my brother David, who was named for Dad. We all sat on the porch, I with my legs up on the railing, in deep silence as the dusk gathered. The silence was more expressive than words. As my thoughts dwelt upon the prostrate figure upon the bed, the philosophy of the words of "Wonderful One Hoss Shay" by Oliver Wendell Holmes flooded my inner self with its real meaning.

"We have lots to talk about, you and I," Dad began as I resumed my seat at his bedside. "And while we talk and wait for the end," he continued, "neither of us must think of the intervening period as a 'vigil' or a 'watch,' as vultures do as they soar above an expiring animal carcass, but as a period within which to cram joyous recollections, the good things received and enjoyed by a united family never separated, except by temporary deaths. I've lived a good, full, rich life, filled to overflowing. I've served my country in peace and in war. I had the best wife that ever lived, and the children she bore me have never been arrested or accused of crime. So, while you are here for this brief spell, let it not be marred by vulgar fear that should only lurk in evil minds. I have but one burning wish and that is that I may pass soon enough not to interrupt or disturb your school schedule."

At first I wanted to say that I cared nothing about returning to school, but he had spoken with such calm conviction and assurance that I thought better of it. Everything about him, his voice and that inner peace that showed in the expression on his face, told me that the final rendezvous with death was his to face alone with his God and was too sacred for the intrusion of strangers, even me, his son and pal. And so to the end, which came on the 10th day of August, we talked about many past experiences we had had together. I recalled the time when I stole Old Button and rode off into the setting sun to get lost, and the anxiety I caused the family before I was found, and the whipping I got from Mother; about the time we went to Guthrie, and our meeting the territorial governor; about our trip to Nocona, then to No Man's Land, and the panther he killed en route, and how scared I was; and dozens of other times and common experiences we shared. But most of all, the things he taught me.

One day when Dad appeared to be better, I rode out to the north ranch. I didn't know the place, four years had wrought such a change. Brother Tom was there, but the big manmade lake, the pasture, feedlots, outer bunks, everything, looked so different from when I had last seen them. I had talked no business with Dad. So I asked Tom about the changes that had taken place. He said that foot-and-mouth disease had visited the ranch, and all the ranches in the southern part of the Territory, and had killed thousands of cattle, and that every species of the botfly had also taken a heavy toll. He said that Dad had lost all interest in business and that the people, blacks free before the Civil War and the freedmen especially, had become scared and discouraged and didn't know what to do since Dad was unable to advise them. In fact, since the lands were soon to be allotted in severalty, they were just about to be stampeded; they were coming into a new age and were completely lost.

I vividly recall that Dad had foreseen such a state of affairs and was prepared to help these people allot their lands on those he had fenced during the time the lands were held in common, and to rent or buy from them, thus preserving the traditional ownership of the lands.

When I returned home that evening, I was sure that Dad would ask me about my trip, but he said nary a word about it, although he must have known where I had been and the discouragement I had encountered. He just lay there and talked on as before, saying nothing about "the things of this world." As I listened, and noticed his eyes and quiet face, I saw in him a greatness I have not since seen in any other human being. The life he had tried to live, his example, showed a fruition in this, his supreme moment. Those words of the Holy Bible, "Man shall not live by bread alone," and "What shall it profit a man if he gains . . ." struck me with such impact that I felt ashamed thinking of the "things of this world." He seemed confident that none of his children would ever bring disgrace and shame upon his name, and that was a sufficient reward for him; he had left them a legacy worth more than money, stocks and bonds, and cattle upon a thousand hills.

He had talked himself out, and I was alone with him when the end came, his swollen hand in mine. He just slipped away, like a tired old man, and he was buried beside his helpmeet in the presence of men and women of every race. The irony is that neither their children nor anyone else knows today where they lie. Like thousands of others interred in the Indian Territory before lands were allotted in severalty and deeds issued to allottees, they were buried on lands held in common, and there was no law to protect and make sacred the burial grounds. Their last resting places have long since been desecrated by the plowshares and the reapers of farmers and landlords unmindful of their presence.

After the burial and ceremonies, I returned home to the house empty of the presence of the man who had been my inspiration and lord since the death of Mother. For a few days I lingered about the place, sometimes halting between conflicting opinions and sentiments. The latter took me up to old Massey Creek one day, to the still-familiar swimming hole where Mother used to fish and where the community boys and I used to swim. There still stood the same old giant oak tree with some of her large limbs extending out above the water. As I sat upon the bank, I remembered what a thrill it was to climb that tree and crawl along these branches and dive beneath the blue water; but I soon aroused myself from such a state. It was clear to me what Dad would have me do were he present in the flesh. There was business to be looked to, financial adjustments to be made. After that, it was back to college.

. I returned to Roger Williams a few days before the fall term began, and piddled about the campus, went out to Colonel Stokes's and down to the publishing house, until the opening. I found in the Boyd household a second home, with the usual fatherly advice and care from Dr. Boyd and the understanding sisterly companionship of Lula, but I cannot truthfully say that school was the same as it had been. I now and then experienced a restlessness that was quite foreign to me. Was it because I felt the absence of my mentor, John Hope, to whom I went more than once with personal problems? Or the absence of Mollie, who even then had become an integral part of my existence? I had already discovered in her certain qualities that uplifted me. Or was it the loss of Dad, who was just about my entire world? Or was it all of these things?

I spent the Christmas holidays at Knoxville College as a YMCA delegate from my school, and took part with W. A. Hunton and Rev. Moorland in the organization of a College YMCA. There is a world of difference between the organization then and now. Then it was almost purely a religious concern, its base of activity evangelical. Now it has been broadened to include the whole man. I enjoyed the trip, and it gave an impetus to the work in Nashville after I returned and made my report.

After the examinations, a few days before the 1901 term of school, I made a trip to Ged to see Mollie. She met me at Brownsville. Clarence Bond lived near there, in Haywood County, and so he went with me, together with Lucy. I had a glorious visit, which was all too short. After I saw my future wife in action, managing the home, looking after the livestock, and overseeing the farm, there was no uncertainty about the kind of wife I wanted.

I had to hurry on to Chicago to find a job for the summer. I did not try the hotels, as it was never my custom to backtrack. I found one at Armour Packing House, in the stockyards. I went in on a strike, which proved to be, at first, very exciting. The union was up and almost at arms. I was taunted, called a "scab," and stones were cast at me, but I stuck to the job. After a few days the excitement was over and I settled down to work for the rest of the summer in the midst of ten thousand or more employees of every nationality under the sun. I found myself working all day side by side with men who could not speak or understand a word of English, nor could I understand their languages. Often we had to swing a large truck of fresh meat from the rails and move it into a chilling room. It was a heavy load, and toward the noon hour, when hunger pains ran through the stomach and tempers got on edge, the foreigner would curse at me in his language and I'd curse at him in English, and neither understood the other.

There was one, though, who never tired or lost his temper. He was the embodiment of fun and goodwill. Strong as an ox, he must have weighed more than two hundred pounds. I guess he was a Swede. He and I became good friends, and he always assumed the heavier part of the work. Sometimes we lifted the green hides of the carcasses from the slaughterhouse, loaded them on flat trucks, and carted them into the drying shed; and he always grabbed the weightier part of the load.

When we carted cooked hamburger to the shipping department, we would, if the many overseers were not looking, steal one and put it in our pocket, under our white robe, to eat with our lunch. I very distinctly recall an episode at this time that almost dissuaded me from further theft. An inspector condemned a whole load of this meat and had it unloaded. I remember this so well, I think, because the inspector was a young colored man. He had a long, sharp, pointed wooden instrument that he ran through the meat, withdrawing it, and then smelling it. That was all he did.

There were advantages in working at Armour's that I had not had before in this city. I could attend church and Sunday school, and become acquainted with Oscar DePriest and Roscoe Conkling Simmons, a near relative of Booker Washington's first wife. I also became acquainted with Rev. Thomas, who was pastor of Mount Olivet Baptist Church at 28th and Armour, and his family. I met and mingled with many more Negroes and really enjoyed myself at different social and religious functions during the vacation season.

On the 6th day of September, while I was working at the stockyard, the news was flashed over the wire that President McKinley had been shot in the stomach by an anarchist, Leon Czolgosz, while speaking at a public reception in the Temple of Music in Buffalo, New York. He lingered, and died on the 14th. On the day of his burial at Canton, Ohio, I became a part of an unforgettable experience. It was high noon, and there began the sound of many shrill whistles signaling the lowering of the body of the president into his grave. At that very moment every worker in the stockyards stood erect with head bowed for a full minute in honor of William McKinley, the 25th president of the United States of America. Thousands of men who could neither speak nor understand English understood perfectly the meaning of it all and stood obediently with those who could. This action struck me as more than a phenomenon; it was nothing short of a miracle.

Just after I arrived at the station in Nashville and was proceeding along the streets, my body suddenly grew taut and excruciating pains pierced every part of me. I fell upon the street, unable to move a muscle and in great misery. Someone, assisted by others, lifted me into a conveyance of some sort and carried me out to the college. I was in such pain that I could not bear to be touched by quilt, blanket, or spread. Dr. Hill was brought over from Meharry, and the first thing he did was to place me in a great vat of hot water, stirred with ground mustard seed, and then cover me up for several hours. By morning every pain had left my body and I was able to take a bath. The doctor said that I had had an attack of inflammatory rheumatism brought on from the many temperatures I had encountered while working in the packing plant.

When school opened, I had a difficult time applying myself. I was low in spirit, and it seemed that nothing could lift me up. My friend Cobb became uneasy but kept it to himself. While out on the football field trying to practice, I could not remember the signals. The coach was puzzled by my lack of attention and concentration. My young white friend Sylvester Mullens, a student at Vanderbilt and the son of J. P. Mullens of Ardmore, formerly attorney for the Chickasaw freedmen, often came over to help placate me and to try to get me to become again the "Buck" that he used to know; but he failed to stir me.

I came to the conclusion that I needed a change; to get away from Roger Williams University and into new scenes and surroundings. I had in mind Atlanta Baptist College, where my friend John Hope was teaching. I wrote him telling him of my feelings of letdown and discouragement, and what I had in mind. He answered my letter at once, but he was careful not to tell me to do it. I could understand why. The two schools were sister schools under the same general board. He said he could not advise me, that I'd have to follow my own mind, and do what I thought best. Then, I wrote Mollie that I was changing schools, that I was going to Atlanta Baptist College in Atlanta, and would write her from there.

Here, I must set down a fact that I've always been ashamed of. It was an unmanly thing to do. I talked with the president, Dr. Guernsey, about my changing schools, and told him a lie. I gave as the reason for my change that I had become dissatisfied over the way the school was being operated, and when he asked me to pinpoint the fault, I'm afraid I failed dismally. I added another lie, that I was not the only one dissatisfied; that others were complaining of the discrimination shown in favor of the upperclassmen. He pointed out convincingly that the thing complained of existed in all colleges. He finally agreed that I should go, but refused to give me a letter to Dr. Sales, the president of the sister college. President Guernsey and Roger Williams had been exceptionally good to me. I have never been able to explain why I told such a needless lie. Had I told the truth, he would have gladly given me the letter I asked for.

5

ATLANTA BAPTIST COLLEGE

I had written Professor Hope my arrival time in Atlanta, and he had a student meet the train and take me to his house. I was glad to see him and Mrs. Hope. Later he took me over to the college and introduced me to President Sales. He had Zack Hubert, who worked in his office and who afterwards became president of Langston College, find me a place to sleep for the night. The next morning I went down to the dining room for breakfast, and among all those students and members of the faculty, I did not know a soul. I, indeed, was a stranger in a strange land and certainly did not feel at home. However, all were friendly enough.

Later that the day, I was abruptly assigned to classes. The assignments did not suit me, but it was all my fault, as I was quick to realize. I had carried no grades, nor had I the common sense to have had them sent on ahead with a written application. I was lucky to even be admitted in the middle of the term. I think Professor Hope had something to do with it, although I never asked him and he would certainly not volunteer the information. My lies, stupidity, and mulishness had overtaken me, and I had no one to blame but myself. I had no intention, however, of sulking or showing discontent. I would take my medicine like a good trouper and not complain. I made friends easily and was soon knocking the ball into every part of the field. Professor Hope saw me often after classes, and gave me fatherly advice and encouragement. My classmates were quick to notice the friendship between us, and they liked it. He was a native Georgian; and having graduated from Brown and having taught school for four years at Roger Williams, he was considered a home boy having made good abroad. He was, therefore, very popular, and it was good to have him in my corner.

Aside from Professor Hope, I think the teacher who made the greatest and most lasting impression upon me was Professor Waldo B. Truesdale, a young man barely in his thirties. He was a graduate of Harvard University and was my science teacher. He was the very symbol of originality in his thinking and in the manner of approach to problems. For that period, I think he brought a new method of teaching his subjects to the ordinary college. He used the lecture system, the textbook, and demonstration that resulted in the use of notes, and problems to be solved. In teaching in botany the circulatory system of the plant, how its tiny root hairs gathered water and food from the soil, and the process of their conversion into food, for instance, he gave one the impression that he was dealing not only with these forms of life, but with human beings as well. Friday evenings, with food knapsacks on their backs and appropriate tools, he and his geology class would trek up to Kennesaw Mountain and study the nature and ages of rocks. He could decipher, explore, and demonstrate their secrets hidden for a billion years.

There were other fine and able teachers at ABC besides Professors Hope and Truesdale. Possibly they were just a little more modern and progressive than those of her sister school. Without doubt, she has produced more great educators, men who have become presidents of other Negro colleges, than any other school created for Negroes following the close of the Civil War. To name a few, Mordecai Johnson, president of Howard University; John W. Davis, former president of West Virginia State College; B. B. Dansby, former president of Jackson College and, incidentally, a former classmate of mine; Ben Hubert, former president of Georgia State College; and Z. T. Hubert, former president of Langston College. To attempt to name its graduates who became principals of high schools would be impossible. Of the twelve children of the elder Zack Hubert and his wife, all the boys—nine, I believe—did their undergraduate work at ABC before going on to graduate work in other great colleges and universities of the North and East. This feat is the more remarkable in view of the fact that their parents were unlettered dirt farmers. John W. was one of my teachers at ABC and afterwards was principal of the Savannah High School for upwards of forty years.

There is no way to calculate or estimate the impact that this great school (now Morehouse College) has made and is still making upon the cultural life of the Negro throughout America. Many of the leading Negroes of the nation, for the most part in business, politics, journalism, the ministry, and in other fields, have been connected in a greater or less degree with this school. Its influence may be likened unto a pebble tossed upon the waters that produces an ever-widening circle.

ABC was born in greatness and to and for greatness. Spawned by the spirit of William Jefferson White in Augusta, Georgia, as Augusta Institute, it came into being while the KKK was riding Negroes to their death and before the deep baying of the bloodhounds had died out in the distance. Later it was moved to Atlanta, where it was rechristened the Atlanta Baptist Seminary and nurtured and tended by the saintly Frank Quarles and E. R. Carter. It started out producing such renowned students and scholars as C. T. Walker, without a doubt one of the greatest gospel preachers ever produced in America; Judson W. Lyons, former registrar of the Treasury; Ben Davis, Sr., journalist of national repute and for years national Republican committeeman of the state of Georgia; William E. Holmes, educator and Christian statesman; and many others. The name of the school was again changed, to Atlanta Baptist College, still supported and inspired by the same great souls, with the addition of Dr. George Sales, who became its president. He held this position for more than forty years, on into the period when the school assumed its last and present name, Morehouse College.[1]

Possibly the greatest president and leader the school ever produced was Dr. John Hope. I think there were many reasons for this. The school and he were born in the same town, with possibly a year's difference in their ages, the school being the older. His mother was feeding the struggling, half-starved infant school from her cupboard while, probably, she was carrying the future president, Dr. Hope, in her womb. While it is true that he was educated elsewhere, he never lost his connection with the famous institution nor with the many great spirits that gave it birth, nurtured, and sustained it.

Approximately seven years before his death, Dr. Hope started a movement to increase the influence and power of education of the Negro by the affiliation of Atlanta University, Morehouse, and Spelman Colleges. His

---

1. The graduates of Atlanta Baptist College and Morehouse College mentioned here, as well as many others, are discussed in Edward A. Jones, *A Candle in the Dark: The History of Morehouse College* (Valley Forge, Pa., 1967).

efforts were rewarded in April, 1929, and resulted in what came to be officially known as the Atlanta University Affiliation. In this new and unique setup, Dr. Hope became president of the graduate school. It is my contention that in this enterprise Dr. Hope demonstrated a genius and greatness in Negro leadership heretofore unknown. I think, also, that the influence, prestige, and greatness of Morehouse College were immeasurably enhanced, although it remained an undergraduate school.

The last time I saw Dr. Hope was at my home here in Tulsa. He had come to Oklahoma to address the Negro State Teachers Association down at Oklahoma City, at the invitation of W. E. Anderson, its president and a former student of his. He came by unexpectedly and remained for dinner. It was a most pleasant and delightful visit. He was both my teacher and Mrs. Franklin's (Mollie, as he always called her) at Roger Williams, and our conversation brought back many memories. Mrs. Franklin told him we had agreed to name our baby for him, and he beamed with a "thank you." He spent much time telling us about his practically new venture, the Atlanta University Affiliation, and what he hoped to do for it. "In time," he began, "I hope to see a School of Medicine and Pharmacy, a Law School, a School of Journalism, and a School of the Social Sciences," and speaking with beaming eyes about his new brainchild, he went on, "I had dreams of this project when I was a student at Brown, and I've never stopped."

The weather was as cold that evening as "blue blazes," and the doctor had on nothing heavier than a light topcoat. I wanted so very much to ask him to remain over for the night, but he was the guest of Mr. Anderson, who would soon come by for him. I've wished many times since that I had offered him my heavy overcoat, because I feared for his health, but I didn't think of it at the time. I realized all too well how justified my fears were when I later received a telegram that the doctor had passed with double pneumonia.

———

There was quite a difference between Roger Williams and ABC, due to the fact that Roger Williams was a coeducational college and ABC was not. At Roger Williams, girls were in our classes; we ate with them in the same dining room; attended social functions together, chapel and church services on the campus; and all day we were passing each other in hallways, classes, and upon the college grounds. There was none of this at ABC, although Spelman was nearby. Spelman was then purely a girls' school, except that there was an occasional exchange of teachers between the two institutions. A young man at ABC had to get written permission to call upon a young lady at Spelman, and on such a rare occasion he met her in the spacious reception room in the presence of the watchful eyes of Miss Harriet Giles, the president, or one of her true and trusted aides. The calling period never extended beyond thirty minutes.

I was not particularly interested in girls while at ABC. If I got lonesome for one's company, I'd write Mollie and read her letter a dozen times when it came. But the boys talked and laughed so much about their experiences while calling upon girls at Spelman that I wanted so very much to share in their experiences. There was a very beautiful girl over there whose home was near Ged and who knew Mollie and all her people, and I secured permission from her preceptress to call upon her. Miss Giles was in command of the "fort," but she evidently soon discovered that there was nothing serious between us from our actions and conversations. We talked loudly about her own people and Mollie's and about the changes taking place in Haywood County, until our guard actually left the room for quite a spell. In her absence, I deliberately kissed the girl full upon her lips. She knew it was in jest and took my sally good-naturedly. I just had to have something new to tell the boys at ABC, although I knew in advance that none of them would believe me.

Seriously, though, Spelman was a great place in those days to train and rear girls, if I'm to believe a brother attorney who was married, briefly, to one of the seminary's products. He laughingly told me that he was miserable the entire time they were married. He said he felt he was not good enough for her, that she was too clean for him. He finally confessed this, and although she did not expect it and in fact kicked against it, he gave her most of his property and paid for the divorce. She was his third wife, and although he and his first two wives had fought like cats and dogs, he and she had never quarreled. When he married his fourth and last wife, they were two of a kind, fussing and fighting. In this normal state they lived happily together until he died from diabetes.

There was another very marked difference between the Negroes of Nashville and those of Atlanta. In Nashville, the religious leaders of the race were the Baptists, and they controlled all the different fields of racial activities. In Atlanta, while the great leaders—E. R. Carter, Peter J. Bryant, John

Hope, the Huberts, Judson Lyons, Henry Lincoln Johnson, and the Nabrits— were all Baptist, as were ABC and Spelman, their emphasis was on politics. The success of this approach was seen in the elevation of Lyons to the position of registrar of the Treasury, and Henry L. Johnson and B. J. Davis to high political positions that enabled them to control many jobs at the disposal of the Republican Party in the South.

I think, too, that there was difference between Nashville and Atlanta in the political treatment of the Negro by the dominant race. I believe there was more tolerance of the Negro in Nashville, notwithstanding the fact that the former owner of the Hermitage had surely planted his spirit there in the hope that it would spring up and abide for all time as a living symbol of resistance to the attempts of Negroes to achieve self-determination.

I don't think Nashville was called the "Athens of the South" in mere jest. I was exposed to elements that gave me the opportunity to meditate upon this and many other things. Sometimes I worked for weeks at the "frat" houses on the Vanderbilt campus and came in contact with the many fine men and boys, members of the different fraternities, and listened to their many discussions upon learned, ancient subjects. More than once I was drawn into such arguments, especially if it involved the frat to which my good friend Sylvester belonged. Often the athletes from Vanderbilt would come over to our campus and assist our coach, Lee Harlan, in training our team. I don't think it was then possible to even imagine such a situation in Atlanta. Then, too, I used to be a Handy-Andy Man in and around Ward-Belmont College, an exclusive college for white girls, and I often heard them discussing learned subjects that would have delighted the ears of the ancient savants. Of course, it's true that I did not see much of the cultural or intellectual side of the white community of Atlanta, and too, I might have been just a wee bit prejudiced in favor of Tennessee in view of the fact that my ancestry on the male side were, for two generations, Tennesseeans.

The state of Georgia had a blessed beginning. No man anywhere in America, at any time, equaled James Oglethorpe as Christian statesman and ambassador of goodwill. But selfishness, greed, and utter lack of vision had rudely upset his applecart and taken over every plan and purpose of this good man, deliberately misconstruing and diverting them into channels flowing in opposite directions. It would be difficult, if not impossible, to find a man in the entire state of Georgia who could faithfully portray the life and character of this most wonderful man.[2] It would seem that his death marked the rise of those evil forces that reappeared in the aftermath of the Reconstruction era, swinging the pendulum so far in the opposite direction that it now operates against the very people it was originally intended to help. And while the Negro threat has been pretty well disposed of, politically, for the time being, the county unit system, in arraying cities against counties, is calculated to produce bad feelings between rural and urban groups.

Meanwhile, in spite of the denial of the franchise, the Negro has been gaining in fields other than politics—in education, business, and the like. There are reasons for this: First, after the Civil War certain religious groups turned their attention to the religious training and education of the newly emancipated slaves. Then training schools, colleges, and seminaries were built for Negroes and teachers employed to teach them. At first, there were racially mixed faculties in a few of these seats of learning, but later on the practice spread to more and more educational institutions. Thus, Negro teachers became a part of the public school system.

A brand new educational star, Booker T. Washington, seemed destined to revolutionize the entire educational thought of the nation. His speech at the Atlanta and Cotton States and International Exposition had riveted the attention of the nation and the world on a new philosophy of educational and human behavior that was so simple and full of common sense that it became the battle cry of men of goodwill everywhere. He had, without seeming to think it through, made himself the leader and spokesman of his race, with an appreciable following from among other races the world over. Few philanthropists would think of endowing a Negro school without the advice of Mr. Washington. Even the president of the United States would not make a federal appointment, especially in the South, without first talking it over with Mr. Washington. Powerful enemies within his own race and the open attacks in the press and public places did not disturb him in the least.

For a long time, Booker T. Washington was the gateway through which Negro schools and businesses had to pass to get support and recognition from other races. Be it said to the everlasting credit of his leadership that he never failed to endorse and support Negro colleges that applied to the

2. The fact that slavery was banned in Georgia at the outset caused many African Americans to bestow generous praise on the Oglethorpe enterprise.

American Baptist Home Mission Society, the General Education Board, or the many Rockefeller foundations. This man showed his greatness in another respect. He surrounded himself with the best brains available to work and plan with him at Tuskegee. He traveled to Iowa State College to influence Dr. George W. Carver to accept the position of science teacher at his institute. It can be said that Dr. Carver and he literally rescued the entire South by introducing a diversified crop system, thus rescuing it from the ruin caused by the one-crop system, which was depleting the soil. Formerly, the Negro, the mule, and the cotton field were the bulwark of the southern oligarchy—"Our Way of Life," as they put it. It was as if they were clinging to a bad dream, a nightmare, that they were afraid to let go. It's to be hoped that the younger generations will take time to survey and analyze the past and lift themselves out of what is nothing more than hollow memories. The trouble with false pride is that it deceives only the ones who possess it.

I have in mind another piece of history that was instrumental in opening the educational door to Negroes in Atlanta and its environs. In 1882, two intrepid women [Sophia B. Packard and Harriet E. Giles] whose faith was boundless, spoke to a small gathering in Cleveland, Ohio, in support of a school for colored girls and women that had just started in the basement of a Negro church in Atlanta. Mr. John D. Rockefeller was at that gathering and heard the appeal of these ladies. After the speech, and when the appeal was made for funds, he emptied his pockets into the collection plate. Two years later, the Rockefeller family visited Atlanta, renewed the acquaintance of these two faithful women, and paid off the mortgage on the school property. In appreciation, the school was named the Spelman Seminary, in honor of Mr. Rockefeller's wife. Since that time, that institution has been a Rockefeller baby and has expanded and grown into a great school, never in need of finance, and under a protective spirit, it seems, that continues to hover above it, two things that are so necessary for the growth and development of educational centers.[3]

It was during this period that the elder Mr. Rockefeller became acquainted with the great Negro Baptist preacher [C. T. Walker] to whom I have already referred, and they became lifelong friends. Dr. Walker was the

3. The early history of Spelman College is detailed in Florence Matilda Read, *The Story of Spelman College* (Atlanta, 1961).

pastor of the leading Baptist church in Augusta. It is well known that on Mr. Rockefeller's winter trips south, he often stopped off in Augusta to attend his friend's church services and to hear him preach. It is conceded that the erection and operation of the Walker Baptist Institute in Augusta was made possible by funds from the Rockefeller family.

The elder Rockefeller was born in the period of rugged individualism and was a product of his time. He was also an ardent Baptist—many say to an extent that he considered no other faith, and that he had decided that no other would be the recipient of his charity. But long before he retired his views had undergone radical change in this and other respects. He sought the friendship of men of other faiths and of goodwill. Many reasons have been given for this. Some say that this change came about through contacts with great educators like David Starr Jordan and William Rainey Harper, and ministers like S. Parkes Cadman and Harry Emerson Fosdick. Others say that the change was due to the mapping out of an entirely new method of operation worked out jointly by the elder Rockefeller and his only son, John D. Rockefeller, Jr.

Personally, I'm inclined to the latter conclusion. In a study of the Rockefeller family, from John D., Sr., down to the last generation, there seems to be a consistency and continuity that sustains a certain pattern of living. "Let this same mind be in you . . ." seems to connect the generations. This family is unique, as if all the generations were the same generation. One generation seems to accept that its goals and purposes should be identical to those of past generations. I predict that whatever field of endeavor—business, politics, or other social aspirations—the Rockefellers enter, they will be heard from for a long time to come.

At the close of the school year, I had grown in favor and in influence with the student body, the faculty, and many strong and influential Negro citizens of Atlanta. As I recall, Raymond Carter (later Dr. Raymond Carter) was one of the seniors to graduate that year. I liked him and he appeared to think well of me. I attended his father's church [Friendship Baptist] and Sunday school and also became acquainted with many prominent members of the Wheat Street Baptist Church, one of whom was the Rev. James Peter Bryant, a rising young minister. President Peter Buell Guernsey of Roger Williams attended the commencement exercises. He was with me as much as possible, and I think he wanted me to return to Roger. I did go there on my way home, with Professor Hope. En route something peculiar, and laughable, happened. Professor Hope and I entered the Jim Crow coach and sat down. Pretty soon, the conductor came to collect the tickets. I handed him mine. Then Professor Hope gave him his. He took it, but said to Professor Hope, "This is the nigars' coach, you'll have to move to the white coach."

The professor said dryly, as only he could, "All right, I want to talk with this young man a while."

"You'll have to make it brief," said the conductor.

We had proceeded up the road many miles before the conductor returned. When he saw the professor still by my side, he became enraged. He yanked the professor by his shoulder and said, "Get up this minute and get out of here before I have you arrested and thrown off this train."

"I'm a Negro," Professor Hope protested, but the conductor disputed him vehemently, and they argued loudly for a good while. Only the porter, who knew the professor, was able to stop it. "You ask him," the professor told the irate conductor. The porter was called in and settled the argument, thus ending a squabble that would have resulted in the professor being thrown off the train.

"We certainly had them guessing," said the blue-eyed, flaxen-haired professor, with amusement written all over his face.

6

FRUSTRATION AND INDECISION

$\mathcal{A}$s I bade goodbye to Dr. Hope and my many friends, including former classmates on the campus of Roger Williams University, I'm sure I had every intention of returning to ABC the next term and pursuing my studies. I had not reckoned with some basic changes that were taking place in the land of my fathers. Would I be able to adjust to the changing times, retain my equilibrium, and move forward to my objective?

What were these changes that had taken place and were still taking place? I had left home six years before and, except for the brief period of Dad's last illness, had remained absent from the land of my birth. All my life I had been used to the great open spaces, where the lands had been held as the common property of the Indian and freedman, who could fence, pasture, and use as much of it as he needed, so long as he did not interfere with land being used or occupied by any other Indian or freedman. All these lands were tax free. Each Indian and freedman was king of his own domain.

There had been moves for some time to prepare the Oklahoma Territory and the Indian Territory for single statehood. Each territory had to be dealt with separately, however, because the sources of titles to land in the two territories were different. It had not been difficult to prepare the western half for statehood. The last and final "run" to open up the western half for statehood had taken place in 1893, when the Cherokee Outlet had been opened to homesteaders. The 1890 Organic Act had prepared the way for the establishment of a territorial government. Every foot of land on the west side had become taxable, and there was a complete educational system, from the

117

University of Oklahoma to the Agricultural College at Stillwater, and Central at Edmond. Public school systems and county governments had also been set up.

On the Indian Territory side (roughly, the eastern half), where the title of the lands was held by the Five Civilized Tribes and their freedmen, Congress had on March 3, 1893, created the Dawes Commission to prepare the Indian Territory for statehood, and by 1902 the final roll of all the allottees, Indians, freedmen, etc. (except as to certain newborns and minors) had been compiled and completed, the lands appraised, and the separate allotments begun. That meant that the holding of these lands in common was at an end. I've elsewhere referred to the many compulsory acts of Congress looking to the preparation of the Indian Territory for statehood. The commission to the Five Civilized Tribes finally wormed an agreement out of these tribes consenting, on March 4, 1906, to the dissolution of all tribal governments on that date, and on April 26, 1906, the Congress enacted a law carrying out that agreement.

I returned home [in 1903] by way of Pauls Valley. I wanted to consult with Dad's old family lawyer, O. W. Patchell. Although he was of a different race, I knew he was honest and could advise me on what steps to take. I had no directions, but I recalled that Dad had outlined to me, in particular, how he would go about having his farm and pasture lands allotted, with a view to buying them from the allottees in the future. During his last illness he did not want to discuss any business, and I did not have the heart to insist. I knew he must have left a considerable sum of money somewhere, if he had not invested it. I thought Patchell would know.

It was noon when my train reached Pauls Valley, and I went directly to the attorney's office. After exchanging greetings, I came directly to the point. "Mr. Patchell," I began, "when was the last time you saw Dad? And do you know anything about his business?" Before he could answer, I told him why I had asked—the talk I had had with Dad when he told me he was going to have allottees file for lands in his pastures and his farm.

Mr. Patchell disclosed that Dad had talked with him many times about the same thing, and he knew that Dad had carried out, or tried to carry out, the scheme. Further, he knew of many freedmen and an Indian or two to whom Dad had paid large sums of money to have allottees file for lands enclosed in his pastures and on his land. He wrote down the names of many of these individuals and gave them to me. I got a lift home that evening from a neighbor, a cousin of mine. Talking guardedly on the way, I became certain that he was one of the men whom Dad had given money to, to file his allotment in Dad's old north pasture, where this cousin told me he had taken his allotment and those of his wife and six children.

Patchell had told me that he was sure Dad had not taken any written contracts from these allottees; it was his intention to do so, but he was stricken before he got around to it. He had told me further: "If David had lived, none of these fellows would have tried to beat him, but now that he is dead, it's very doubtful that any of them come forward and do the honest thing. And if any of them get scared and convey their patents to an innocent buyer, without notice, all chances to recover anything will be gone by the board."

When I reached what had been home that night, it was a desolate place. David, two years my junior, was there with his new wife. He had filed on the old homeplace. I was glad of that. Fisher, only nineteen years of age, had married and was living with his father-in-law, and Lydia had moved away with my sister Hattie down near Springer, forty miles from the old homeplace. My oldest brother, Walter, and my brothers Andrew, Tom, and Matthew were all married and living off to themselves. Sister Dolores had passed for some time.

The following day I told my brothers what I had learned from Mr. Patchell and asked them point-blank if they would try with me to salvage something from Dad's vast loose investments. I did not tell them what I knew of Dad's scheme. Of course, that would have made no difference. They were never jealous of us. Good old brother Walter was never a businessman, and he had nothing to offer. Brothers David and Fisher were more inexperienced in such matters than I. Brother Tom had a complicated business matter and told us that it meant so much to him that he would not have the time to take on any other matter. Andrew and Matthew, being both shrewd businessmen, had already bought so much surplus land that they actually did not want any more. In the future, they intended to breed pure-blood cattle and horses and other registered livestock, and emphasize quality rather than quantity.

And so nothing had come of the conference, and as I took leave of my brothers, I had a sinking sensation. I'd reached the end of my rope, and everything about me had begun to look strange. Everywhere I turned it seemed that a thousand strange hands were reaching out to me and every finger on each hand had a mouth that was saying, "Don't do that. Don't touch this and don't touch that." In a spirit of defeatism, I threw up my hands in frustration and exasperation.

Looking back, I recall now that I'd never in fact been on my own, in the real sense. All the experiences I'd had in Chicago and elsewhere, seeking and attempting to hold jobs, were absolutely useless out here. This problem had no counterpart in any experience I had had. I thought I had experienced the dawning of many new worlds; but none of them was like this one. This one was an old world made new. All the physical objects about me were the same. Old Massey Creek, with its silent blue hole, and Eight Mile Creek flowed in the same direction. Wild Horse Creek flowed to the Washita River, mingling its water with that river, and the two flowing into the Red River, and thence into the "Father of Waters," on to the Gulf of Mexico and to the oceans of the world. Inwardly, though, I was a stranger in mine own land. "There had arisen a king"—many kings—"in Egypt that knew not Joseph."

I decided I'd go again and consult my dad's old faithful friend and attorney. "I've been thinking," were the first words the lawyer said when we sat down to talk. "All these men know that I know David advanced the money and that he selected their allotments for them in his pastures. I believe that I can get some of this money back by putting pressure on them." He outlined his procedure, and I was satisfied. Neither of us believed that the money could be fully recovered, not a fourth of it. He had to labor against one disadvantage: he did not know how much money Dad had advanced these allottees.

He did have one advantage that was to weigh heavily in his favor. He was the oldest attorney in the town by many years. He had come there when my brother Walter was born and had been Dad's adviser ever since. Ninety percent of the old settlers went to him for legal assistance. No one ever questioned his honesty, whether he be white, black, or red; whether he be judge or jury. And no one would want Patchell to think he was dishonest. Mortgages, notes, and other written evidence of debts were not used then. If one's word could not be trusted to secure payment of an obligation, he could get no credit. I returned to Homer, promising the attorney I'd keep in touch, while he went off in his buggy. Often, I'd hear of him in different parts of the community, rushing here and there, always in his buggy, in the early morning, at midday, early and late evening.

I got busy salvaging that part of the property that had fallen to me. It was scattered among my brothers and sisters, which meant that some of it was as far away as Springer, where my sister Hattie and her husband lived. What was I to do with the livestock? I had no place to put them, but I had to decide. I had no land save 20 acres—raw and unimproved and, according to the U.S. government appraisal, worthless—which had been allotted to me as a Choctaw freedman. Had Mother lived until the enrollments, she would have been enrolled as a Choctaw Indian by her old friends who brought her up and who had always recognized her as one of them; but it was not to be. Her Choctaw Indian kin were allotted 160 acres each, a homestead patent calling for 40 acres and a surplus, or allotment, patent calling for 120 acres.

About the middle of July, I went to Springer at the urgent request of my brother-in-law, Hence Cohee, to look at a small farm that he thought I could buy. It contained fifty acres of rich, open bottomland. A small stream ran through the center of it. It had a makeshift fence around it and a three-room box house. I looked the property over without agreeing to buy it. Two days later, I made a trip to Tishomingo, the capital of the old Chickasaw Nation, that served as a turning point in my life.

At that time some of the work of the old Dawes Commission, such as final enrollment and selection of allotments, had been transferred to the capital from Muskogee. The little old tribal capital was full of people of all races, excited people running here and there, trying to get on the final roll so that they might share in the allotment of lands of the Chickasaw and Choctaw tribes. My good friends Mr. and Mrs. James Seay operated a roominghouse and restaurant, and I had no difficulty in getting accommodation. The town was so full of people that most of them were camping in wagons and on the ground.

There was a woman there at the time who was trying to get on the Chickasaw Indian roll, Eliza Harris. She was introduced to me by my friend James, who said he had known her all her life and that she was an Indian. She was fair, and the coarse black hair and prominent nose were absent. However, I'd learned that the absence of such features was not always a sign of the absence of Indian blood, and my friend said she was more than half Chickasaw and that there was an old full-blood who said she was his grandniece.

I had a permit to represent applicants for enrollment before the commission and decided to do so. Another thing that influenced me to try and help the lady was the fact that Bill Murray was against her. He was about the biggest thing in the Nation at that time. He was not only an attorney but general counsel for the Nation, and the son-in-law of the governor. He had no use for Negroes, especially those who claimed they were not Negroes. On the day of the hearing, I made a good case for her. She finally prevailed, after more than a year.[1] Awaiting the outcome of Mrs. Harris' case settled forever the question of my returning to college. The experience had done something to me: it had awakened and aroused something that had been asleep in me since that late evening when I had driven Colonel Stokes back home and he had said, dryly, "The experience will help you when you become a lawyer." Then, too, I've always been stubborn. I've never liked to see little people being picked on by big people. And I've always hated racial prejudice. The thoughts I had about Mr. Murray's opinion of the Negro proved to be well founded, as shown in all of his future political life in Oklahoma.[2]

On my return to Springer, I stopped off in Ardmore for a visit with my old friend Sylvester. He had a great office, or rather offices, with many rooms, and a great force of men and women assisting him. The general businesses were land titles, land litigations, and probating of estates. He wanted very much for me to become a part of his organization. When I finally refused, he couldn't understand and he seemed hurt. But I knew such activities involved cut-throat competition, cutting corners to carry points, and other things that my makeup didn't agree with. I don't mean to imply that my friend was crooked or even basically dishonest. He was just a product of his time, and he didn't see anything unnatural—or wrong—in what he did. Even now, I cannot say that he was wrong and I was right.

1. For a discussion of the tangled problem of freedmen seeking allotments, and the author's role in this effort, see Daniel F. Littlefield, Jr., *The Chickasaw Freedmen: A People Without a Country* (Westport, Conn., 1980), 200–201.

2. As president of the Oklahoma Constitutional Convention in 1906, William "Alfalfa Bill" Murray declared that the Negro was a failure as a soldier, doctor, and lawyer. He should be in separate schools, railroad cars, and waiting rooms. When Murray became governor, he was an advocate of total racial segregation and achieved some of it by executive order. William H. Murray, *Memoirs of Governor Murray and True History of Oklahoma* (2 vols.; Boston, 1945), II; Keith L. Bryant, Jr., *Alfalfa Bill Murray* (Norman, Okla., 1968), 55–56.

Looking back, even today—looking about me—I can see men whose millions have fed the hungry and clothed the naked, but whose millions I could have never acquired because I'm of a different mold of clay; I've been shaped by a different pattern. I think that the most dangerous individual in the entire world is the man who is untrue to himself. Paraphrasing the well-known wise saying, if one is true to himself, it follows as the night the day that he cannot be false to any man. What I'm trying to say is that if one truthfully believes that what he is doing is right, then I'm inclined to believe he is right, and in some way beyond human understanding, he is justified in the sight of Him who looketh into the heart. An old, unlettered Negro philosopher once said to me, "Frank" (as he always called me), "you know that there is always three sides to every question or problem." "How is that," I asked with deep interest. "Well," he expostulated laconically, "there is your side, my side, and the right side."

When I returned to Springer, I wrote Mollie that I had started something in Tishomingo that would not be completed for some time, possibly a year; that I felt an obligation to watch it and see it through; and that because of this and other reasons I would explain later, I had decided to drop out of college. I told her that if she would have me, she could set the date for our wedding. I suggested the latter part of the following March as allowing me sufficient time to prepare a home for us. She had already accepted a school job in Mississippi, and my letter was forwarded to her. We finally set our wedding date for April 1, 1903.

I went to Pauls Valley to check with Patchell on his success or failure in the effort to regain the money Dad had advanced certain allottees. As this was before the days of the widespread use of the typewriter, stenographer, and the like, I sat in his waiting room for some little time before he peeked out of his private office to discover me. He came forward all smiles, grabbed my hand, and patted me in such a way as to bring back the feeling I had when another man thus greeted me. "Come in," he said. "Have a seat, and let me get the records."

Spreading them out on the center table, I on one side and he on the other, he commenced to read, and in amazement I listened. He went on and on. "You'll notice that to everyone who paid anything, I gave a receipt in full. He wanted it that way, and what else could I do?"

"I understand," I answered. "You had to take each person's word for it. You didn't know how much Dad had advanced them."

"That's it. We were in no position to dispute any of them."

"You did far better than I expected," I told him. He had collected $11,350 and some odd cents. I was looking for him to charge a fee of at least 25 percent, but he only charged 10 percent, and nothing for the use of his horse and buggy.

My older brothers and sister Hattie refused to accept any of the money, so I divided it equally among David, Fisher, Lydia, and myself. After I'd sold off my livestock, except for a team, a saddle horse, and two milch cows, I had upwards of $3,500. Of all things, Old Coaly had been killed by a mountain lion, or some other carniverous wild beast. The irony of it—killed by an animal he had always been able to scent and escape. I traded Flag to Matthew for two brood sows that were soon to farrow. I sold my allotment and purchased the fifty acres I had looked at and commenced improving it.

I worked hard for the remainder of the year getting my living quarters in shape. I committed one costly error in putting around the farm a hogproof wire fence. I committed additional costly errors in building cribs and filling them with corn, and buying hogs, putting them in the pasture, and feeding the corn to them, over a hundred head. For good measure, I dumped the two sows that I had gotten from Matthew, and their pigs, into the pasture. My farm had not been cultivated for years, it seemed, and the soil being rich, everything grew luxuriantly in it. I noticed patches of cockleburrs here and there but thought nothing about them; I knew nothing to think about them. I had not been advised.

During the remainder of the fall and winter, I fed my swine and watched them grow. I kept Mollie informed about everything, the improvements, the hogs and their growth and development. They were sights pleasing to the eye. Spring came early with rains and hot sunshine. March appeared to be a real summer month, and all plant life commenced to sprout and grow. I had two of my nephews, Otis and Dock, with me to assist in the farming. We were waiting for the earth to get dry enough to plow and plant corn and other crops, even a big garden we had separated for that purpose.

Then it started. The hogs, big and little, began to die. They died swiftly, all through the day and night. I was in a panic. I didn't know the cause of the deaths, and no one else around seemed to know. I rushed to Springer to find a vet, and was told that there was one in Glenn, another little rural town three miles to the north. I found him and took him to observe my hogs. One glance was sufficient. "They have eaten sprouting burrs," he announced with finality. "I could tell at once from the way their carcasses swelled and from the green saliva exuding from their mouths. When these burrs are sprouting, they are poison and bring on certain death as if your hogs had been shot in the head." This was a stunning blow to me. Not one hog survived. Hundreds of dollars including the investment in the hogs, for feedstuff, and for labor had been wiped out almost overnight. My wedding day was just a few days off, but I'd make that. The trip would have to be shorter. She would understand. I would not write about the disaster. I'd see her in a few days and she would learn firsthand, and we could plan together. My sister Hattie and her husband did not live so far away. They could have Lydia stay with the boys and drop in daily and see how they were getting along.

That was a rainy spring everywhere. Mollie was teaching in Shelbyville, in Bolivar County, Mississippi, down in the Delta, as it's called.[3] The old "Father of Waters" was on a rampage. Changing trains at Memphis, I could see its swollen dark billows as my train crept south toward my destination. I was more frightened on the train than were the inhabitants of the swamps, leading their livestock to higher ground. My soon-to-be wife was boarding with Rev. Williamson and his wife, who was a graduate of Roger Williams and had taught school there for years, up until she and her husband had grown independent. They lived in a beautiful roomy house and owned property all over the little Delta town.

This part of Bolivar County has always been a typical "black-belt" area. Just eight miles farther on is the all-Negro town of Mound Bayou, dominated by the great Isaiah T. Montgomery.[4] Through the years, it has not only survived and grown in influence and respectability, but it has served as a buffer to absorb, dissipate, smooth out, and render harmless what might otherwise have been disastrous conflicts between the races. This may not always be possible. It could be, however, if the better elements of the two races would try to understand that there are evil men in both races, recognize them for what they are, and join together to see that such troublemakers are firmly dealt with according to justice and the law. Almost everywhere, racial

3. The current name is Shelby; the place is about eight miles north of Mound Bayou, Mississippi.

4. Montgomery's role in the politics of post-Reconstruction Mississippi is treated in Vernon Wharton, *The Negro in Mississippi, 1865–1890* (Chapel Hill, N.C., 1947).

tensions and conflicts arise out of situations where the good people of each race are strangers to the other. Therefore they are suspicious of each other, and the bad elements of the two races take advantage of this situation to the ultimate injury of both.

My train reached the little town about the middle of the afternoon of March 31, and the wedding took place on the afternoon of the following day. I had time to tell Mollie of our great loss. I told her about the amount of money I had left; that I had been offered a government job to teach at We-woka; and that I could get a teaching job for her if she wanted it. We were in agreement on everything.

We spent a few blissful days together and I hurried back home, stopping off in Ardmore for an interview with George Beck, the supervisor of federal schools for the Seminole and Chickasaw Nations, under the auspices of John Benedict, the general superintendent of federal schools of the Five Nations. I opened and organized the first public school at Wewoka the following week. Mrs. Franklin didn't join me until her summer school closed.[5] We were at home together about once a month until she accepted a job that fall at Tatums under the same federal system. She was made principal of this school and enjoyed her work immensely. The school was in the community of my people, and she had a chance to make weekly visits among them to get to know them.

When I commenced teaching, I started to study law under a correspondence course put out by the Sprague Law School of Detroit, Michigan. I purchased a set of saddlebags and carried my textbooks with me everywhere I went, studied hard, and devoted myself to it as never before. I had decided to make the legal profession my life's work.

In 1904, I took a similar teaching job at Milo, and my wife taught at Springer. That was a little better. She could be home, and I every weekend. My nephews were still with me, and we were able to carry on some semblance of farming. And by working sometimes night and day, we were able to make the farm pay. I bought my wife a fine saddle horse that she rode to and from school, while I took the buggy. The following year, 1905, my wife

5. Once they were married, the author seemed to derive special pleasure in referring to his wife as "Mrs. Franklin"; this usage also protected her from whites who might condescendingly call her by her first name.

continued to teach at Springer while I farmed and continued to read and study law. The Harris case was decided by the Interior Department in 1904, but I didn't realize anything from it. I had lost trace of the Seays and my client, and never heard of either again. Well, after all, not being a lawyer, I knew I could collect no fee, and so I didn't let it bother me.

I enjoyed my year on the farm. I became a great sweet-potato grower, and my wife and I would take a load every weekend to Ardmore to sell. Sometimes we would resort to street peddling. Once I was almost arrested for engaging in the trade without a license. In my experience of potato growing, I learned to produce a double yield. How? Very simple. When the vines began to run, I'd run my sweep through the center of the rows, thus covering up the ends of the vines, and in the fall there would be as many potatoes in the middle of the rows as in the rows. We grew plenty of corn and roughage for the stock, Kafir cane for the chickens and turkeys, and sorghum cane from which our molasses was made. I gave my nephews a cotton patch, but they didn't care enough about it to gather it in. Mrs. Franklin loved it and could pick 250 pounds a day and cook three meals. I learned to do everything else on the farm, except picking cotton.

But farming was not for me. I was dedicated to the legal profession, and to keep up my interest, there were then four colored lawyers in Ardmore, whom I visited on an average of once a week. Then they would drive out to my farm on Sundays for dinner and a visit. Among these lawyers was J. Milton Turner, former minister to Liberia, great constitutional lawyer, interpreter of treaties, an expert on Indian and freedmen land titles, and one of the greatest orators I have ever listened to. It was both instructive and inspiring to sit at his feet and hear him tell about his many and varied experiences. There was Sherman Tecumseh Wiggins, a graduate of Ohio State University and of Ann Arbor, Michigan, a great lawyer and scholar in his own right. Turner and Wiggins maintained offices in Washington, D.C., and worked for legislation on behalf of the Chickasaw and Choctaw freedmen that would give them preferential right to enough land at the government-appraised value to make out 40 acres for each. In this they succeeded, thus increasing these freedmen's acreages to more than 50,000 acres. Then there were Josiah Clark and T. S. E. Brown, self-made lawyers, but good ones. My contact with these men before and after I moved to Ardmore meant more to me than I can ever know.

I had an experience on the Springer farm in 1904 that I shall never forget. I was returning from Ardmore one Saturday evening near dusk. As I reached the top of the last hill, possibly about two hundred yards from home, I heard two shotgun blasts a few seconds apart. The shots came from our home, there was no doubt about that. I rallied my horse and in a dead heat started for home. My heart was in my mouth. But what could I do? I had no firearm, about which I never thought. Just as I reached the front gate and before I had time to dismount, my wife came from behind the henhouse, shotgun in hand with the barrels still smoking.

"What was it, darling," I asked her between breaths.

"An animal of some sort disturbing the chickens," she answered with a calmness that shamed me.

"Did you see it? What did it look like?" I pursued.

"I only caught a brief glance of it, possibly a lobo, the same one that's been seen in the neighborhood for some time."

"I didn't know there was a timber wolf in the community."

"Yes, several people have seen it," she said.

"Do you think you hit it?"

"I don't know," she said. "I tried, but the shot was not a good one."

On investigation the next morning, there was no doubt but that the brute had been hit. There was plenty of blood on the ground and along the path that the beast took. I knew that animal would not return.

Rains were seasonal and my crop yields were good. The neighbors planted many acres of cotton, and I recall that my wife taught two summer months because the children would pick cotton in the fall. About the middle of September, I received a letter from J. Goody Johnson of Wewoka urging me to come there for an important conference. He offered no hint as to the nature of the business, and I was unable to hazard a guess. Yet I knew it was something important, coming from such a man. Mr. Johnson was one of the few highly educated freedmen and a man of vast influence throughout the Territory among all the races. He was the chief legal adviser to the Creek and Seminole tribes, whose languages he spoke fluently—he had been constantly used as an interpreter in Judge Parker's court and in other federal courts more recently established at Muskogee and Chickasha. He knew the treaties of these tribes with the federal government from the first to the last. I had met and admired him when I organized the public school at Wewoka. In fact, I selected him, with Dr. Coffey and others, as trustees of my school.

His offices were large and well appointed, lined with the latest lawbooks. I recall that he used some law students in his office; one I particularly remember, a young white law student, Guy Cutlip, who afterward made his mark in the profession. He was to assist Mr. Johnson in the organization of his Black Panther Oil Company that became so powerful in the oil business. Possibly Mr. Johnson was the greatest and best-known attorney of his time in the Indian Territory.

My wife and I read the letter together and discussed it. We were completely agreed on the fact that I could not ignore the invitation, coming from such a man; and as her school was on vacation for the cotton-picking season, we decided we would make the trip together. He appointed the hour when I should be in his office. At the time, I didn't think this strange. I knew how busy he was; such a man had to work by schedule. He was here today and some other place tomorrow, in court or conference, attending Indian council meetings, and so forth. I took it that he did not want me to make the trip and miss him. We timed ourselves, figured how long it would take to get there in our buggy. We missed it by one hour.

Our talk (actually his) had not proceeded very far before I discovered I did not know this man—his other side. He had met with me in the trustee board meetings. There he had listened to me and the school program I'd outlined, and seldom asked questions. Here, he rattled on, although always concisely, telling me about his organizations, his many interests, who was at the head of this one and who managed the other one; then what he wanted me to do and the pay I'd receive, and where I'd have to live. He would spend a certain time to "break me in." He saw I was a married man but never once asked me what I had been doing, whether I had any business, and if so, the nature of it; whether I could leave it, or arrange to leave it; or how much time I'd want to arrange things so I could get away from it.

I broke in to tell him about what I was doing and that if I accepted his offer, I'd have to have time to work out something. It was out of the question to pull up stakes and come to him at once. I could see that he was impatient and displeased. Soon he interrupted, "What you are doing amounts to chicken feed. I'm offering you the chance of a lifetime. When I was on your board, I trusted your judgment and did not try to tell you how to run your business." What he had just said was so unreasonable that I did not argue the matter. In fact, he had arisen and would not have listened to anything I may have tried to say. I arose too and said, "Mr. Johnson, it has been nice talking to you. If you will give me two weeks, I will give you a definite answer." We descended from his office to the sidewalk, into the sinking sun. That was a strange conference, or interview, or whatever was the proper name for it. Both my wife and I were flabbergasted, and we needed time to collect our wits. We were soon settled on one thing: Here was a man who evidently had always had his way; who moved men around in his organizations like men on a checkerboard.

We returned home by way of Hennepin and spent the night with my people. I have wondered a thousand times whether I made a mistake in writing Mr. Johnson declining his offer. I'm sure of one thing: that if I could have gotten into such organizations as he had then, where men trusted and respected each other and discussed the affairs of the businesses on an equal footing, I think I'd be a very rich man today. Someone has said that comparison is odious, but I have thought of what this man might have done for his people and humanity, with such organizations in a virgin country, had he been able to surround himself with men his equal, or his betters. He could have built an empire of strength, power, and ever-encircling influence fed by roots of charity, tolerance, and mutual understanding.

The fall season was well upon us. My wife had reopened her school, and I was busy harvesting and storing the crops, grinding the juices out of the sorghum cane and making molasses, storing some of it in kegs and marketing the balance. Every weekend my wife and I hauled to the Ardmore markets a wagonload of produce including vegetables, fresh and juicy, and new sorghum molasses. We had two good milch cows and sometimes we brought pounds of fresh country butter and eggs to the market, as well as crates of young turkeys. I followed Dad's policy of deep fall plowing, and therefore the hot, sometimes dry, weather never cut down on our crop yield. We raised more than enough corn to feed, fatten, and market our hogs. For me, work never ended. At the end of the day's work, I sat up until midnight many nights poring over the legal questions my school had mailed, and preparing the answers to be returned.

In the fall of 1905, my wife became pregnant, and our first child was born on the 10th of August the following year, a girl. We named her Mozella

Denslow for Mrs. Franklin's Latin teacher at Roger Williams University. My wife was attended by Dr. Higgins of Glenn, an English doctor. There were no Negro doctors nearer than Ardmore. Before the child was born, several of my friends jokingly remarked that I should name and enroll the unborn infant under the name of Jesse, Willie, or Johnnie, as those names applied to both male and female. You see, the last date of enrollment had been extended by Congress to April, 1906. I never considered the matter.

———

Meanwhile, intrepid forces were driving hard for statehood, single or double, *i.e.*, separate statehood for the Oklahoma Territory and separate statehood for the Indian Territory, or failing that, single statehood for the two Territories. As a matter of fact, there had been introduced in the Congress in 1902 an Omnibus Bill seeking the creation of separate states for Arizona, New Mexico, and Oklahoma; but this bill failed passage in 1903 and again in 1904. Other bills had been introduced in different forms and different modifications, seeking the same end, all of which likewise failed to pass.

In 1905 a meeting was called and an organization was formed, which was called the Sequoyah Convention. Chief Pleasant Porter of the Creek Nation was made president and C. N. Haskell elected vice-president of the Creek Nation; Chief W. C. Rogers, vice-president of the Cherokee Nation; Chief Green McCurtain, vice-president of the Chickasaw Nation; and Chief John F. Brown, vice-president of the Seminole Nation. A proposed constitution for the new state of Sequoyah, to include the Indian Territory only, was written and an election was called for November, 1905, for its adoption or rejection.

By this time, Congress had passed an Enabling Act which, among other things, provided for a single state of the two Territories. The proponents and advocates of the Sequoyah Convention idea, seeing that public opinion was in favor of single statehood, faced about and began working tooth and nail for this more popular idea. In fact, the Enabling Act foreclosed definitely the idea of single statehood expressed in the Sequoyah instrument. Therefore, the provisions and steps to be taken as set forth in the Enabling Act, in order to secure statehood, were followed to the letter. The delegates elected to the constitutional convention which met on November 20, 1906, at Guthrie, Oklahoma, were overwhelmingly Democratic and white. During the long session, which finally ended in July, 1907, the influence of two men, C. N. Haskell and William H. Murray, stood out over and above all others.

Personally and racially, I grew more and more interested in what was taking place politically in the Indian Territory. I had watched every movement looking toward statehood. I knew that neither the Indians nor the freedmen were ready for it—that is, the vast majority of them—and that if it came then, it would be only a question of a very short time before they would have nothing to subsist upon. I made several trips and spoke in many places over the Territory against it at that time. Unfortunately, all that the leading Indians were interested in was keeping liquor out, if statehood came, which was very good and with which I agreed. The majority, however, were densely ignorant and did not have any training in industry and economy. It's true that the full-blood was protected by treaty and acts of Congress against the alienation of some of his allotment; but I knew that would not last long and, too, this protection was full of loopholes. The freedman was worse off. He had scarcely an opportunity to get an education which might have fitted him for business or industry. Unfortunately, the Negro from the states had the vague belief that statehood would be a good thing, although intermarriage was going on daily between him and the freedman, and he and his children were benefiting immensely by such marriages. Some shrewd members of the other race had some of the state Negroes believing that the freedmen disliked them and that they could get along better with the white man than they could with the freedman.

I was against the constitution offered by the Democrats. It was a "Mother Hubbard" document, covering everything, full of untried legislation. I liked the one offered by the Republicans. Then again, I was against certain all-powerful leaders in the Democratic Party, shrewd men in a way, but without culture and refinement. How correct I was in this has been overwhelmingly borne out by history.

If the Republicans had rallied around the constitution offered by Henry Asp and a few others, and had made an open and earnest effort, Frank Frantz, the Republican candidate for governor, would have been elected with his ticket. He lost by only 27,280 votes. That was a small margin in a state-wide election. I don't believe the slogan, a sort of battle cry, of Mr. Haskell, "Let the People Rule," was considered by them. Had the people actually been informed, I believe they would have ruled. The campaigns for the election of delegates to the constitutional convention and for the adoption of the proposed constitution, and for the election of a governor and state and congressional officials, were heated. Especially was this true of the campaigns to elect delegates and for the adoption of the proposed constitution.

I spoke at a half dozen or more rallies where the going was both rough and dangerous. Crowds of partisans from the opposition camps would come into our meetings demanding the right to speak, and if told that they would be permitted to speak later on, they would attempt to strong-arm their demand to speak at once. In such situations I had to use my wits to avoid the shedding of blood. If I had lost my head once, there is no telling what might have happened.

Norman Pruitt, whom I had known for a long time, was the leader of the opposition. He became so persistent that I challenged him to a debate on the issues, which he accepted. I reserved the right to open and close the debate. Being a prominent criminal lawyer, he was always popular and brought his supporters to the meeting to root for him. I opened the debate in a pleasant and conciliatory tone, which I maintained throughout my initial remarks. I referred to the attorney as "Brother Pruitt" and added that we were all brothers under the skin. Using those wise words of Thomas Jefferson, I said that difference of opinion may be tolerated where reason is left free to combat it; that if we Americans could not discuss the present issues without losing our heads, then that in itself proved we were not competent or prepared for self-government; and that therefore we were not yet prepared for statehood.

There came thunderous applause from my opponent's section, and when the hot-tempered attorney got up to speak, his sail was completely punctured. I learned in those experiences what I think is true today and will continue to be true to the end of time: that most great issues are moral, not political; are human, not racial; that the statesman can never be displaced by the politician without harmful dislocations of natural evolutionary processes; and that the entire world is both mentally and spiritually ill today because of this derangement.

7

ARDMORE

*I*n the fall of 1906 we sold the farm and all our livestock, except the horse and buggy, and moved to Ardmore, to a home we bought in the northwest part of the city. This house consisted of four rooms, with a kitchen and dining room, and was set upon a lot 100 by 150 feet. It was a beautiful lot, as level as the floors in the house. But the house was not modern. None of the homes were modern then, except for those of the few rich families living in that part of town, among them Lee Cruce (the banker and later governor), Ben Colbert, and Westheimer. On our lot was a fine young orchard with fruit trees of several varieties and a few rows of berries. In the northeast corner there was a small barn, large enough to accommodate the horse and buggy and crib.

When Mozella was born, there began in me the fear of insecurity, which stayed with me, off and on, throughout my life. This was one of the things that hastened my abandonment of rural life. Too, I knew I would not be able to prepare and maintain the proper environment in a rural area for the growth and development of my family or opportunities for travel, communication, fellowship, and education. I had the faith to believe that, while my education was limited and not formal, with the aid of rigid self-help, by the right contacts and absorption, I might yet be able to fortify myself and family against haphazard living.

On November 12, 1907, I left by train for Purcell to take the examination to practice law in the new state of Oklahoma. The federal judge, J. T. Dickerson, was holding court. He appointed a committee of practicing attorneys to examine me and other applicants, a score or more. The test was very rigid and lasted all day (the examination was oral) until midnight. Many or most of the applicants were graduates of well-recognized law schools, such as Ann Arbor. But the result showed that mine was the second-highest grade, as I later learned from the clerk, O. M. Campbell, when he mailed my certificate. On August 8, 1908, I was admitted to the bar by the Supreme Court of Oklahoma, which meant, of course, that I could practice law in any state court in Oklahoma. It was then only a question of form, and my certificates to practice law in all federal courts of the different districts were secured in due time.[1]

At Ardmore, I connected myself with a church for the first time in my life, a C.M.E. church in a small, poorly painted building on an eastern spur of the Santa Fe Railroad. The C.M.E. was my mother's and all her people's church. It was the weakest of all the denominations in town. My friends and my father's kin thought I'd made the biggest mistake of my life, considering the fact that there was not a member of the church who had enough business to need a lawyer. But it wasn't sentiment that influenced me to join the church, even if it was my mother's church. There has always been a stubborn streak in me, a desire to team up with the underdog. I've always thought that it was there where I was most needed.

I recalled my dad's attitude toward denominations. He didn't care a hoot for them, as such. His idea about sects was that they had nothing to do with whether one was a Christian, that Christianity consisted in living it. My old friend, then and for fifty years thereafter, Tom Gatewood, was the pastor. He was too poor get out of town, and went hungry many a day, along with his wife, who was a schoolteacher without a job. I had no money to speak of, but many friends. Mrs. Niblack—a former school superintendent—and superintendent Tucker helped Mrs. Gatewood to get a school, and that for a time eased the financial burden of the pastor and his wife.

At the same time, I was getting before the people and trying to build up my own practice. I was well known, through my father's name, from Marietta in Love County north to Purcell in McClain County; but that was no

---

1. He was admitted to practice before the United States Supreme Court on January 31, 1949. The certificate hangs on the wall of the law offices of his grandson, Waldo E. Jones II, of Tulsa.

assurance that these people, most of whom were relatives, would employ me as their attorney in a lawsuit. If the opposition hired a Negro lawyer, they might hire me to oppose him, but if the adversary employed a white lawyer, then they were sure to hire a white attorney. This was not unnatural, when it was a fact that colored lawyers on this frontier were rare and, except for those in Ardmore, few and far between on the old Indian Territory side of the state. In fact, I cannot recall another, except Goody Johnson down at Wewoka. But, as in all things, there was an exception to the custom of Negroes hiring white lawyers.

Mother Simmons, once a very prosperous and shrewd colored lady, was that exception. She had a son, Knox Simmons, who never worked. He lived entirely off his mother and had reduced her almost to poverty. He was a good-looking man, just about pretty, and he thought that every woman wanted him. Trouble was his middle name, growing out of gambling, whiskey, fights, and women. He would take his mother's stock and sell or mortgage it to pay his debts, until she refused any longer to stand for it.

Mother Simmons owned a beautiful registered paint stallion worth several hundred dollars. Knox took him from his stall one night and allegedly sold him to a fellow named Pruitt to pay, it was claimed, a gambling debt. His mother came to me to recover the horse for her, and I brought an action in replevin. It was actually the first lawsuit I had had since admission to the bar. Pruitt employed a prominent firm of white attorneys. I asked her if she still wanted me to represent her. "Yes," she said emphatically. "We have God on our side. We are right and He makes the majority." She was deeply religious and her faith sustained her even if it did not reassure me.

On the day of the trial, I went to court with my heart in my mouth. I had no practice in court procedure and was almost as green as a gourd. The opposition was on its toes with motions and demurrers, all of which were overruled by the court. The court, over the objections of defense counsel, permitted me to introduce newspaper clippings to show that Knox had been in court before for trying to dispose of his mother's property, and a long news item and editorial in a paper of general circulation concerning the trouble the son was giving his mother about her property. This line of testimony was to show that the defendant could not have been an innocent purchaser for value without notice. One other thing in my client's favor was the fact that the defendant was a constable and had been for years.

Before my client took the witness chair to prove ownership, I had a brief conference with her in an effort to have her testify to certain facts that I thought were material. They were not lies, but she thought they were. Again when she was seated in the witness chair, I whispered my request to her. She blurted out, above a whisper, "No son, I wouldn't tell a lie for a thousand stallions. If I can't win with the truth, he can have my horse." In exasperation and forgetting where I was, I told her to pray while I lied like hell.

The defense attorneys refused to put on any evidence and rested. Then a thing happened that greatly surprised me. Judge Pullium, before whom the case was being tried, refused to hear arguments on either side and rendered judgment for my client, with a scathing denunciation of the defendant. He left the bench abruptly, calling the defendant into his chambers and telling the plaintiff to remain seated, that he wanted to see her later. I left the court mystified and returned to my office. The strange behavior of the judge was cleared up when Mother Simmons came to my office. "He knew me," she said, "and my entire family, and made me remember him. My parents were his father's slaves, and he remembered me as soon as I entered his court. He said no Simmons servants ever told a lie, nor were any of us ever deadbeats; that he had been reading about the trouble my son had been giving me; and that he had told Pruitt that if he appealed the case or gave me any further trouble, he would make the affair his personal business."

This was one case I wanted to win. My family had increased, and I had one more mouth to feed. B. C., Jr., had been born on December 23, 1907, and the attending physician, Dr. Drizzle, had not yet been fully paid. I wanted to pat myself on the back over the outcome, but it seemed that maybe I had not done so well after all. I have thought many times since of what might have been the outcome had not the previous relationship existed between the judge and my client. Anyhow, the many Negroes who witnessed the trial never knew about this part of the courtroom drama. My practice increased very noticeably, which gladdened and encouraged me.

I don't believe that I ever enjoyed the practice of law more than I did the first two years in Ardmore. At first, all five Negro lawyers occupied the same building, at 311 South Main Street, and we had the habit, while idling in the building, of engaging in what might be called seminars. We would discuss all branches of the law, its growth and development; define "The Rule in Shelley's Case," and whether that rule had been enlarged or modified. Toward the end of that period, T. S. E. Brown moved to Oklahoma City and Clark gave up the practice to live with his daughter and her husband in Pine Bluff, Arkansas. Turner and Wiggins were spending more and more time in their main offices in Washington, D.C., looking after the passage of a bill they had had friends introduce in the Congress, to increase the acreage in the allotments of land to the Choctaw and Chickasaw freedmen. At the end of the two years I moved my office to the second floor of the Love Building, across the street diagonally from my old office.

All the judges and many of the lawyers were friendly. The judges were absolutely impartial on the bench. If a colored man went into their chambers for advice, they would invariably tell him, with patience but with emphasis, to "confer with one of your own lawyers. They are able men and will be treated with the same respect as any other lawyer." And if a Negro employed me or another colored lawyer to represent him, and then attempted to change to another attorney, that attorney would call the colored lawyer and clear it with him before he would have anything to do with the case. More than once, the Cruces, for instance (A. C. and Will, brothers of Lee Cruce), would persuade the client to come and see me.

All my life I've been unlucky in investments and in taking chances. Here is what I mean: I used to buy at churches tickets to win a turkey or a big juicy ham, and in dozens of attempts, I never won anything. I actually believe that if I had purchased all of the tickets but one, that one would be the lucky number. I recall two times in Ardmore when I could have gotten rich if I had been lucky, or known a good thing from a bad one. An agent came through Ardmore selling interests in a mine. He offered me a certificate, or as many as five, for almost nothing, but I turned him down. He set up lawyer Clark as his agent there and went on to Muskogee, where he sold a few, and then moved on. A few days later, Clark got a telegram from him canceling the agency contract, telling him to cease all future effort to sell certificates, and instructing him to forward all blanks to him. A few days later, the Muskogeeites who had made investments were wealthy. I had had another flop.

I've referred to the bill that Turner and Wiggins succeeded in having introduced in the Congress giving the Chickasaw and Choctaw freedmen the right to purchase at government appraised value enough land to make up forty acres. Well, I had a client who needed twenty more acres. Under the bill, a third party or parties could purchase this additional acreage from the allottee, taking his deed therefor, and file same in the Register of Deeds Office in the county where the land was located. Rev. A. Hill and I bought from the allottee twenty acres out in the Arbuckle Mountains about fifteen miles from Ardmore and two miles from Dougherty. One evening soon after we had acquired the land, there appeared in the *Daily Ardmoreite* bold black headlines announcing that the richest zinc mine had been discovered upon our holdings. This fact was verified by a comparison of the description in our deed and the numbers in the paper. The next evening the paper played up the find more daringly. It went on to state that an old zinc company, which name I can't recall, had agents out looking for the owners, and that as soon as they were located and deeds secured from them, the company would run a spur into the mines from Dougherty and commence operations at once. Almost before the paper was off the press, a businesslike man called at my office to inquire if I was B. C. Franklin. Upon learning that I was, he then asked where he might locate Rev. Hill. I told him I was looking for him to stop by at any time.

Soon the preacher came and the agent made us an offer of six thousand dollars. We retired to the next room to discuss the offer. My partner wanted to take it. He said, with sound common sense, "It only cost us ten dollars apiece, and let's take it." When I think of what was to follow, I can still see the plaintive, pleading look in the poor preacher's eyes. "Let's put him off until tomorrow," I answered. "That will give us a chance to see and talk with some of our business friends uptown." My banker did some telephoning around and said, "I believe you can get ten thousand dollars." My Jewish friend said, "I'd gamble on a little more if I were you. Certainly you can always get more than you paid for it." That wasn't the question, in my judgment, but I thought we had done the businesslike thing in seeking advice from our business friends. The banker should know more about it than either of us, I thought.

The agent did not return the following evening, nor the next, nor ever. The paper had little to say; but the following Sunday issue carried the whole story, even with photographs of the entire layout, quoting in scientific language the descriptions of the deceiving formations and ending up with the statement that nothing like it ever existed before in the ore-mining business; that after the top layer was excavated, nothing appeared below except the bare earth. I believe I was more sorry for the preacher than for myself. We had a chance to make a clear profit of five thousand nine hundred and eighty dollars, and muffed it.

One outstanding thing happened in Carter County that gradually changed the entire financial and economic status of the county, particularly Ardmore, its county seat. There had come to Ardmore a great geologist and scientist, but so eccentric that, at first, no one of note paid any attention to him. He walked all over the western part of the county, especially around Healdton, and reported that he had come across great underground pools of oil. He spoke with authority to the oil companies and convinced them to lease and block off thousands of acres for drilling. In the operations, the great Healdton oilfield was discovered.

I believe Ardmore had more great lawyers at the time than any other town in the country, and these men became legal advisers for the companies and allied businesses, such as railroads, express, and other transportation companies. It created such widespread interest that S. T. Bledsoe wrote a textbook on Indian land titles, and W. A. Ledbetter rose to great heights as a land title attorney.[2] These activities were good for the white population but veered business away from the Negro citizens, because not one Negro owned any real estate where oil was discovered. In the course of time, I was the only Negro lawyer in the county. From that experience, I learned the bitter lesson that one Negro lawyer in a white community will starve to death; that the more colored attorneys there are in a town or community, the better each will do—unless, of course, there are too many. That was true then, at any rate.

Ardmore then was a clean town and a pretty good business center. It was served by three railroads. The main line of the Santa Fe ran through it, one new road ran east into Tishomingo, and one west into the Healdton oilfields.[3] There were red-light districts, but they were not near the churches, the residential parts of the town, or the schools. It could and often did get rough in the slums, and sometimes uptown, when cowboys and oilfield workers visited

2. The impressive array of lawyers in Ardmore can be seen in *R. L. Polk's Ardmore City Directory*, 1907.

3. The Gulf, Colorado, and Santa Fe Railway was the line that ran through Ardmore. The Chicago, Kansas, and Nebraska Railway ran a few miles north of town from northwest to southeast. The third railway was doubtless a spur of one of the two and went into the Healdton oilfields.

the speakeasies and gambling joints and ran amok with the card sharks and city outlaws. I vividly remember one incident in particular that happened on Main Street not two blocks from my office.

Near the spot where this trouble took place, there was a drugstore, which ran a speakeasy and gambling joint in the basement. One morning when the sun was as yet young, there emerged from this basement two brothers, whose names I well remember but will not give for the reason that they might still be alive. Presumably they had in mind to go home to sleep, as they allegedly had been gambling and drinking all night. It was never clear just what happened then between them, a man named Collins, and a tough guy called "Wobbling Willie" because he had been shot so many times in arguments that he could scarcely walk—he swayed and wobbled when he moved about. Despite his physical condition, however, Willie was still fast on the draw and an accurate marksman.

At the corner of Main and Caddo Streets, the men apparently renewed an argument, and it became more heated. Bullets began to fly, and in no time Collins and one of the brothers lay upon the ground in pools of their own blood. As I recall now, the other brother had left for home before the new squabble started. Buck Garrett was sheriff then and one of the greatest peace officers of his day. Someone called him at his home, and soon he was on the scene making inquiries. He was told that Blue, otherwise known as Wobbling Willie, was in the basement of the drugstore. The sheriff started down the steps to the basement, calling to Willie.

"Don't come down for me," Willie called to the sheriff. "I'll kill you. I'll not be arrested. I'll kill you. I'll not be taken alive."

"I'm unarmed," said the sheriff, moving all the time down the steps. "You wouldn't shoot an unarmed man."

The huge crowd that had gathered was silent, scarcely breathing, listening for shots and expecting to witness the death of a popular officer; but no shots were fired, and soon the sheriff and the prisoner appeared at the top of the steps. The sheriff had Willie's gun in his belt, helping the prisoner up the last step to the street.

During the time we lived in Ardmore, the changes in professional and business activity had been gradual, but in it I could discern a trend, a pattern that would, unless changed or modified, eventually lead to a ruinous end for me as a lawyer. I was reluctant to accept the portents that I saw dimly taking shape from many directions. There was, possibly in my subconscious mind, the vision of some great octopus, with a thousand tentacles, reaching out to entwine and crush its adversary.

The specter of insecurity that came into being at the birth of my first-born rose up to haunt me; I told myself, though maybe not convincingly, that I could conquer it. Why not? Was I not born in the southern part of the old Indian Territory? Was I not the son of David Franklin, the most beloved and, with his large family of five brothers with their own large families, the best-known man in the area where he lived? Surely, I thought, my dozens of kin would give me their business and lend me their influential support. I did not want all of their business, however. I only wanted to succeed in the normal way in my profession. Too, there was Irvin McCain, a progressive man, who founded and was then living in the little rural town of Ran, not twenty miles away. He had one daughter, Mary, a schoolteacher, with whom I had attended Dawes Academy. And there were several of the Douglas brothers living and doing well at Lone Grove, with whom I had ridden the range. All around Berwyn (Gene Autry) were many old classmates of mine at the academy. If one-tenth of them would give me their business, I'd be able to laugh in the face of impending financial disaster. At any rate, we would not starve while I was trying to build up my practice.[4]

Weekends we would put our two children in the buggy and visit different communities, for instance, to Ran to visit Mr. McCain and his daughter; to Lone Grove to visit the Douglas brothers (Uncle Bill, their father, had passed); to the Dawes Academy settlement to visit with so many who knew me. In all these visits and many others, I often spoke in the churches, presenting my case, and taking care to tell the people that all I wanted was to be treated just like any other lawyer, no better and no worse.

On one of the trips, possibly next to the last, we learned that certain white lawyers had Negro runners in the different communities seeking clients—in some cases telling the people that a Negro lawyer had no standing "in white courts, before white juries." Of course, that would amount to nothing now, but back then—in a new country—when everything was in the

4. *R. L. Polk's Ardmore City Directory*, 1907, p. 70, lists Buck C. Franklin as publisher of the *World*, an activity to which the author does not refer in his autobiography. The same source lists Mollie L. Franklin as milliner and dressmaker.

rough, where so many people were coming from different states, and mistrusting or afraid of others, it made quite a difference. I was soon to see some results of such sustained, insidious campaigning.

Looking at the situation more closely and remembering that the freedmen of the Five Tribes now owned hundreds of thousands of acres of the richest and most valuable real property in the old Indian Territory part of the state by allotment and homestead deeds, it dawned upon me that the ongoing struggle was always an economic one, possibly more economic than racial; that such a struggle was by no means new; and that in similar situations geography was always incidental. Here, many thousands of Indians, and one tribe in particular, had, under the constitution of the state, been classified as Caucasian, thus preventing social contact and intermarriage with the Negro and making impossible the enrichment and predominance that intermarriage would have brought to him. I know of but one Negro who could have coped with such a situation, and that man was J. Goody Johnson. I've wished many a time that he had tried, not because I necessarily advocate the mixing of the blood of the races, but for the sake of sanity, reason, logic, morality, and clarification.

For instance, the Dawes Commission, a quasi-judicial body created by Congress to fix the legal status of allottees on the final roll, classified and defined the Indian according to quantum of blood and ancestry, with emphasis upon the ancestry. This body was simply carrying out the tribal law and customs which, in the case of the Cherokee, originated with their ancestors, the great Iroquois, who not only cast their descent in but also counted their generations through maternal ancestry. This was true of the Muskhogean tribe and its offspring, the Choctaw, Creek, Chickasaw, and Seminole tribes. But the Oklahoma constitution changed all this by the flat and wholly nonbiological and unscientific statement that if a person has one drop of Negro blood in his veins, such a person is of African descent, and is therefore a Negro. This is not, of course, a direct quotation. I only translated the statute to give its plain meaning. Such a statute not only flies in the face of ethnology but is unscientific, illogical, and senseless, and its end is ridiculous.

I know of one American commonwealth that has had to amend or change its statutes three times in order to secure enough citizens of pure Anglo-Saxon blood to run its state and county governments. I'll point to just one example to show how a loose definition of race can lead in the final analysis to complications and contradictions, and to the substitution of propaganda to excuse a misapplication of a decision of the law. Take the case of *Plessy* v. *Ferguson*, 163 U.S. 537.

Plessy, a citizen of Louisiana, and seven-eighths white, purchased a passenger ticket in that state to another point within that state. The railroad had its starting point and terminus within that state. In his opinion, Justice H. B. Brown stated that no federal question was involved in the suit, not even the interstate commerce clause of the Constitution. If anyone, especially the legal profession, would twist a local state action and make it apply to every sovereign state in the Union, and by sheer propaganda create the fictitious phrase "separate but equal accommodations," I knew it would eventually lead to confusion and contradictions that the Court would have to clarify. It did have a longer run, without interruption or discrediting, than I first thought possible.

The propaganda about me and other Negro lawyers was false, insofar as the courts' being prejudiced was concerned, but true or false, it's a thing that is hard to discredit, if well organized. So, I found myself losing out, no matter how hard I worked and hustled, and by 1912 I was at the point of throwing in the sponge and yelling quits. There were two things that hastened my decision.

A man from the little colored town of Rentiesville visited Ardmore, and by chance I met him. He was loud in his praise of his town. He said that it had a population of a thousand; that it had a splendid school system in the form of a school built of brick, with seven teachers and an enrollment of perhaps five hundred pupils; that it boasted a cotton gin, a sawmill, a large post office, and churches of most faiths; that it was located on the main line of the M. K. & T. Railroad, about seventeen miles south of Muskogee; that the county seat of McIntosh County, Eufaula, was seventeen miles or so farther south; that the town was incorporated, and that its officers were colored, as were the justice of the peace and the constable. In a word, it was a Negro town situated on the banks of Elk Creek, with fine rich farms on both sides owned by colored farmers. In fact, the entire community from every direction was composed of colored farmers who owned their farms. He emphasized the fact that the people were like one great loving family.

My wife and I discussed the matter after our friend had left. It sounded like a land that was flowing with milk and honey. The man was a good salesman; he said nothing about there being large giants in the land. The seed of the missionary spirit planted in me by my mother, and that old example set before me by my dad, "do for others," commenced to urge me on. Then I remembered the words of Miss Dawes that she hoped I would become a minister; that my young race needed trained Christian preachers to lead it in this probationary period. And had not every school I had attended been consecrated for, and devoted to that very purpose? The wild, strange notion began to form in me that I was born for that purpose.

Up till then, I had not displayed any great or startling legal ability. The fact was, I had been a much better farmer than a barrister. I couldn't see much future for me as an attorney. At best, all of my clients would be Negroes. In almost six years I'd never had but one white client, a lady bootlegger at Chickasha that Judge James M. Shackleford asked me to represent. She was without funds, and no other lawyer would take her case. It terminated in a mistrial because some of the jurors became intoxicated while deliberating. You see, it was a "possession" case, and in those days the jury was permitted to take the evidence to the jury room.

My wife and I agreed to make the change without investigating, and listed our property for sale. We would drive to Rentiesville in our buggy and have the transfer man haul our furniture and other belongings.

Almost five years had passed since statehood, and everything that I and others had predicted had happened or would happen. In the very first legislature, the freshmen legislators began to introduce and pass a series of hostile and discriminatory laws aimed directly at the Negro, such as the Separate Coach Law (known as the Jim Crow law) and the Separate School Law. In 1910 the governor convened a special session of the legislature to introduce and enact into law the infamous Grandfather Clause, spawned in little minds and nurtured by twisted brains that never conceived that, although heathens may imagine vain things, this is a moral universe; that there are certain moral laws so fixed that the final certainty is "the wicked shall be caught in his own devices."

The first governor of the new state, Charles N. Haskell, during whose administration these obnoxious statutes were enacted, was an Ohio Republican turned Democrat, an opportunist of the first water. He never vetoed any of these pieces of black legislation. Before any of them became law, I made a trip to the capital to seek an interview with the chief executive concerning these proposed laws. I saw him twice, once during the first legislative session and again in 1910, during the special session that had for its chief purpose the enactment of the Grandfather Clause. I had no trouble seeing him each time. This was the first time I'd met him face to face, although he had heard of me. To talk to, he seemed a fun-loving, pleasant enough man.

In the questions of separate schools and coaches for the races, he said he thought it was really for the best. I pointed out to him how the law had worked in certain southern states, but he argued that the inequality in equipment, teachers, and so forth was due to those in authority and not to the law; that during his administration he would not put up with such foolishness. I pointed out the tremendous expense involved in such double standards, and also the lack of facilities to educate and train colored teachers. He pointed to Langston College (the state Negro college). I told him that it was infested and controlled by politicians, white and colored, and that although we had an able president, his hands were firmly tied and he could do nothing constructive. He said he would look into that at once, and if what I had said was true, he would recommend a house cleaning and have the president's hands freed. Of course, I knew he couldn't do any such thing. I was not sure he would even try.

When I returned to see him during the 1910 special session, I was a different fellow, and so I found him to be. He admitted me, after a long wait, and was gruff and cold toward me. "You again? And what is it this time?" I came to the point: "I came to see what you intend to do about the grandfather proposal."

"Nothing, nothing at all," he answered emphatically. "I'm the governor and have no intention of trying to control the legislative branch of the government."

"Even if the proposed law is unconstitutional?" I inquired.

"I don't know if that's a fact," he said.

"Governor, you have lived in the state about ten or twelve years, I believe, and you know the meaning of such a proposed law—just what is at the back of it. If it is enacted into law, the Negro will have lost all. He will cease to be a citizen, and a voteless man is a hopeless, defenseless man."

He said, with irony, "Maybe your friends can help you. You were against the constitution, against statehood, and now you come to me for help."

I replied, "I'm not seeking any help or favors for myself, but for the help-less. I think there is a moral issue involved here, and politics—partisan poli-tics—has nothing to do with it."

I was rising to go, and I saw that he was not at all sorry. When I reached the door, he turned around in his chair to bid me goodbye and said in a more friendly tone, "I'm really sorry I cannot help you and your people, Franklin, but I just can't." I never met the governor again.

I saw all of these discriminatory bills enacted into law, and I have been fortunate to live to witness every one of them declared unconstitutional, and of no force or effect whatsoever, by the United States Supreme Court. The Grandfather Clause statute was given its death blow in 1915 in *Guinn* v. *United States*, 238 U.S. 347, and by a later decision (1939) in *Lane* v. *Wilson*, 307 U.S. 268. On the question of discrimination in transportation, the plain-tiff would have obtained equitable relief had he pleaded facts sufficient to en-title him to same (see *McCabe* v. *A.T. & S.F.R. Co.*, 235 U.S. 151). Since that time, and before, proper and equitable relief has been uniformly granted when the bill was sufficient to secure it. The decisions affecting the Separate School Law of Oklahoma are found in *Sipuel* v. *University of Oklahoma*, 332 U.S. 631, *Sipuel* v. *Board of Regents*, 332 U.S. 631–632, *Fisher* v. *Hurst*, 333 U.S. 147, and *University of Oklahoma* v. *McLaurin* and *McLaurin* v. *Oklahoma State Regents*, 339 U.S. 637.

Before these nefarious statutes could be declared unconstitutional, how-ever, they had succeeded in accomplishing their purposes. They had un-manned the freedmen, destroyed their dignity and self-respect by making them much less than second-class citizens. They stood humiliated without legal recourse. They had never experienced such before and did not know how to cope with it. Having no trained leadership, there was no Moses to lead them through a dense wilderness infested with unscrupulous enemies lying in wait to cheat them of their possessions, the accomplishment of which would be easy, when we reflect on their previous life and history.

The freedmen, like their former masters in the Five Civilized Tribes, were a happy-go-lucky breed, with very rare exceptions. Their servitude had never been harsh, nor inhuman, as was that of their brethren whose masters were of the Caucasian race. Theirs was a life of indolence, idleness, and in too many instances, crime. They hunted the buffalo with their masters and gave chase in frivolity without thought of tomorrow. There was this significant difference, except in the case of the Seminole, who never gave them free access to the tribal schools (and this restriction was more and more pronounced as the older heads of the tribe died off).

Referring briefly to these restrictive statutes, one Oklahoma historian gave as the reason for the passage of the Jim Crow law that the freedmen were impudent and did not show the proper respect for their white brothers in the matter of transportation facilities. It was true that the freedmen had never been used to treating people differently because of color, but the enactment of the grandfather statute had for its primary purpose the destruction of their civil rights, including property rights, which the courts would not feel obliged to protect because of their poor standing in the community.

At the same time the Jim Crow law was being enacted, there arose a simple scheme to secure the record title to much of the freedmen's allotments without their knowledge. This is how it worked. Conveyances would turn up on record to a freedman allotment in favor first of, say, the Iowa Investment Land Company, and a few days later the record would show that this company had conveyed the same land to a third person. The deeds were regular in every respect. The third party would appear and claim the land, threatening to sue for possession unless the land was delivered to him at once. The true owner, ignorant and baffled, did not know what to do. He would consult an attorney, and possibly nine times out of ten the lawyer would exact a fee of one-half interest to try to recover the land, with the freedman paying all expenses. Possibly the freedman couldn't even pay the court costs to institute the suit. The freedman would compromise for a mere pittance, give up possession of the land on which most of his children had been born, and move off.

You are saying that he was a fool not to fight for his land. Maybe yes, maybe no. More than likely, such a land company did not exist, and if it had been sued, it would not have put in an appearance in court. But what of the third party? He would likely have claimed to be an innocent purchaser for value, without knowledge of any fraud. You are saying that the freedman could prove that the signature on the deed to the land company was not his signature. But where is the deed? In every such case, the "land company" withdraws the deed as soon as it is filed and recorded, and destroys it. That's the way it was done back then, before the method of photostat records was used. I've had two such experiences. I was fortunate to represent allottees who had the intelligence, the courage, and the money to carry it through. If the freedman's allotment had prospects of oil or other minerals, his title would probably have a thousand clouds on it before he knew it, and to clear same he would have to institute a suit, joining many defendants, before he could get a clear title again, in which case the suit would be costly and long drawn out.

Not only was the freedman allottee affected by this kind of fraud, but the unrestricted Indian as well—though not as many of them, because the grafter had the right to intermarry with the Indian and did not have to resort to fraud to acquire a right to the Indian's allotment.

Another means of securing title to the freedman's allotment was by tax deed. Not being used to paying taxes, he would forget to do so, and in the course of time someone would have a tax deed to it. The freedman's ignorance of business and the lack of trained leadership, stemming from two hundred years of slavery, gave the grafter an unbeatable hand in the deck from which he dealt himself wealth, prestige, and prosperity.

Unlike the Indian, the freedman was never a ward of the government, and he never had legal recourse in the federal courts to protect his allotment. This fact, together with others I have tried to enumerate, will, I hope and believe, place his plight in proper perspective in the future.

Dawes' Roll No.	NAME.		Relationship to Person first Named.	AGE.	SEX.	Year
	RESIDENCE: Chickasaw Nation COUNTY.					Chocta
	POST OFFICE: Homer, I.T.					
2418	1 Franklin, Andrew	32		28	M	
2419	2 " Thomas		Brother	25	"	
2420	3 " Matthew		"	21	"	
2421	4 " Buck		"	19	"	
2422	5 " David		"	17	"	
2423	6 " Fisher		"	14		
2424	7 " Luena		Sister	12	F	
	8					
	9					
	10		No. 1 — is husband of No. 3 on Ch			
	11 Nos (1) (2) (3) (4) (5) (6) (7)		Children of Davis F			
	12		For child of No. 7 see Minor Choc Freed			No
	13					No
	14					m
	15		For child of ♥			
	16	ENROLLMENT OF Nos 1,2,3,4,5, 6 & 7 APPROVED BY THE SECRETARY OF INTERIOR JUN 11 19				
	17					
	18					
6—1044						ADDITIONAL

Extract from Choctaw Nation Freedmen Roll listing the names of Buck Colbert Franklin and his brothers and a sister, who were entitled to land allotments based on their mother's part-Choctaw heritage. The roll gives their place of residence as "Chickasaw Nation" and their post office as "Homer, I.T. [Indian Territory]."

AL ENROLLMENT.		SLAVE OF —	REMARKS.
County.	No.		
k Natu	83		
"	84		
"	86		
"	87		
"	88		
"	89		
"	90		

Card 50

On Chickasaw Freedmen Cards # 245.

the husband of Catherine Franklin
aw Freedman Card no. 288. March 21. 1901.
Minor Choctaw - Freedmen card No 482
"   "   "   "   489
"   "   247
Choctaw   "   " 400

Date of Application for Enrollment 9-12-98

Buck Colbert Franklin (right) and his older brother Matthew, *ca.* 1899. This is the earliest known photograph of B. C. Franklin, who was about twenty at the time.

Class of 1903, Morehouse College (then known as Atlanta Baptist College).
The author is seated second from left.

Mollie Lee Parker (right), future wife of Buck Colbert Franklin,
and her sister Lucy Medlock, *ca.* 1903.

John Hope as president of Atlanta University. Professor Hope taught both Mollie and B. C. Franklin at Roger Williams University and was the namesake of their first son.

B. C. Franklin (right) and other African American lawyers in front of the building that housed their offices in Ardmore, Oklahoma, 1910.

Inside the Ardmore law office. The author sits at left. Note the photograph of the incumbent president of the United States, William H. Taft.

Greenwood Street, Tulsa, *ca.* 1920—about a year before the great race riot of May 31–June 1, 1921. The main thoroughfare of Tulsa's relatively prosperous African American community, Greenwood Street was sometimes called the "black Wall Street."

"Captured Negros" being taken into detention by vigilante whites on June 1, 1921, during the Tulsa race riot. The riot began after a black man making a delivery accidentally stepped on the toe of a white female elevator operator and rumors and "news" accounts blew the incident into an assault.

Partial view of the destruction in Tulsa following the 1921 race riot. Thousands
of armed whites attacked African Americans on the streets and burned virtually
every home and business in the thirty-five-block black section centering
on Greenwood Street.

The author (right) and fellow attorney I. H. Spears (left), with secretary Effie Thompson, in the tent that functioned as their office following the Tulsa riot. Lawyers like Franklin and Spears fought to keep the property of burned-out black residents from takeover by real-estate developers and other opportunists operating with the aid of new city ordinances aimed at preventing the riot's victims from rebuilding their homes.

The Franklins in 1925

Mollie Parker Franklin, *ca.* 1929, six or seven years before her death

Waldo E. and Mozella Franklin Jones on her seventy-fifth birthday, 1981

The author on Greenwood Street near his office sometime in the 1940s

John Hope Franklin (left) and B. C. Franklin, Jr., Tulsa, 1944

Franklin (left) with Amos T. Hall, activist attorney and at one time grand master
of the St. John Masonic lodge in Tulsa. The photograph is *ca.* 1950, about a year
after the author was admitted to practice before the United States Supreme Court.

Attorney Primus C. Wade presents a testimonial plaque to B. C. Franklin at a
dinner honoring him on April 3, 1959. At left is daughter Anne Franklin McEwen.

8

RENTIESVILLE:
A PERIOD OF CRUSADING

*T*he evening before we moved to Rentiesville, all my office fixtures were crated and stored in the moving truck and taken to our home for the night. Early the next morning, the household furniture, kitchen utensils, and clothing were loaded into the truck. Then the driver was on his way to what was to be our home for almost eight years. Mrs. Franklin, the two children, and I followed in the buggy, but we soon overtook the driver and took the lead. I had never been to the little town, but years before, Dad and I had traveled to Fort Smith over a part of the route. I suppose the natural thing to have done was to first visit the town, look the place over, meet the leading citizens, and arrange for living quarters. However, with the spirit of the pioneer in our bones, and being acclimated to the rough and tumble of the Old West, we ventured on with no thought of the morrow.

Mrs. Franklin and I were in full agreement that the children needed such experiences as we might encounter. We wanted them to get a taste of the best traditions of the pioneer life. We made good time, crossed the Canadian River south of Eufaula, and near midnight reached Checotah, which is about four miles south of Rentiesville. We had not stopped en route except to water the stock in the streams we crossed. Mrs. Franklin fed the children from the lunch basket as we drove along, and gave them water from the jug. In Checotah we got specific directions to our destination from the night marshal, and it was well that we did; otherwise we might have passed Rentiesville and gone on into Oktaha, or even Muskogee.

It was past midnight when we finally reached our destination,[1] and the little town was fast asleep, except for my friend Jim Stevenson and the town marshal. Jim was there to meet me at the depot. We spent the night with him. He had already secured a nice four-room bungalow for us, and I had the trucker dump my things in the yard. This was the first, and last, rented house that we ever occupied. After we moved in, I spent the rest of this first day in Rentiesville meeting people and getting acquainted.

On all sides of the town the soil was rich and fertile, especially to the west along Elk Creek bottom, as my friend had said. And it lay in the middle of a dense Negro population. The town proper had then a population of about one thousand. Its well-built brick school had about five hundred pupils and five teachers, including the principal, William A. Hill. It had a cotton gin, owned and operated by H. O. Frederick, and several stores. The largest, a general store, was owned by F. P. Brinson, who, with his wife, had been educated at Wilberforce, as were three of their daughters. R. P. Hudson was the postmaster and Jerry Alberta was the depot agent.

All the people were colored and all the businesses were owned and operated by them. The only doctor was J. J. Lowe, and the town had never had but one doctor at any time.[2] There was one Negro lawyer in the county (McIntosh), who maintained offices at the county seat, Eufaula. In time, he and I formed a limited partnership. The town also boasted an up-to-date drugstore, with P. S. Thompson, a graduate in pharmacy at Meharry Medical College, in charge. Like the college, which I was soon to learn was a denominational institution, the pharmacy was a partnership based on one-denominational ownership.

At this time, the population of the county was half white and half colored. Aside from Rentiesville, there were two other colored towns in the county, Huttonville and Vernon, each of them surrounded by farmlands owned by Negroes, Creek freedmen, and state Negroes who had intermarried.[3] There was at this time living in the county a Negro, Queenie Jack-

---

1. The distance from Ardmore to Rentiesville is at least 120 miles. In all likelihood, the family spent several days making the journey.

2. In 1920 the town had two African American physicians, Lowe and Durham.

3. *State Negroes* was a term used in reference to African Americans who had settled in the Territory or Oklahoma from some other state.

son, who was reputed to be worth a million dollars, and about whom I shall have more to say further on. There were but two Negro businesses in Checotah, a cafe owned by my cousin and a four-chair barbershop owned and operated by A. J. Temple, whose customers were white, red, and colored. In those days the Creek Indian, particularly the full blood, paid absolutely no attention to the color of a man's skin. A millionaire full-blood Creek Indian then living in the county, Eastman Richards, had built his own town, Richardville, and he associated with freedmen and Indians far more than he did with whites. It was no doubt because of situations like this that legislators, when framing the state constitution, defined an Indian as a white person, and then enacted Jim Crow laws. It takes a long while, however, to change the habits and customs of a people, even by fiat. Thus, it took a long while to stop the full blood from taking his meals at Garland's cafe and getting his hair cut at Temple's.

In Eufaula there were more substantial Negro businesses. Aside from cafes, a tailor shop, shoe shop, and the like, there was the Brannan and McGee meat market, about the best in town, whose trade was not restricted by color. Brannan had been a rancher for a long time, raising and marketing registered cattle of many strains. He was one of the few men I knew who could guess the weight of cattle on the hoof within a pound or two.

While the Negro school at Checotah was a small frame building with only two teachers, Eufaula boasted a large brick school building with a principal and six teachers. The town had one colored physician and one dentist. They were brothers, Cooper by name, and they practiced their professions in their own two-story brick building. Attorney O. B. Jefferson, a graduate of Howard Law School in Washington, D.C., with whom I formed a limited partnership, had his offices in the Cooper Building.

In a very short time, I came to know many real leaders of the white race who were to become lifelong friends. Such lawyers as Charles Freeman, Claude Niles, and William Duffey of Checotah, along with McIntosh county superintendent R. J. Mullens and former county school superintendent Cheesie Graham were clean, honest, and upright, and won my respect. I learned that they were the kind of men who favor reason and sanity and stand apart from the actions of the mob against minority groups. They were staunch friends who could always be depended upon to uphold justice. Looking back and recalling the part they played in exposing the wrong and defending the right, I now know that had it not been for these men, there might have been many conflicts between the races and possibly much bloodshed.

As my wife and I became more acquainted with our neighbors, we discovered that Rentiesville was torn right down the middle by petty jealousies based on religious differences, spelling doom for the promotion of harmony and goodwill among the inhabitants. My wife and I tried hard to adopt an attitude of strict neutrality, but we were to learn that we could not avoid involvement, unless, of course, we hid our lamps under the proverbial basket and refused to "let them shine." In order to escape the strife, bitterness, and turmoil about us, we had to accept the status quo, material and spiritual, and never express a new thought or idea that might better the community and its people. We sized up the situation, believing it stubborn to change and that it would worsen in the future.

Both factions commenced courting me and, indirectly, trying to pressure me to commit myself. One faction sent my friend to consult me. He said, "I invited you to come here, and I regret the rising storms. I don't belong to either of these factions, nor do many of the good people here. They are peace loving but are being used, indirectly, to bolster the causes of the partisan leaders."

"We don't know what it's all about," I told him. "It all looks like child's play to us. We thought that all of you loved the community and wanted to see it grow and live in peace. We shall never join either faction."

About two weeks later my friend returned, deeply agitated and disturbed, as I could plainly see. Hardly waiting to say "Good morning," he blurted out: "Lawyer, are you a Democrat? I was told you are."

I was stunned and at first didn't understand the meaning behind such a question. I did not answer him or attempt to answer him for quite some time. I was searching my memory. Then he asked again, more emphatically, "Are you a Democrat?" looking me straight in the face, half doubting, half believing. I could see by the expression on his open, honest face that he was begging me to say no.

Then I recalled that in December, 1907, John R. Hogan, Caesar Simmons, C. C. Buttram, and I met in Chickasha and organized a statewide "Jeffersonian Democratic Association," and he must have heard about it. I remembered the proceedings were printed in the *Daily Ardmoreite*, and how the colored people of the city had shunned me and refused to speak to me, even on the street. He had learned about that meeting in some way. I had never bragged about it. Possibly he had learned about it through Professor Buttram, for many years principal of the colored high school in Eufaula. He was proud to be a Jeffersonian Democrat and often bragged about it. I was just as proud as he was but didn't boast about it.

I told my friend about the organization at Chickasha. "It's no secret," I said. Then I asked him if he had ever read and studied the life of this great statesman. This was like adding insult to injury. He rose to go. I said, "Please don't leave until you hear me out." My request was almost too much. He had arisen and stood fidgeting; and then he sat down uneasily on the side of the chair. "I'll be brief," I told him.

"My oldest paternal uncle, Alexander, was a free Negro, like my grandfather, his father, and the entire family, and came and went as he pleased. He was in Virginia almost as much as he was in Tennessee. He was acquainted with many of the slaves of Mr. Jefferson's wife. He hated slavery because he was convinced that it was sinful and a moral wrong. He believed in the dignity of man and the human soul; that basically all men are equal in the sight of God; and that this will eventually be recognized by man, when knowledge and enlightenment shall become diffused throughout the earth. Speaking of the unrighteousness of slavery, he said: 'When I reflect that God is just, I tremble for my country.' His preamble to the Declaration of Independence reflects this thought. His entire life reflects it.

"Tradition, which is often more of an index to man's thoughts, has it that the bitterest quarrel he had with his wife was on the question of slavery. You see, Jefferson was no ordinary man. God had endowed him with a wisdom that enabled him to be a philosopher, scientist, artist, among other things, as well as a prophet. As a prophet, he was on a par with Isaiah and the other prophets of the Old Testament who foretold the coming of Christ. Great men, truly great men, whether prophets in the ordinary sense or not, do not belong to any age or era; but to the ages. Their feet are astride generations and their foresights are as accurate in prediction as their rear-sights; and just as the major prophets were able to foresee the Christ child, his growth, manhood, crucifixion and resurrection, so it was for Thomas Jefferson to make predictions about this nation that have come or are coming true. Understand me, I have no relationship with nor sympathy for the great mass of so-called Democrats who kid themselves about perpetuating what they call the good old way of life. I have never voted for, nor will I ever vote for them."[4]

After I had finished justifying my position, my friend quieted down but asked me to deny the rumor that he had heard about my being a Democrat. "I've just told you that you heard a rumor that is a fact, and I cannot deny a fact." My friend liked me very much, but he just couldn't see how a Negro could be a Democrat. His trouble was, of course, that he thought all Democrats were the same, just as he did not know the difference between the Abraham Lincoln Republican and the Lily White Republican. Be it said to the everlasting credit of my friend that he never forsook me, but I lost friendship and popularity from the two factions—because I was a Jeffersonian Democrat. In those days a colored man who was a Democrat was considered a traitor to his race.

In both factions, however, there were a few neutrals, and they loved and respected my wife, if not me. Then, as time passed, I made friends in many of the towns of the county and in Muskogee. By hustling, I made enough money to break just a little better than even, so that we didn't have to interfere with our nest egg as yet.

The challenge to remain in Rentiesville and help the people there was a very great one, but could I do it? That was the question—and problem. It was just about a closed corporation to an outsider like me, without friends on the ground able to assist me or to whom I could go in confidence and discuss the problems. This was a little town in a paradise, with plenty and more to spare, its inhabitants sitting on a hogshead of meat. All they had to do was to knock in the head of the barrel and eat their fill. If they were together, they could easily establish a trade territory by creating a variety of businesses and interests that could draw customers from afar.

I had already spent much time in setting up a Business League. H. O. Frederick, the owner of a large farm lying along Elk Creek, was elected as

4. The author was not exposed to such revisionist writing as William Cohen, "Thomas Jefferson and the Problem of Slavery," *Journal of American History*, LVI (December, 1968), or Paul Finkelman, "Thomas Jefferson and Antislavery: The Myth Goes On," *Virginia Magazine of History and Biography*, CII (1994), or Conor Cruise O'Brien's iconoclastic *The Long Affair: Thomas Jefferson and the French Revolution, 1785–1800* (Chicago, 1996). All of these and more appeared long after his death.

president; Richard Ferguson, another prosperous farmer, as treasurer; and J. H. Higgs, secretary of the school board, as secretary of the league. Care was used to select real businessmen who could not be controlled by either faction. In fact, that was the move that triggered trouble for me. About midnight, not long after the league had been set up, my horse, mooching fodder in the lot, was shot, though not fatally. I don't believe that the hoodlum intended to kill him, but just to notify me that if I wanted to do anything worthwhile, I'd better get the consent of the powers. At any rate, that's what my friend told me it meant. This made me mad. It's possible I would have moved somewhere else; but now I found myself and my wife beginning to make bigger plans, which were to keep us there for approximately seven more years.

Before the end of the year, my agent had sold our Ardmore home and, with a part of the money, we bought an eighty-acre farm on Elk Creek, the southwest corner of which lay against Honey Springs, where General Blount had defeated the Confederate army on July 17, 1863. The following year, I farmed. I had four horses, one a fine saddle horse, down at my sister's, which were brought up to me before the farming season began. With two law offices and a farm, I'd have to organize my activities. I wanted the farm very much for experimentation and demonstration in agriculture. I needed a farmhand or sharecropper. I finally settled for a farmhand. The farm was without a dwelling, and we still had either to build one or rent, the latter alternative costing so little that we found it good business to pay rent.

Although we attended to our own business, we were friendly, visited the churches, and my wife attended the sick; and we diplomatically ignored the ostracism. I worked almost literally night and day. I cut and hauled my own firewood, except when I bought some from the Frederick mill. We raised our chickens and turkeys and hogs on the share. My wife had become acquainted with a Rev. Jones and his family living in the Pine Hollow settlement about eight miles east of town, who had agreed to raise the hogs, chickens, and turkeys for us.

On November 18, 1913, our third child, Anne H., was born, and on January 2, 1915, John Hope was born. Meanwhile, we had moved steadily forward, not so much financially, but in making worthwhile friendships all over the county. I had continued to look after the farm and to spend from two to three days a week in my office at Eufaula. The train schedules were just right for me to be in my office before nine in the morning and home before evening. I had been contemplating for some time establishing a newspaper, and on July 5, 1913, the first issue made its appearance on our little streets. It struck the sleepy little hamlet like a thunderbolt. Every copy sold like hot-cakes. Presumably people whose consciences were bothering them wanted to see what, if anything, had been said about them. There is power in the press, and from then on, the Rentiesville *News* was consulted weekly.

The old regular postmaster died, and the vacancy had to be filled by competitive examination. There were a half dozen or more applicants for the job—not that it amounted to much from a financial point of view, but in a place like Rentiesville, it carried great prestige. I took the examination, not that I wanted the job, but I figured that my wife and the two older children could take care of it. And there was the station agent, Jerry Alberta, a special friend of ours, who took the outgoing mail to the depot and brought back the incoming mail. We knew we could depend on him for help when neces-sary, and we were not mistaken. As I made the highest mark of any who took the examination, I became postmaster.

There were so many things I had pledged myself to undertake that I found out I would be a complete failure in accomplishing my purposes un-less I adopted a rigid schedule and followed it to the letter. My schedule ran something like this: Each weekday except Saturday I'd spend in my Eufaula office, unless I could arrange to do business elsewhere; on Saturdays I'd find work to do on the farm, often working from daylight to dusk, as well as gath-ering wood and charcoal for fuel.

In 1916, when the Business League commenced early plans for a county-wide fair, F. P. Brinson and I conferred. He was a leading merchant, and nei-ther of us knew anything about such matters. We called F. L. Rounsevel, county agent at Checotah, for information and direction. He was officially connected with the Extension Division of the Agricultural Department of the A. & M. College (now Oklahoma State University). Through two good friends in Washington, R. L. Owen (then U.S. senator) and W. W. Hastings, we received at once enough garden seeds of all kinds to plant the entire county, and some corn and cottonseed. Meanwhile, I had written Emmett J. Scott at Tuskegee for literature on how to set up a community or county fair. Hence, within a very short time we had all the information and material we needed to start with.

The fair that fall was a huge success. Every officer of the First National Bank of Checotah, including the president, R. D. Martin, the vice-president, Jackson Thompson, and the cashier, E. M. Hill, as well as other businessmen in Checotah and Rentiesville, contributed liberally to the prize-money fund. We had judges of livestock, hogs, and birds from the state university; and judges in the domestic science department from outside Rentiesville.

However, this first effort could not be called a county fair. No schools or teachers outside of Rentiesville were represented, although they had special invitations to take part. The state school's officials did not understand this and made mention of it. But we were not discouraged or dissatisfied. Mrs. Franklin had decided to reenter the schoolroom and had spent one month teaching to enter the fair. A state official suggested to me before leaving the fair that I should take the examination for the position of farm demonstration agent for the county, pointing out that it would give me an official status over the colored schools. Of course, that was in the days of separate schools.

The fair of 1917 was more representative but fell far below par. Mrs. Franklin and her school had worked hard to make this fair more representative, and were rewarded by the many prizes they carried off. Again, my friends stood by me and encouraged me. I had started this thing, or more accurately, the Business League of Rentiesville had started it, and I could not turn back, not yet at any rate. I must first give it all I had. I took the examination for county farm demonstration agent, and the first of the year I circulated throughout the county the following letter, taking care not to indicate my official designation. I had known from the start that jealousy would lead to lack of cooperation. How glad I would have been to turn the whole thing over to the objectors and fall in behind them.

Rentiesville, Oklahoma
February 23, 1918

To the Colored Teachers
McIntosh County, Oklahoma

My Dear Co-Laborers:
 Among the manifold duties connected with the office of Industrial Supervisor of rural Negro schools of this county is that of emphasizing the importance of school gardening in the scheme of education in the public and secondary schools. Hitherto, we have been concerned in

school gardening from purely civic and cultural points of view. We have been telling the pupils that school gardens help to rid our vacant lots and plots of weeds; that they beautify the home and school and furnish healthful recreation. But now, in view of the fact that our beloved nation is engaged in a bloody grapple, a terrible death struggle, school gardens mean doubly more than they have heretofore meant. They mean now the possible conservation and utilization of greater amounts of foods for our own soldiers and those of our allies. We should use every possible vacant lot and plant it to corn, peas, beans, onions, and other vegetables and sell these things if possible and buy thrift stamps, baby bonds, and other government securities, and articles for the Red Cross and other war necessities.

In our county we have 32 schools and 48 teachers actively engaged in the profession and we should be able to do quite a bit for Democracy. I know we can and I know we will. I, of course, know of the many handicaps that girdle and slow down you in your desire and effort in this matter, such as low salaries and short terms; but even these handicaps can be overcome by will power and determination to feed and sustain our valiant soldiers at the front. . . . In every community you should organize neighbors' clubs for the purpose, among other things, to can vegetables, knit socks, sweaters, and other garments that our soldiers can use. Call the Home Economics teacher in care of the County Superintendent of Schools when you need her or me at Rentiesville and appointments will be set up for you. She is able and will be ready to instruct you in all domestic science works— Arrangements are now being made to purchase all your surplus foodstuff if properly canned, or you can donate it and it will be sent direct to the proper army headquarters, as will the money you derive from the sale of the articles you have made and the canned goods, if that is your wish. . . . Food is going to be an important fact in the winning of this war and we cannot afford to sell short our golden opportunity to help.

Yours for America and Humanity,
B. C. Franklin, Supervisor

Approver,
R. J. Mullins, County Superintendent.

This circular letter did not meet with universal friendly approval, and not without reason. You will recall that our country was in the midst of World War I, our soldiers were locked in a death struggle to make the entire world

"Safe for Democracy." In the muddy foxholes white and Negro soldiers slept and bunked together, and with numbed hands and frostbitten feet they marched abreast facing the enemy, what was supposed to be the common foe, and at home we civilians of all colors were tightening our belts in order to save and preserve food for our men in arms.[5] And yet at such a time Governor R. L. Williams had called the legislature in special session, in January, 1916, to try and salvage some remnant of that nefarious Grandfather Clause of the statute that the United States Supreme Court had declared unconstitutional in June, 1915. Many people asked me, "Why should we deny ourselves and make sacrifices to assist a government that denies us citizenship and treats us as mere chattel?"

I tried to meet their arguments and answer their questions in the only way I then knew, and in the only way I now know. It was simple and, I trust, straightforward: that Oklahoma is not the United States, nor are the other states, all put together, the United States; that we the people, the whole people, in all the American states, constitute one nation, indivisible, and that I believed, as I now believe, that America is going to sink or swim with all her peoples intact and that we have got to fight it out, as the immortal general said, "on this line if it takes all the summer"—and, I added, "if these summers stretch into eternity."

I might also add here that it is a part of me to believe that we, the nations, tribes, and of many tongues, inhabiting the entire universe, live in a moral universe and that there is a Divine Creator, or Personality, or First Cause, call this Entity what you will, that shapes and fashions it and that, in the end—the final consummation—this Entity is going to have the last word. If I didn't entertain such a belief, this life of mine would be meaningless and without purpose. And because I have such a belief, I'm unmoved when the "heathens rage and imagine vain things." This belief makes us patient and tolerant. Patience and tolerance, of the commonsense variety, are the complements of works, faith, and love.

And so I moved on undisturbed, even though that special session of the legislature in January, 1916, enacted a law requiring all qualified voters to

5. The author was apparently not aware that the African American soldiers were largely under French command during World War I and were not fighting alongside white American soldiers. See John Hope Franklin and Alfred A. Moss, Jr., *From Slavery to Freedom: A History of African Americans* (New York, 1994), 330–39.

register, and submitted an amendment to the constitution limiting the right to vote or register to those who could read and write any section of the state constitution, excepting persons who had served in certain wars in the past, which exemption was adopted in a special election the following August. My comment at the time was, "The wicked shall be caught in his own devices," and "he that digs a ditch for his brother, shall fall therein himself."

During the spring and summer of 1918, it would be a conservative guess to say that I slept an average of three hours a night. I looked after my farm, attended court almost every day at Eufaula, except Saturday, and visited the schools throughout the county. This necessitated traveling at night and being away from home some nights; for if I visited the Vernon, Huttonville, and other schools in the southern end of the county, I'd drive into Eufaula, spend the night there in my office, and look after my legal affairs. If I finished before the noon hour, I'd drive through to Rentiesville, visiting schools en route.

Late one evening something happened to me that I've never been able to explain satisfactorily. I'd just left the Brush Hill school and started for home when two unmasked hoodlums, two brothers, jumped from the bushes on the roadside in front of my buggy, grabbed the reins, stopped my horse, yanked me out, and proceeded to beat me over the head. They were large, strapping fellows and I was no match for either of them. They offered no explanation for their outlawry, and after they were done with me, told me to leave the county.

I knew both of them and of their reputations as toughs, but I never could understand why I was the victim of their assault. They dared me to have them arrested, which would have meant having to arm myself for protection, and that was unthinkable for me. I'd never carried concealed weapons and had sworn I never would. Or I could drop the matter, which I did. My pride was about the biggest injury I sustained, and I decided to swallow it. The news reached Rentiesville almost as quickly as I did, and I discussed it with Mrs. Franklin. A friend offered an explanation but advised me to let the matter drop. As a matter of fact, I considered what I was trying to do for my people, the county, state, and nation so much larger than I was that I was determined to allow nothing to interfere with it.

I have only been able to guess the reason for the assault on me. The principal, who had served the school for many years, had been displaced by a new man, Frederick Sharp, and many thought I was the cause of it. But only the school board had the authority to make this change, and I certainly did not have the influence over the board to cause this change, even if I'd wanted to. The old principal and I were good friends, and he was an able man. He did not take sides in what I was trying to do or what the Business League wanted to do, but I don't believe there was any hostility; I think he just wanted to be neutral and remain free to do his job without any entangling alliances. But certain extremists regarded me as Peck's Bad Boy. I had preached as hard as I knew how the value of industry, economics, and business as a foundation on which to build a life for a people, nation, or government. I'd done this so effectively that the other races in the county had undergone quite a change in their attitudes even toward education in the public and secondary schools.

C. A. Buford (principal of the separate school at Eufaula), Professor L. McNeal, Professor W. G. Patterson (principal of the separate school at Vernon), and I issued a joint call for a meeting at Eufaula on July 20, 1918, to organize a County Farmers' Conference. The delegation was not very large but quite representative. Several Negro farmers and ranchers attended, as well as a representative from our State Agricultural College and the county farm demonstrator, domestic science teacher, and others. Seminars were conducted and lessons were given in canning, the care of meats and other foods, judging of livestock, etc. All of these things were in preparation for the county fair to be held at Checotah in November. There was sufficient interest generated to make possible a thorough follow-up that covered every school, white and colored, throughout the entire county. The meeting closed with the common understanding that no color line would be drawn in exhibits or in the awarding of prizes. And everybody, delegates and nondelegates, went away to work to that end, happy in the thought that, amid black legislation and racial bias so thick all over the county, the Negro would be the first to extend the olive branch and to make the occasion a common fight for the success of our armed forces overseas.

In October, 1918, there appeared a strange and hitherto unknown malady which in no time reached epidemic proportions. No community in the county or adjoining counties escaped its vicious and often deadly consequences. In fact, it laid its heavy hand upon the entire state. It was diagnosed by the medics as the Spanish influenza. People, the big and the little, the old and the young, died like flies caught in the first frost of autumn. The health authorities were scared and the people were in a panic. The schools that had started were ordered closed, and gatherings at churches and other public places were forbidden. To make matters worse, there was a scarcity of doctors and nurses, due to duty in the armed forces. An attempt at quarantine was ineffective. The people simply disregarded the orders and went to the rescue of sick neighbors. My wife, as well as others who had not been stricken, worked night and day attending the sick and afflicted, and these attacks lasted until the first of the year. Each recurrence, however, was a little milder than the preceding one.

It was a phenomenon (strange in the sense only that it was not understood) that always appears and draws people together in every common disaster. Before this common enemy appeared in our midst, our governor and the legislature were spending all their time in efforts to keep the Negro disfranchised, and in some instances white American citizens had resurrected the old KKK's watch on foreign-born whites to keep them in line. It was a common thing to hear of one of them being flogged for an alleged unfriendly expression against the government.

How ridiculous such hate can become when carried to extremes. I recall one instance in point. A well-known worthless Negro in an adjoining community stole a half dozen bananas from the fruit stand of a foreigner, and the merchant had him arrested. At the mock trial (and that is what it was), the culprit pleaded innocent, and when he was asked why this merchant would want to tell a lie on him, the thief answered, "Judge, I kin think of but one reason," and when the judge asked him what was the reason, the Negro, without blinking, said, "It's because he was bragging on Mussolini, saying what a great man he was and how he loved the Negro. I knew he was lying and told him he was lying, and told him he otter go back to Italy and stay there and not try to prejudice my people against their country. I knowed at once that was what he was trying to do."[6] "Case dismissed," said the judge, and turning to the Italian, he said, "I'm going to fine you $10.00 for disturbing the peace, and if I hear anything more against you, I shall turn you over to the federal authorities for sedition." And there were other instances

6. The author perhaps was confused between experiences of World War I and World War II. Mussolini had no prominence during World War I, and besides, Italy was on the side of the Allies. The incident might have involved the kaiser and Germany.

where, if the foreigner did not voluntarily buy bonds, some of his property would be confiscated and sold to buy the bonds, and what was left over would be returned to the victim.

Now, however, in the face of this common enemy, with its trillions of invisible deadly germs riding on the wings of every wind, slaying the whites, reds, and the blacks, the big and the little and the rich and the poor, all this wild racial hate, prejudice, and discrimination ceased temporarily, and in its stead appeared a common bond of protection. Racial differences disappeared. The races attended each other's sick and helped to bury each other's dead. The colored doctors at Rentiesville, at Mattison, and at Checotah attended as many, if not more, white patients as colored, and vice versa with the white physicians.

There was one other thing that lent emphasis to the importance of the Farmers' Conference at Eufaula. It was the fact of Oklahoma's entry into the war in 1917 and the setting up of a Defense Council, the appointment of Dr. Stratton Brooks as state food administrator, and the rationing of certain foods and commodities. This rationing operated very effectively against the honest and law-abiding citizen but was almost a complete failure against the lawless. For instance, the moonshiners and bootleggers were always able to get plenty of sugar to make their liquor, while the housewife and farmer had to skimp and save to have enough for home use, and there was the same discrimination in the rationing of gasoline for home and farm use.

The Oklahoma soldiers reached the battlefront near the close of the war, unprepared, and the few battles in which they became engaged had a disastrous effect. A National Guard organization, which we called the State Militia, had been formed some ten years before, during Haskell's administration as governor, but it was no more than a state decoration. Before being sent to Europe, it had had no sustained training in the science of soldiering. (Some of them may have given chase to Pancho Villa.) Of the divisions of Oklahoma soldiers shipped to Europe, none were Negroes. Our state had been and still was too busy putting the "Oklahoma Negro in his place" and had overlooked the fact, if it ever knew, that the American Negro is by nature and disposition a natural-born soldier.

This is not to say that there were no Oklahoma Negroes who fought in World War I. By voluntary enlistment and the draft, they had arrived early upon the war fronts, and some of them had become seasoned veterans by the time the state commenced sending soldiers to war. I recall that in August,

1917, there were many violent protests against the draft and many bloody clashes between the resisters and army officials; but not one Negro defied his government in attempting to do his duty.

Most of the famed 9th and 10th Cavalries and the 24th and 25th Infantries were called out from Fort Sill earlier for active duty. These are the great bronze soldiers to whom reference has heretofore been made regarding the part they played in taming the Indian Territory wilderness and making it possible for countless westward-bound pioneers to get through No Man's Land on their trek to the Arizona and New Mexico Territories and the state of California. To single out any particular racial group to display their heroic deeds to the exclusion of others just as brave and heroic is not American; but I justify these repeated references because in the histories, in the books that all our children must study, no mention is made of them, which in a free and democratic country is lamentable and inexcusable. I've therefore no apology to make. If I made these references through prejudice or foolish fear, I'd apologize.

On the 11th day of November, 1918, the Armistice was signed and there was unrestrained world rejoicing, although it would be approximately a year before our victorious armies would return home. Many thought that the world had been made safe for democracy; but there were others who knew history with its record of ambition, covetousness, jealousy, selfishness, and inhumanity; knew all too well that the Armistice meant only a lull, a truce between wars, a sort of respite to prepare for another war, more deadly and devastating than the one just ended.

The war and the epidemic killed all efforts at a county-wide fair; the people generally lost all incentive for one. But we did prepare for a 1919 community fair, and it was locally a good one. Mrs. Franklin had taught a part of two terms in the Pine Hollow District and was now a member of the Rentiesville school system. That gave me a chance to look after my farm and my law practice more diligently. I'd also bought a four-acre tract just outside town and moved onto it. It was well improved and we had plenty of room for trucking and experimenting with garden seeds and shrubbery and plants.

Meanwhile, I'd given up the post office job, and my friend Brinson, being the second highest in the original examination, was named to take my place, for which he was well prepared. He moved the post office into his general store, which served as an effective magnet in drawing trade and increasing his business.

A few days later, while attending court at the county seat, I called upon the chairman of the County Central Committee of the Democratic Party and complained bitterly about the shabby treatment the Negroes of the county and state had been subjected to at the hands of the party. I'd known him well since coming into the county and didn't believe that he favored such treatment. He told me very frankly and, I believe, honestly that he did not. After discussing the matter at great length, he suggested that I put my complaint in a letter to him and he would see what he could do about it. Upon my return home, I told my wife about my conference with the chairman and asked her if she had any suggestions about what I should put in my letter.

Looking back, I don't think it was right to have asked her. We had both had honest but significantly different upbringings in religious and political beliefs. Both of our fathers had served all their lives as Baptist deacons, but my father-in-law, Harry Parker, was a staunch, uncompromising Baptist, as the elder Rockefeller had been. For years Mr. Parker had been a trustee of the Howe Baptist Institute of Memphis, watching over it and nurturing it with the care due a blood offspring; and until his death, he had been a consistent and devoted Abraham Lincoln Republican. During the Reconstruction period, he fought undaunted for the party's principles, without fear of the hooded nightriders with white pillowcases over their heads, and he taught his children of the sacredness of his religious and political principles. I recall when I visited his home to see my future wife, he talked feelingly about the sainted Lincoln and his own daring exploits during the period following the Civil War.

As I was then attending a Baptist school, he took it for granted that I was of his faith. He said little about the church except that it was the only church ordained of God. Since he was my elder and I was his guest, and since I was afraid that he might think I was unworthy of the hand of his daughter, I listened and kept silent. On the other hand, my dad, also a Baptist, never emphasized sect in his home, and he always stood ready to defend and protect my mother in her Methodist faith and practice. And while he had been a Union soldier and fought for the freedom of his people, he leaned strongly toward the beliefs of Thomas Jefferson as they had been taught to him by his brother Zander. He believed in the greatness, the honesty, and the consecration of Lincoln. He respected President Grant, Secretary Seward, and a few others, but he had no respect for President Hayes or for Senator James G. Blaine. He had been raised to believe that it was Blaine and a few other Republicans who were responsible for the amendments to the early civil rights bills that caused the United States Supreme Court to declare them unconstitutional. Many Negroes of that period reasoned that an enemy in your house is more dangerous than many on the outside. They also believed that General Grant would never have become president had it not been for the Negro vote, especially in the South; that many so-called Republicans voted against him because they thought he would be fair to the newly enfranchised Negro.

I wrote the chairman the letter as I'd promised. I have a tattered copy, now rotten and yellow with age. In that letter I first reviewed all the black laws enacted since statehood that had the single purpose of belittling and degrading the Negro and reducing him to a state of helplessness by taking from him the right to vote, which was his only means of self-protection. Thus, I pointed out, he was being taxed to support a government that only regarded him as a mere piece of property on a par with other chattel. I told him, in substance, that he must know as an intelligent man that in a democracy, no state or nation can long survive with half of its people enfranchised and the other half disfranchised; that I believed in social evolution because it is ordained of God, and no earthly power can permanently stop the inevitable without being ground to powder and blown away by the winds of Him who, in the beginning, established the bounds and habitations of man and decreed that such bounds shall never be moved; and that, while the Negro was in no position to fight against the power to tax without representation, I was convinced in my own mind that a Supreme Power was fighting the battle for him.

I told him further that after having read everything Jefferson had written, and having heard what other unprejudiced and fair-minded people had said about the life and works of this man, I was convinced that I was expressing his philosophy of life, and that it was not only a shame for anyone to think that he has a right to be a Democrat because his ancestors owned slaves, but that such people do Jefferson a grave injustice by putting him in a class with them. I concluded by saying that we needed Christian statesmen as leaders instead of mere politicians in our government, and appealed to him to try and do something about it.

The chairman was a very cultured, broad-minded, and well-read man. He was always fair, honest, and true, and I have every reason in the world to believe that his intentions at the time of our conference were good. Later on, however, he became a candidate for national office, and only in a vague—very vague—way did he in his public utterances refer to injustices. Looking back, I do not, even now, judge him too harshly. No one in a race for political office would commit political suicide by siding with a voteless people.

Before the 1919 community fair, I spent a good deal of time in an effort to unite the warring factions of Rentiesville into one harmonious whole insofar as the economic and business life of the town was concerned. I first disclosed this desire to a few members of the business league before I made the attempt. Each of them agreed with me wholeheartedly that such a move was not only timely but mandatory if the community was ever to be able to rise up and claim its just heritage. My next step was to have the president of the Business League invite the heads of the two factions to a special meeting for a general discussion of ways and means of interesting the townspeople and those of the surrounding communities in a united and sustained effort to realize their vast potential. The president sent out the invitation, and at the appointed time and place these men with a few of their followers presented themselves. I arrived a bit late, as if I knew nothing about the gathering. There was no trick in such a situation. It was a perfectly normal step in such surroundings.

The meeting had already started when I arrived, and I took a back seat. The president, Mr. Frederick, was speaking, stating the reason the meeting had been called, which was for the express purpose of exploring the possibilities of a united effort by the town. He pointed out that the race owned 80 percent of the rich farmland surrounding the town, and that there was no reason why Rentiesville should not be as large as Checotah, with its own bank, hardware stores, ice plant, meat markets, and the other things a thriving, progressive town should have. When he had finished speaking, he called upon the leaders of the factions, and each in turn endorsed the president's speech. After hearing from some others, he presented me, emphasizing what I had tried to do for the good of the town and the community. He said I had given the town a new life, an uplift, and a boost since settling in it; that new settlers had benefited his own business and those of others.

I made a few observations, first saying that I heartily endorsed all that the president and others had said, and that he, the president, might use me in any way he saw fit; that I had cast my lot with them and I would be glad to help open jobs and positions for our children. I said further, "The only good reason we can give for existing as an exclusive Negro town is to prove to others that we can build and conduct business as well as they can; that we too can have a beautiful town, with well-laid-out playgrounds and parks for our children, and beautiful paved streets, fringed with shade trees; that we can keep the peace and make our town as fit a place as their own in which to raise our children." I concluded by suggesting to the president that he appoint a Committee on Ways and Means, or a Town Planning Commission, to assist him in instituting and carrying out these objectives. He said he would do that before the next regular meeting of the league, as he wanted time to pick and choose such an important committee. I thought that was the right thing to do.

The president talked with me about a week after the special meeting and told me he had appointed, among others, the leaders of the two factions on his committee. I was glad to hear that. He himself was a fellow church member of one of these leaders. I knew he could not be influenced by this leader, but that he might interest him in our cause. It wasn't very long before my friend, whom I could also trust, told me that this leader had expressed himself very frankly. He told my friend that he had no intention of using his influence in our effort; that he thought it was good strategy to join in order to keep up with what we were trying to do; that in this way he could sabotage the movement; that he intended to fight a delaying battle all along the way; and that he did not intend submitting to other denominational leaderships. I never told the president about this conversation. I trusted him to find out for himself, and in no time he did. That leader never attended another meeting, simply because he was never notified.

During this year J. H. Higgs resigned as justice of the peace, and the county commissioners almost demanded that I serve out his unexpired term. As there was not much work involved, I accepted the appointment. R. D. Hudson, who had once been justice of the peace, was then the constable. If there were any arrests, the defendants would make bond for their appearance in court on Saturday, the day on which I'd conduct court. In that way, the job would not interfere with my other duties. After the term of office expired, I did not seek election.

There was but one exciting case that came before my little court. A party was brought before me charged with petty larceny. The evidence was purely circumstantial except for that provided by bloodhounds, who had allegedly picked up the scent of the defendant at the victim's home, from which the goods were stolen, and followed it back to the defendant's home. The case was tried before a jury, and that body acquitted him.

I must confess that I believed the dogs, and had the accused been tried before the court, I would have found him guilty. I always believed that the constable influenced the jury from what he said to me after the trial. He said, "I'm glad the jurors believed as I did. I'd never convict a Negro on the scent of a damned bloodhound. They are trained to be prejudiced against a colored man." I looked at him sharply and asked him point-blank, "Did you tamper with that jury?" He answered, solemnly, "Why no, judge, you know better."

I was not satisfied, and called in the jurors. All said it was their verdict and Hudson had nothing to do with it. In these little cases, it had been my custom to allow the constable to select the jury, but after that I selected them myself. However, I don't believe he would have thought of tampering with a jury in the absence of the evidence of bloodhounds.

Two things made me decide against standing for election as justice of the peace. Toward the end of the term, there broke out a rash of petty lawlessness, and the office would take too much of my time. Besides, I never liked criminal cases, although since coming to Tulsa I've had great success in defending persons charged with the commission of crimes. The other reason was that I had been planning for some time the organization and incorporation of a Rentiesville Improvement Company. I had come to the conclusion that only through such an organization could we carry out the aims and purposes of the Business League.

The organization would need sizable capital. I had no cash to speak of, but some officers and members of the league were in pretty good financial shape. Never having had any experience with such business, I did not know how they would take to such a corporation. I had in mind a very rich friend of mine, Eastman Richards, a full-blood Creek Indian. Also, my wife had formed a warm acquaintance with Queenie Jackson, a very rich freedwoman who owned many oil wells and other properties. I had broached the subject with Eastman, and he had half consented to partially back the undertaking. There was one fly in the ointment: he was building a town west of Checotah, Richardville, and putting a great deal of money into it. I might be too late to enlist his assistance. At the time, I didn't see how we could fail in the creation and operation of such a corporation. But as I pursued the matter further, I was not slow in discovering that there were many complications and insuperable obstacles ahead.

Richards was one of a few Indians whose social contacts were with his own and with the colored race. No amount of propaganda or prejudice had been able to affect his sympathy and respect for the Negro race. But Richards was a full blood and, therefore, restricted Indian. Despite his vast capital, he could make no investments or even transact any sizable business of any kind without the consent and supervision of the Indian agent through the county court. In such matters he was like an infant, a minor, laboring under legal disability. The authorities put their feet down on such an investment in no uncertain terms, and that was that.

On first thought, one would not have supposed that such a thing could happen. Richards, like all other restricted Indians, always had money to burn. He owned a fleet of high-priced automobiles and had a retinue of servants and hangers-on and useless properties and other things from which he never expected any financial returns. But on second thought, one would have to recall that the sacred (?) state constitution had said Richards was no longer an Indian and certainly not a Negro, and he must have no social contact with the Negro, who had been classed as untouchable by the Organic Law of the state. In common practice, this meant that the red man of Oklahoma was henceforth and forever more prevented from having business or social contacts with his former slave or any other Negro, and from reaching down, lifting him up, and encouraging him in business matters. Richards tried hard to make good his promise, but every legal avenue was tightly closed against him.

Queenie, although not laboring under any constitutional or statutory restrictions, had absolutely no business experience and with very little educational background had become so involved that she was unable to extricate herself. And never having had business dealings with members of her own race, it is likely that she doubted our ability to carry on such business as we explained to her. Whether it was that or dark and selfish motives of others, or both, she finally took cold feet and balked at venturing.

There is one thing that we did not know—that in just a few years Queenie Jackson, with her oil wells, fleet of cars, and millions of dollars, would be teaching at a backwoods country school and would die almost penniless. Eastman Richards, too, at one time the richest man in McIntosh County, died almost penniless. The town he built with his millions is now inhabited by bats and owls.

After Mrs. Franklin's and my failure to secure assistance from Queenie and Eastman in the effort to create and incorporate the Rentiesville Improvement Company, I discussed the matter of capital, not once but many times, with each of the principal officers of the Business League. I never revealed to them my effort to interest Eastman and Queenie, only because I thought it was not the businesslike thing to do. I told each of them that we should incorporate with a capital stock of no less than $100,000. To this they agreed, and each of us decided to get busy and see how many shares of stock we could sell to our friends at ten dollars a share. We did not intend filing incorporation papers until we secured pledges for that amount. We agreed that each of us would subscribe for $1,000 worth of shares. We could no longer keep our effort a secret.

Never did men work as hard and as earnestly as we did, but in the end we just could not make the grade. We encountered all kinds of excuses and opposition. Weekly boosting in the Rentiesville *News* was not enough to stem the tide of opposition. The secret forces against us were the hardest to confront. If only we could have forced them into the open—but we couldn't, although we dared them. We challenged them to joint debates, allowing them to speak last. If we went to the fellows we knew were sabotaging the movement, they would deny it without blinking; and if we asked them to make public statements endorsing the effort, they would just say no. Figuratively, I crawled on my knees begging these enemies known to me, if not to the general public, to recant for the sake of the town, the community, and their children, but my pleas were met with ironic, self-satisfied smiles.

In the long days and nights of my life that have unfolded and become a closed chapter, I have had few successes and many failures; but this one at Rentiesville was the bitterest and hardest to swallow. It blotted out and made blank eight years of my life, and it left me prostrate and bleeding, hurting me more than any other failure I'd ever experienced before—or since. The other failures had given me only physical discomfort. This one hurt deep down inside me. It was as if I'd lost a long link in my chain of life, and it made me weak all over, and sick in the pit of my stomach. In my groggy state of mind, one thing stood out clear in the mist: I'd reached my nadir, and everything that I might attempt there would be an anticlimax. My wife's Federation of Colored Women's Club had a motto, and that is yet its motto, "Lifting as We Climb." I'd be unable to lift as I climbed, for my climbing days were over.

Why was this undertaking a failure? Looking back from this distance, I think I can now coldly analyze the cause. I believe the fault was largely mine. Had I carefully examined the situation beforehand, I would have concluded that it was impossible to form such a company at that time. In the first place, Oklahoma had been established and admitted as a state that would make it possible to completely separate the Negro and his Indian friends not only from social contacts but from business relationships; and this was made doubly secure by the constitution and the speedy enactment of discriminatory and prohibitive laws which, inherently, made second-class citizens of Negroes and Indians.

In such an extreme situation, there was scant possibility that a trained, unselfish Negro leader with vision could have saved the day; but there was a total absence of such a force. On the contrary, there was the selfish, uneducated, vindictive, and ignorant religious leader who had vowed, in so many words, that if he could not lead, he would destroy. There is hardly a limit to what an intelligent, dedicated religious leader can do in lifting and saving a people if he approaches his problem in prayer and supplication, and with faith and hope. Such a leader has always been in the forefront of an ignorant, suspicious and superstitious people since time began. Moses was such a leader, and Joshua, Peter, and Paul, and all the disciples and apostles.

America is founded upon trained, religious leadership. It was the trained ministry who founded our greatest colleges and universities and who trained religious leaders to lead a young nation into peace and plenty. Every time I have had occasion to think on these facts, I recall the remarks of Miss Dawes: "Franklin, I'd like to see you train for the ministry. Your race is in great need of an educated, consecrated, unselfish clergy." And that was what she had in mind when she spent so much time during her lectures at chapel and vespers explaining the Christian virtues. That was why all the colleges

I attended made the study of the Bible a requirement. That was why Princeton, Yale, Harvard, and the first American institutions were founded by religious leaders, in the belief that no young nation or people can survive unless founded on Christian principles. No one knew this better than the federal government, and no one knew better than the federal government that it was a cruel mockery to turn over to these freedmen allotments of rich lands and property without legal safeguards. In practice, it amounted to government complicity in confiscation of these valuable holdings without just compensation.

When my term of office as justice of the peace expired, another local citizen was elected and the town grew progressively lawless. It brought about a condition greatly desired by the element that wanted no progress. That element went deeper underground and became more secure in opposing anything that stood for progress, new ideas, or anything that might replace lawless, static leadership. This is not to say that this element was immoral or lawless per se, but that it produced a condition inviting lawlessness, with its inherent evils.

Having seen, first through a glass darkly and finally a mirror crystal clear, what the future of the little burg held in store for me and my family, I began to cast about for another and different location. Too, my wife for the first time became more anxious than I to get away. It was chiefly because we thought our oldest child was entitled to be brought up in a different environment. I had an idea where that would be, and we at once commenced to plan to that end.

P. S. Thompson and I came to Rentiesville about the same year. He was a pharmacist, a graduate of Meharry, and he came from there to operate the Rentiesville drugstore. I did not learn until two years later that his wife was Effie Bryant, an old schoolmate of mine at Roger Williams University. They were then living in Muskogee, and she came down to teach at a rural school at Soda Springs, out in the Warrior settlement about three or four miles from town. They had one child, not a year old, Bryant Thompson. Mrs. Thompson had already developed into a real pioneer. She drove a large sorrel horse and would put her little son in the back seat of the buggy when driving to and from school.

Among my many bitter and anxious moments at Rentiesville, there were a few moments of sweet and pleasant relaxation. These precious few were spent with Dr. J. J. Lowe and his wife, Thompson, J. H. Higgs and his wife, and Mrs. Franklin and myself discussing things that never were to be—not there. Drs. Lowe and Thompson were always neutral, and studiously and righteously avoided controversial subjects. They stuck strictly to their knitting and never lifted a hand to help our dreams come true.

P. S. Thompson was the first person to plant the seed of doubt in my mind about trying to make Rentiesville my home. "This town is not the place for you," he would say in his quiet way from time to time. "Visit Tulsa sometime," he would urge, "and look the place over." I pondered his advice over and over. And if my condition has been made better by moving to Tulsa, I owe it largely to him.

After I had failed in creating and organizing the Rentiesville Improvement Company, the Rentiesville *News* lost much of its punch. In fact, I had no heart to fight a newspaper battle when I saw no advantage to be gained by such a conflict. I had many close friends there, the Fergusons, the Bohanans, and many others; but they were not of the fighting kind. They were independent and wore no man's collar, and if anyone said in their presence that I was selfishly ambitious and only wanted to divide the people, take over and enslave the inhabitants, they would emphatically say that that was a lie. But they would stop there. They were not of the crusading kind. They were peaceful and wanted, above everything, to live in peace with their fellow men.

There were two spots on me that were vulnerable. I was a Jeffersonian Democrat and was denounced as a traitor to my race. No Negro could possibly be a Democrat, they would argue. Well, back then, my old friends didn't know just how to meet such arguments, for a Negro Democrat was just about as rare as a hen's teeth. Lamely they would say that no man who had tried to do the things I had undertaken could be a traitor. I have lived through that smear, even in the lifetime of my traducers: I returned to Rentiesville during the second presidential campaign of FDR, and Negro Republicans were as scarce as Negro Democrats had been in 1912 through 1929. Whereas I had been scorned and shunned as a leper during my stay in Rentiesville, upon my return I was wined and dined and called a prophet. I had been completely vindicated within a space of a few short years.

My other weak spot was the fact that I was a member of the poorest church in town. In fact, it was only a one-room mission with not more than fifty members. The pastor lived in Muskogee and came down once a month to conduct services, and we had a hard time raising his fare back home; many times I'd pay it out of my own pocket. Say what you will, membership in a strong church is an important factor in business, politics, and any avenue of activity. No one has a right to know this better than I, but I've always regarded such things as trifles when placed against principle.

I had lived through many different experiences in many environments since leaving home and the ranch; but none of them was like those experiences through which I lived in Rentiesville. This was a separate world, and it was difficult to prevent its stifling influence from engulfing our family and our home. It was fortunate for us that we were able to draw upon our heritage as a prop, for sustenance, and above all, as an ever-present consoling inspiration. Naturally enough, this influence came from Mrs. Franklin. Our youngest child, John, not yet five, with more sense than his years, insisted on doing, with his own little hands, his bit to help. The next older, Anne H., was also brave and thoughtful; and B. C., Jr., barely twelve, like the others, took his lead from their mother and gave the family reassurance. Mozella, the oldest child, was away at boarding school and escaped some of the darkest hours that the family experienced. I think our togetherness, our clannish spirit, served to keep us united physically and spiritually. I recall the many times we gathered together in our home at the end of the day, away from the roughness outside, finding solace and comfort until morning came again.

9

TULSA, 1921: BLOODY RACIAL CONFLICT

I had made two trips to Tulsa and had discussed with my wife the matter of moving there, and she agreed it was the thing to do. Before leaving Rentiesville, however, there were several details to attend to. I had one or two undisposed-of cases at Eufaula. I vividly recall my last trip there. I took John Hope with me. Although just past six, even then he loved to mingle with great crowds of people, preferably grownups, and if he could, he would strike up a conversation with any one of them.

It was Saturday, the regular court motion day for settling pleadings. Lawyers were there from all over the county and adjoining counties. The boy was all eyes and ears—nothing escaped him. He sat beside me within the bar. When my case came up on the docket and I arose and approached the court to present my motion, John Hope also arose and stood beside me. Every lawyer in the crowded courtroom noticed it and laughed. The judge, Harve Melton, looked pleased and, after my pleading had been disposed of, beckoned him to the bench. "How old are you, and what do you intend to be when you grow up?" the jurist asked. "I was six years old last month," John Hope answered in a matter-of-fact way. "I intend to be the first Negro president of the United States when I grow up." The judge could hardly stop laughing. I was too startled to laugh or do anything. When court recessed, the judge told the lawyers about his conversation with my son, and they all laughed and enjoyed it.

When we returned home, I told his mother about our son's talk with the judge. She was as startled and surprised as I had been.

I arrived in Tulsa, the oil capital of the world, on February 20, 1921, leaving my family behind for the time being. I sought temporary quarters in the L. W. Thompson Rooms, the proprietor being a brother of my good friend P. S. Thompson. I fully intended to stay there for only a few months. At Rentiesville we had a good home, and expenses were not a problem. In any case I wanted to be properly located and substantially placed before bringing my wife and children. I knew I had to start from scratch, getting acquainted, making friends, and building up a practice to sustain a family.

I worked hard at building a practice. It was not exactly ethical, but I had professional cards made, visited the churches, sought introductions to the congregations, and handed out my cards as if running for election to a political office. Not only that, I attended public gatherings and functions, whether invited or not, and if no one else introduced me, introduced myself to all present. I did not intend keeping this up, but only until I had established a law practice.

To be able to meet my office and room rents, as well as eat, I lived frugally. I had dozens of near relatives in the community, and many times I was invited out for meals, none of which do I remember ever refusing. I walked everywhere I went. I ate a late, light breakfast, except when I had to meet an early court trial or some other early professional appointment. If the noon hour caught me at court, my meal consisted of roasted salted peanuts, which I coaxed from the vending machine with a few pennies, followed by a drink of ice water. That made for a good, healthy, sustaining meal.

I had a few cases from time to time, and I'd sit up nights in my office as long as it would take to prepare for trials. Sometimes I spent the entire night there. When I had finished briefing a case, if it took until past midnight, I'd go to the cafe two doors away, get a sandwich, return to the office, eat my lunch, stretch out on the couch and sleep until daylight. Then I would get up, wash my face, arrange my toilet, and walk leisurely down to the courthouse, ready to try my lawsuit. At the courthouse, when I was not engaged in the trial of a case, I spent most of my time in the county law library browsing over points of law involved in some future case in my office docket. In those days there was no law librarian. The janitor who cleaned and kept in order every office in the building became one of my best friends.

Once, I had an occasion to put that friendship to the test. I had a lawsuit coming up in the next few days involving many points of law with which I was not too familiar. It was a murder case, and the state was relying, for the most part, upon circumstantial evidence. The case also involved the question of venue: whether the deceased was killed in Tulsa, Wagoner, Muskogee, or Okmulgee County. Hence, the state would have to prove that the homicide was committed in Tulsa County and that the defendant committed the offence. My friend the janitor slipped me into the library after courts had adjourned and everybody else had gone home. There I spent the rest of the night, with blinds drawn. About 2 A.M., after I had finished briefing my case, I stretched out upon the sofa and slept until the defendant's father came in from his home in the country and took me to my office, where the defendant's witnesses were waiting. We had a hearty breakfast and returned to court just as the docket was being sounded.

This was an important case for me. It was the first real case I had had since coming to Tulsa. My client's father was a successful farmer, well known and liked, and he was able to pay a decent fee. I had an ace up my sleeve on which I depended as a last resort: my surveyor had in his files a chart and map of the location where the four counties were joined.

When the case was reached on the docket, I read into the record a motion to dismiss on the ground that the offense, if committed, was without the jurisdiction of Tulsa County. The state was taken by surprise and was ill prepared to meet this definite defense on a jurisdictional ground. After considerable wrangling and evidence offered by the state, the prosecution was not able to fix any point in the county where the murder took place. The state put the driver of the ambulance on the stand, but on cross-examination he had to admit that he didn't reach the scene until more than two hours after the shooting, that someone had moved the body, and that the ground was so trampled that no one could tell from where it was moved. The case was finally dismissed. This was not the final disposition of the case, but I had established that I was not a bad trial lawyer. After that, the county attorney, sensing that the state's case was not as strong as he first believed it to be, agreed to admit the defendant to bail, which he made at once. After two years, the case came up again for trial in another county, and he was freed by a jury because, as one of the jurors afterwards told me, they were in doubt as to the county in which the murder took place. That was not the issue, but as jurors often do, they went outside the issue.

I'd gotten a halfway decent fee out of this case but had accumulated a few debts. I'd also made a little reputation, but it was not easy to build a reputation as a lawyer of note in a new state where the ethics of the profession were too often worn loosely, and where truth was too often considered a stumbling block. Too, there was the ambulance chaser, as in Carter and McIntosh Counties, a human vulture who always singled out the injured in accidents or the bereaved in fatal accidents and followed them until contracts were secured from them on behalf of some absent attorney who had promised the "runner" a takeoff on whatever amount he might recover through a compromise settlement or legal procedure, should a lawsuit become necessary. The chaser, not being an attorney, worked under a disadvantage and in many instances never realized anything for his services.

I remember vividly one such case because I was on the opposite side. It was not a personal injury or wrongful death case, but an intermeddler was involved. Strictly speaking, the case involved an estate worth millions of dollars and had been brought against certain major oil companies on behalf of the known heirs of a deceased allottee for cancellation of a deed, oil and gas leases, royalty transfers, and for an accounting thereof. This intermeddler secured a contract for an attorney from certain individuals claiming to be heirs of the estate. He not only secured this contract, but turned over to the attorney many hundreds of dollars to be used for expenses in prosecution of the claims of the client with whom the contract had been made. After nearly twelve years of litigation, the case was compromised. The intervenor client got more than $250,000 out of the settlement, but the intermeddler did not get one penny, although he brought suit in an effort to recover. This sort of action simply has no legal basis to sustain it. No lawyer would make a contract with a layman for a division of his fee, for fear of being disbarred; and I know of no way in which an oral contract, or an alleged oral argument, between an attorney and a layman, as in the case above cited, can be enforced.

———

May 31, 1921. I sat in the courtroom that afternoon among other attorneys. There was a short recess. The judge had gone to his chambers to settle some legal matter. Close by, I heard some lawyers in serious discussion. I heard one of them say, "I don't believe a damn word of it." Another said, "It does not seem reasonable." The first speaker said, "Why, I know that boy and have known him a good while. That's not in him." Then the judge emerged from his chambers and assumed his docket.

When my matter was disposed of, I left for my office, not dreaming that there were dark, threatening forebodings riding the air. Then, as I walked leisurely along the sidewalk, I heard the sharp shrill voice of a newsboy, "A Negro assaults a white girl." At the next newsstand, I purchased a paper and hurried to my office. I came across the article broadcast by the paper vendor. Then it dawned on me that this was what the lawyers at the courthouse were talking about. Even then, I was not disturbed. I simply dismissed the whole matter from my mind, secure in the belief that the man had already been arrested and jailed, and that he would be properly and legally punished, if found to be guilty. Then my mind turned to my family and our reunion. The girl would come in from college, and I'd be done with eating in restaurants.

I was just about ready to close my office and go to my room for the evening when some fellow came in and said that there was going to be a race riot; that as he was coming from his work across town, he saw hundreds of men coming into the city and heard them cursing and swearing, saying they were going to "git that damned nigar." I went on to my roominghouse and up to my room. It was dusk when Mrs. Thompson knocked on my door. I opened it and admitted her. In great excitement she said, "It sure looks ugly out on the streets. There is talk of taking Rowland from jail and lynching him, and that some young Negroes say it won't be. There is a crowd on the corner and more are coming."[1]

I rushed from my room, went down the steps in double quick time, and crossed the street where a huge, menacing crowd was congregating. I soon spotted the leaders, one white and a Negro. I stood in the outer edge of the

1. There are several accounts of the Tulsa riot. Not much is known about the author of the only published contemporary account, Mary E. Jones Parrish, *Events of the Tulsa Disaster* (N.p., n.d.). It contains much information that seems valid and reliable. The best account is Scott Ellsworth, *Death in a Promised Land* (Baton Rouge, 1982). The seventy-fifth anniversary of the riot, June 1, 1996, inspired several extensive accounts of and reflections on the tragedy, such as in the Tulsa *World*, the Washington *Post*, and the New York *Times*. An exhibit in 1993, "Greenwood: From Ruins to Renaissance," at the University of Oklahoma museum, gave considerable attention to the riot.

crowd and listened. There was no doubt that these men had seen active service in World War I; they fired up the crowd by telling about their exploits in
the different battles; how they spent nights together in the same foxholes; that
winning a battle did not always depend on numerical strength, but on strategy
and surprise attack. That's when the white soldier suggested that someone
should proceed across town immediately and set fire to houses in different
parts of the city; that would take the pressure off the Negro part of the city and
cause the governor to immediately dispatch soldiers to the scene. He said, "If
you don't do this, they are going to burn you out before this thing is finished."

That's when I moved to the center and warned against such a move with
all the persuasion at my command. I must have made a strong appeal because
the crowd commenced to melt away. Not one white home was burned. As
the two departed together, the white soldier paused to remark, "This sort of
battle is as much mine as it is yours. A great mob is forming, and you are at
a disadvantage you can never overcome in an open fight." I had never seen
either of these men before, or since.

I tried hard to reach Sheriff McCullough for several hours but was unsuccessful, and I learned that the wires were cut. At daybreak I went to my
office, still believing that I could get to the sheriff's office. But I saw I was too
late. Hundreds of men with drawn guns were approaching from every direction, as I could see as I stood at the steps to my office, and I was immediately arrested and taken to one of the many detention camps. Even then, air-
planes were circling overhead dropping explosives upon the buildings that
had been looted,[2] and big trucks were hauling all sorts of furniture and
household goods away. In these camps I saw pregnant women, and one was
so heavy that a doctor was called in to deliver her baby.

Soon I was back upon the streets, but the building where I had my office
was a smoldering ruin, and all my lawbooks and office fixtures had been consumed by flames. I went to where my roominghouse had stood a few short
hours before, but it was in ashes, with all my clothes and the money to be
used in moving my family. As far as one could see, not a Negro dwelling-
house or place of business stood. Soon thereafter, as if by magic, there arose
tents erected by the Red Cross, the greatest human institution that has ever

2. The bombing is discussed in Parrish, *Tulsa Disaster,* and described in Ellsworth,
Death in a Promised Land, 63.

existed. It furnished food and clothing for the adults and milk for the babies. Negroes who yesterday were wealthy, living in beautiful homes and in ease and comfort, were now beggars, public charges, living off alms.

While the ashes were still hot from the holocaust, certain questionable real-estate men influenced the mayor and city commissioners to enact an ordinance with an emergency clause prohibiting owners of lots in the burned area from rebuilding unless they erected fireproof buildings. At the time, I had formed a law firm consisting of attorneys I. H. Spears, T. O. Chappelle, and myself. We erected a tent as an office at 605 East Archer and employed Mrs. Effie Thompson as temporary secretary, since she and her husband had lost their drugstore in the fire. We immediately filed an injunction action against the city to enjoin and prohibit it from enforcing the ordinance. Among other things, we alleged that the fire was not the fault of our client, Joe Lockard; that to enforce such an ordinance would be equivalent to confiscation of property without due process; and further, that for all practical purposes, it would make the city a party to a conspiracy against the plaintiff and others similarly situated to despoil them of their property; it would be using the city for the selfish purpose of arraying citizens against each other; and such acts were outside the legitimate police power of the city.

In the end our client prevailed, but while the case was pending, a friend of ours was arrested a dozen times because he persisted in rebuilding his home and place of business. We also instituted dozens of lawsuits against certain fire insurance companies who had insured properties of families and firms in the destroyed area, but in all cases where the policies did not insure against "riots, civil commotion," and the like, no recovery was possible—fully 95 percent of the cases.

As this book is supposed to tell of my experiences during my lifetime, I've for the first time told the complete story of the incidents that happened near my roominghouse on the eve of the trouble. I was never as sure of anything as I was that that white man and his dark companion were soldiers and had no doubt seen action in the war that had just ended; but I've always been puzzled about how he knew that the Negroes would be burned out. Too, I have often since believed that had I known anything about mob psychology, I might have been able to prevent the things that happened. If I had paid attention to what I heard at the courthouse and had had sufficient foresight to get the name of the fellow who had said, "I don't believe a damn word of it," I would have been able to contact him later, and maybe he would have found a way to nip this trouble in the bud.

You see, the accused was the son of Dave Rowland, one of the best-known and respected men of his race in the city, one of the very few Negroes in Tulsa who had purchased a family burial plot at the cemetery at Eleventh and Peoria, where his remains now rest. I had been in Tulsa not quite four months when the trouble came, and although I knew the elder Rowland and his daughter, Damie, slightly, I did not know the name of the accused or his connection with the senior Rowland and his daughter.

The accused had lived in Tulsa a long time, worked as a janitor and shoeshine boy downtown, and as I learned later, was one of the best-known and best-liked Negroes by his patrons. Had he committed an assault? No. Here is what happened, according to Assistant County Attorney [Samuel] Crossland. The boy was on his job and, boarding a very crowded elevator, he accidentally stepped on the lady's foot. She became angry and slapped him, and a fresh, cub newspaper reporter, without any experience and no doubt anxious for a byline, gave out an erroneous report through his paper that a Negro had assaulted a white girl. What was done to the Negro? Nothing. After a most thorough and painstaking investigation, Crossland reported that the alleged assault was untrue.

Out of this vast, needless slaughter,[3] only two prominent Negroes were killed: Edward Howard, a realtor, and Dr. [A. C.] Jackson, a well-known and highly respected physician. Howard was killed behind one of his rented houses as he was supervising a repair to his building, and Dr. Jackson was killed as he ran from his home into the street, in his shirt sleeves and with both hands lifted high above his head. Let me add that there was never the slightest evidence that any responsible white resident of the city had anything to do with these murders. I don't think, however, that the city and county officials handled the situation with the degree of intelligence, firmness, and care that they should have. I learned valuable lessons from my personal experience of this frightful and bloody incident—far more valuable than my property loss.

Some years back, Tulsa had become voluntarily a sharply segregated city. In the beginning, there was no segregation or apparently any thought of segregating the races. They lived together and were buried together. This was

3. There is much disagreement regarding casualties during the riot. The Tulsa *Tribune*, June 1, 1921, said that 9 whites and 68 blacks had died. The next day it revised its figures and reported 99 white and 22 black dead. Ellsworth, *Death in a Promised Land*, 60, says that estimates of total deaths ranged from 27 to more than 250.

due, mostly, to the fact that the Indians and freedmen owned most, if not all, of the land. The federal government was in sole control of the titles to these lands, either directly or indirectly, and did not concern itself with the separation of the races. In those days, I recall that Negro lawyers maintained their offices in downtown Tulsa and employed a white stenographer. There was at least one Negro barbershop, as well as a real estate office. At Archer and Cincinnati there was a roominghouse patronized by both races, and on the surface at least, no one thought anything about it.

A few years before statehood, however, there came to Tulsa two very rich Negroes, O. W. Gurley and J. B. Stradford, who immediately invested large sums in large acreages of real estate "across the track." Gurley bought some thirty or forty acres and had it surveyed, plotted into blocks, streets, and alleys, and put upon the market to be sold to Negroes only. Then adjoining land was purchased by real estate men of other races, plotted and surveyed, streets and alleys laid out, and placed upon the market to be sold to Negroes only; and ever afterward the same process was repeated. In the end, Tulsa became one of the most sharply segregated cities in the country.

I've often thought how easily our racial troubles here in 1921 could have been solved with common sense and understanding between the decent elements of the races. As I have said, I believe I might have done some good in that direction, had I then understood mob psychology. That was my shortcoming. Suppose I'd had then a knowledge of the working of the minds of a mob, and the foresight to keep my mind, eyes, and ears open to everything about me. Who can say that I, singlehanded, would not have been able to marshal an alert and righteous force of law-abiding citizens that would have stopped the mob encircling the Negro inhabitants across the tracks?

I long ago reached the conclusion that it is mandatory upon law-abiding citizens of every community to consult regularly with other communities, if racial and religious disturbances are to be checked. Of course, I think that, meanwhile, it must be diligently taught in the schools and preached constantly from every pulpit that ours is a government of laws and not of men, and that in a democracy such as ours there is no way of preserving our republic except by orderly, legal processes.

It has taken the Negro, in fact the entire city, a long time to rise from the embers of that disaster. In fact, the Negro has not yet attained his former financial condition. He has done as well as he has because he never indulged in self-pity. Added to this, he has been constantly encouraged and assisted by responsible members of the opposite race, and although here the Negro has never occupied a position of influence and trust, he has been a constant ally in voting bonds and pushing projects that have enabled Tulsa to grow and prosper.

Following the great holocaust, there was a great letdown in faith, ambition, hope, and trust. The immediate future was blank. Two of the greatest leaders, O. W. Gurley and J. B. Stradford, pulled up stakes and moved away, the former to California and the latter to Illinois. Many followed their example, in the belief, no doubt, that if men like them were afraid to remain and face the future, then the weaker could not hope to survive. Not only had homes been destroyed, but all places of worship, chief among them Mount Zion Baptist Church, modern, imposing, and beautiful, recently completed at a cost of over a hundred thousand dollars. Only piled debris and twisted steel marked its former site.

As for me, I had nothing but mistrust and misgivings for the future, and that old sense of insecurity I had had at the birth of my firstborn returned with more intensity. I had planned for my wife to resign her teaching job at Rentiesville and move with the children (except Mozella, who was in Lane College, in Jackson, Tennessee) to Tulsa. Now, however, we both agreed it was better for her to hold on till we could see our way more clearly.

There were many faithful, courageous ministers who stood their ground, counseling faith and trust in ourselves and in God. Chief among them were the Reverends R. A. Whitaker, pastor of Mount Zion Baptist Church that had been destroyed; J. H. Abernathy, pastor of the First Baptist Church, North; and J. R. McClain, pastor of my church. Denominational differences were forgotten in the crisis. They issued a joint call for a common meeting where the watchword was "stand fast and be not moved." This was like a tonic, and I have since wished a thousand times that I had had my wife with me. She always had faith in every trial. She always had trust, the remedy for every fear, for every crisis.

Mob violence and lawlessness have never done a community any good and never will. Tulsa had been given a black eye in 1921, and the entire city felt the aftermath of the riot. This was especially true of the colored section. Negroes from Tulsa traveling elsewhere or abroad were taunted and ridiculed about what had taken place. As is too often true, people everywhere of all races thought Tulsa was an unsafe place in which to locate and do business, and most of them thought there was not a good white person in the entire city.

To offset this widespread, entirely erroneous belief, there was a movement started early in 1925 to bring the National Negro Business League to the city. The idea was first discussed and actually started by my wife and others in the Federated Colored Women's Clubs of the city, and communicated to the local Negro Business League.[4] The idea grew and became popular. The white section of the city, chagrined and still smarting under the almost nationwide misrepresentations of the good people of the city, thought the idea a good one and pledged their united support. Organizations were formed and committees appointed to carry forward the thought, and the national league accepted the invitation to hold its national gathering in Tulsa during August of that year.

Never before or since have the races in Tulsa been more determined to put forth a united front, and the undertaking succeeded to a degree hitherto unknown or since. The national meeting opened on the 19th day of the month and continued until the 21st. Negro business and professional men from all over the nation were present, including Dr. R. R. Moton, who had succeeded Booker T. Washington as principal of Tuskegee Institute, and who spoke at the meeting. Many other notables, among them Governor M. E. Trapp, journeyed to Tulsa to welcome the visitors. The city was properly represented by its mayor, and many remained to attend and participate in the seminars. Throughout the meeting, in committees and in seminars, there was a pervasive atmosphere of friendly fellowship, and the huge gathering came to a close with a feeling of goodwill and a sense of the interdependence of the two races.[5] There was one unfortunate happening that temporarily marred the success of the meeting. A jealous and drink-crazed man gunned down his talented and popular wife. This, however, as I have just remarked, had no permanent effect on the results of the meeting.

4. This is an error of fact. The author's wife and the remainder of his family did not move from Rentiesville to Tulsa until December, 1925, several months *after* the National Negro Business League had met there.

5. Visiting Tulsa in February, 1926, W. E. B. Du Bois praised the city for the recovery it had made from the riot. "Thank God for the Grit of Tulsa," he wrote. *Crisis*, XXXI (April, 1926), 269.

I have always believed that the meeting in Tulsa of this great body of businessmen had another effect upon the relationship between the races in Oklahoma. It must be remembered that the Ku Klux Klan had been very strong in the state since before World War I. Immediately following the 1921 trouble in Tulsa, they had become strong enough to prevent temporarily two of the judges from functioning. Some of the starch had been taken out of their arrogance and bigotry by the foreclosure of their local meeting place; but they were still powerful over many parts of the state. They had succeeded in impeaching Governor J. C. Walton because he dared to defy them. Had he not been impeached, he would have represented the state at the league meeting instead of the lieutenant governor, Trapp. I'm inclined to the view that this meeting of Negro businessmen from all over the nation, and the favorable publicity that resulted from it, served to show the uninformed that the Negroes, as a whole, were good, decent, and dependable citizens; and gave the good white citizens added strength to support their already good intentions.

In the latter part of 1925, I received a letter from a friend at Wewoka telling me that a group of citizens had met and organized an association to ensure honest government; that oil had been discovered in Seminole, and that Negroes and Indians were being fleeced out of their allotments; and that it had been unanimously voted to invite me down to protect them. I first made a hurried trip down there to look over the situation, and found it as depicted, if not worse. After returning and discussing the matter with my wife, I decided to open a branch office down there.

There were several colored lawyers there, but I was very fortunate in selecting a young attorney just out of Howard Law School, R. P. Boulding. I preferred a young lawyer so that I could give him the proper start in the actual practice of the profession. As to his qualifications, I had no misgivings. I'd known many graduates of that famous law school—O. B. Jefferson, Spears, Chappelle, Corbett, and many others—and I'd never met a dumb one. I was, therefore, convinced that the school would never turn out a poor scholar upon the public. In addition to being a brilliant law student, Boulding was accomplished in shorthand and in taking dictation. He could do more in the records and in research work on land titles than a dozen lawyers who had never had shorthand.

Oil production was in full force. From almost every other well drilled, the black liquid gold spurted out and leapt into the sky. Following the discovery of oil and gas, there appeared a thousand agents seeking leases, royalty deeds, and often, straight-out title deeds to these productive lands. Naturally, sharp practices sprang up among these competitors, many of whom had no scruples about forging deeds and other claims to land. And as there was then no method of making and recording photocopies of the originals, the forgeries were difficult to prove.

These land titles were complex and intricate. In some instances, the McMurray's *Arkansas Digest* or the Wilson *Oklahoma Digest* controlled them, or the Original Creek or Seminole Agreement or some treaty or act of Congress; in each case, it depended upon the time the title was cast. Then there was the question of the legitimate heir or heirs. Here again arose the question about the number of common wives by whom the deceased had had children, when title was cast, and the particular law, treaty, or act in force at the time of his death. The matter of heirs almost drove me crazy. I remembered often the story of a former college president's daughter who went stone crazy trying to understand the root of a Greek verb. And I had doubts about whether the great Harry Rogers, the best authority I ever knew on Indian land titles, or S. T. Bledsoe or Lawrence Mills, authors on Indian land titles, actually understood all these titles.

We opened offices in Dr. Coffey's building, almost in the center of the business district and within two blocks of the courthouse. I had a distinct advantage over the other lawyers in getting business. I had taught there years before and my pupils were now adults, some of them married. Most of them were freedmen, had allotments, and were vitally interested in what was going on around them. In fact, they were the ones who had started the movement to get me to open a branch office there. They had never known me as a lawyer, but they had confidence in my honesty. They also knew I was a freedman, and naturally thought I knew more about Indian and freedman land titles than anyone who was not a freedman; and they thought, because of this relationship, that they could trust me to safeguard their interests.

It was several weeks before we filed our first suit. There was the business of seeking out the rightful heir or heirs when the title was cast, and applying that information to the case. We first made a takeoff of the land involved, then ordered an abstract, and thoroughly investigated the title from it. Then we engaged in more research and applied the facts to the casting law. In these preliminary matters we just could not make a mistake. Many times we did not depend altogether on the records and documents but sought verification from our client and his people, his oldest kin and remaining ancestry.

I vividly recall with satisfaction the first suit filed. Our client was Charley Johnson, a World War I veteran and the surviving spouse of the deceased allottee. He had tarried so long in France after the close of the war that his wife thought he was dead. In fact, he was reported dead, and she had remarried. Of course, there were other heirs. We made her second husband one of the party defendants in order to litigate his marriage. There were dozens of defendants, including a district judge and an unincorporated association. I'm sure that the cost to the defendants of the abstract, publication, and service costs ran above one thousand dollars, not including stationery, stenographic work, and other costs involved in exhausting, painstaking research.

We had been engaged for two months in the preparation of this suit, and when it was filed, it struck the city and the county like a bomb exploding. The newspapers, of course, were the first to publish it, and because so many prominent people had been made defendants, the news spread like wildfire and excitement ran high. Fully 75 percent of those who had purchased some interest in these titles knew that they had done so on a gamble. They knew that most of these land titles were not clear, that they were bad, very bad; but many had thought that the statute of limitation would run out and secure their title. Now they no doubt thought that this action would arouse those who had been beaten out of their land, and that a rash of lawsuits would follow. By the time the defendants in our case had been brought under the jurisdiction of the court and pleadings were settled, we had been bombarded by all the interested defendants seeking a compromise, an out-of-court settlement. Meanwhile, we had filed two other very important actions, to which I will refer later.

When we had dickered with the defendants and had gotten the best possible offer, we conferred with our clients, and they agreed to the offers of settlement. An agreed judgment was then signed by the judge and entered on the record. We were reasonably sure that we would have won the case in the end, but considering the time and cost of litigation—and there is always that element of chance—we figured that a just and reasonable settlement was the best thing for all parties.

The speedy and fair settlement of this case made it possible to settle the other two. One was the Peter Lincoln case. Lincoln had been allotted land that afterward proved to be oil-and-gas-bearing, and therefore extremely valuable. He was an incompetent and had been all of his natural life. When he lost his land he had no guardian appointed for him, and it was generally known that, although now very old, he had the mind of a child. If the matter had gone to court, we would have been able to prove the allegations contained in our petition: that the defendant had the mind of a five-year-old child; that he did not know the value of anything, much less of land, and that this fact was known by all the defendants; that he was born in the county and had lived in it all his life; that all the defendants had known him all his life and knew he was incompetent, or could have found out by the most ordinary and casual investigation; and so forth.

In the other case, I'll not mention our client or the defendants involved, because most of the parties to this action still live and because of the fraud involved. Too, as the case was settled out of court, without the ugly facts being known, I see no use in exposing them now. On the face of all available records and documents, this action was clearly barred by the statute of limitation, and my only chance to bring the case back within the statute of limitation was to prove that there had been a fraud committed against plaintiff and that the defendants had mutually agreed and did enter into the commission of this fraud, jointly and collectively, and so forth.

Now, there were certain earmarks, if one read between the lines, that tended to prove a common fraud; but that was not good enough. I knew one of the bunch had been dropped because he could not come up with a certain sum of money, and something told me to go and see him. He was sore clear through, and I told him about the fraud that I thought had been committed against my client. He admitted that I was right and offered to produce written proof that I was right. I told him if that was so, then I'd have my client pay him a reasonable amount for the information. We agreed to meet the next day. Meanwhile, I saw my client, and we went together the following day to see the disgruntled erstwhile common swindler and Judas. He had the proof, signed by the defendants, but took cold feet and did not want to deliver the original instrument. When I told him I'd have a photostat copy made and return the original to him, he agreed. In the next day or so, I mailed the original to him.

In the meantime, defense counsel had filed a motion to make plaintiff's petition more certain. The motion was directed to that part of our petition wherein we alleged a common fraud on the part of the defendants. When the case was reached on the docket, and one of the defense counsel presented his motion, the judge asked me what I had to say about it. I hesitated, and then asked the court if I might confer with defense counsel in chambers. He consented and we withdrew to the chambers. I presented the defense attorney with the photostat copy of the agreement purported to have been signed by all the defendants. I told him I thought the instrument was genuine. The color drained from his face as he scanned the paper, for he knew the handwriting of most of his clients. Finally he said, "I'll investigate this thing. In the meanwhile, we will agree to have the motion passed by mutual consent." This was agreeable with me. I begged him then not to believe that I thought even for one moment that he was a party, or any of his associates, to this ugly thing, or that they even knew anything about it.

Of course, the case never came to trial, and the settlement was the best I had ever made. In this case, we had a certain advantage. Our supreme court has held that, in a case similar to this one, defendants shall lose, in addition to the cancellation of instruments, all oil rigs and improvements made on the premises.

Looking back on my activities at Wewoka and Seminole County, I recall a strange experience. In the case where our dragnet took in one district judge, there was an outstanding federal injunction enjoining everyone from filing a lawsuit or action that might disturb the title to the property included in our dragnet action. We had not been party to this federal suit and paid no attention to the injunction. After filing our suit and refusing to dismiss it, in spite of threats by certain parties claiming an interest in it, they had our evidence man arrested and jailed on the ground that the federal court injunction had been violated by the filing of our action. The writ had not been issued out of the federal court, but a state district court; nor had the writ been based upon any pleadings in the state court. It was never known who caused the issuance of this void instrument.

As soon as I discovered that our evidence man was in jail, I went immediately to see him. I learned that two men, strangers to him, had arrested him, telling him it had been ordered by the federal court. They claimed to be deputy U.S. marshals. Of course, I knew their representations were false, and I called the district judge included in our lawsuit, explaining the matter to him. He was very angry and assured me that he would have our man released by the time I reached the jail, which he did. He did not stop there. He spent much time making a personal investigation in an effort to find out who had impersonated a federal officer. He didn't have a chance. These men were outside men sent in to do the dirty work.

Late in 1926 we closed our branch office at Wewoka and I returned home. Possibly never before or since had two Oklahoma Negro lawyers created such excitement in so little time as Boulding and I had created in Wewoka, or been as successful in putting money in the pockets of Negroes and Indians. While we had, in fact, filed only four lawsuits, there had been dozens prepared for filing, but they had been compromised and settled out of court. These settlements were made upon stipulations and agreements. Thereafter, friendly actions were brought by claimants, based upon those stipulations, agreements, and conveyances executed by our clients for satisfactory cash settlements. Where minors or incompetents were involved, settlements had, of course, to be made through the county court upon proper probate proceedings.

I garnered greater satisfaction than ever before or since from my labor in Seminole County, not in the monetary sense, but because I had been needed to help people who were totally unable to protect themselves. I thought I had responded, in a small way at least, to the lessons Miss Dawes had tried to instill in me at the academy. She used often to say to me, "If your race perishes, it will be because of the lack of dedicated, honest, and intelligent leadership." Then, too, I'd been given the opportunity to return, in the nick of time, to the very community where I'd toiled almost a quarter of a century before in an honest and patient effort to impart to pupils, now grown, principles that, if nurtured and carefully tended, would ripen into enduring assets.

What we had done down there in Seminole County was but a drop in the bucket. I had, after all, helped to save only a few. What of Queen Victoria Jackson, Creek freedwoman, enrolled opposite Roll No. 1899; Zeke Moore, Creek freedman, enrolled opposite Roll No. 1809; Sarah Rector, newborn Creek freedwoman, enrolled opposite Roll No. 261; and Luther Manuel, newborn Creek freedman, enrolled opposite Roll No. 312, all of whom I knew personally? Their combined wealth in oil, gas, money, and properties amounted to many millions of dollars. They all either died paupers or are eking out miserable existences in hunger and rags. There were dozens of others I did not know. Zeke Moore's allotment was, if my memory serves me correctly, in the great Cosden oilfields, near Tulsa. It was said he used to light his cigars with ten-dollar bills. No! I'm not an idealist. I recite these facts to show what little I did in and around Wewoka, and to show how much Negro wealth went into the building of Oklahoma. It is exceeded only by the worth of the sweat, toil, and tears of American slaves' free labor of more than 250 years.

When the federal government sent me to organize and teach the first school for Negroes, among the first freedmen I met and became acquainted with was the Reverend Davis Jackson. As I now recall, Saturdays we used to sit in the shade on the sidewalk in Wewoka for hours and talk, talk, talk. One of his children, Raymond, had run away from home after a whipping, and his father did not know where he had gone. Weeks, lengthening into months and years, had slipped by. In time, an oil company wanted to lease the boy's allotment for mineral exploration, and so, to validate the lease, the father had to have himself appointed guardian by the county court. Drilling tools and rigs were moved in and, after a lapse of time, the first producing oil well was brought in, and then others, until the absent allottee was fabulously rich. Feverish searches were made for the allottee by dozens of oil companies and individuals, but he couldn't be found. And, as his twenty-first birthday approached, the search was augmented.

Later it was said that there was an agent or lessor or royalty purchaser in every city and village in America searching for this boy nearing manhood. It seemed that he had completely disappeared, as if swallowed up. It is said that one oil company spent a cool million dollars trying to find the lad, but to no avail. It was nowhere reported that his dad had tried to find him. In the meantime, guardian reports to the court became irregular, few and far between. What made this game of hunting for the missing allottee so dangerous was the fact that if anybody found him after he had reached his majority, and secured a deed from him, that someone would be in the driver's seat. This game was not only dangerous but became more and more desperate as zero hour approached.

His age of manhood came and passed, but still there was no Raymond. Then the statute of limitation commenced to run. If Raymond did not appear and claim his wealth within three years after reaching his majority, he himself would be barred from instituting suits against innocent purchasers for value, excepting provable fraud of a certain kind. As the time passed, lawsuits were piling up in both federal and state courts, from the lowest to the highest tribunals in each, filed by attorneys of various parties jockeying for advantage.

Three days after the twenty-first birthday of the missing allottee, Reverend Davis Jackson, strangely enough, received a telegram from Arkansas stating that a Negro hobo had been thrown from a freight car, dead, and that he resembled the newspaper picture of his long-missing son. Reverend Jackson appeared to identify and claim the body, returning it to Wewoka for burial. Neighbors and boys and girls of Raymond's age, with whom he had played, said that the body of the hobo was not Raymond's. Some years back, there had appeared in the federal court two different plaintiffs claiming to be Raymond Jackson. The federal judge ordered both held for perjury, and they were afterward tried, convicted, and sent to the penitentiary.

Later there appeared another man claiming to be Raymond Jackson, and a host of people believed him. Men and women from the same community came forward and swore that the claimant was the real Raymond. They had known him from childhood. He told the same stories that they related of common childhood experiences. But Reverend Davis stuck to his story, that the dead hobo was his son. For some strange reason, his wife never took the stand to testify as to whether the last claimant or the dead hobo was her son. As for me, I believe that this last claimant is the true Raymond. He walks the streets of Tulsa as this is being written, downcast and bitter against the whole world. I've spent hours with him, and he has told me the story of the life he led while a whole continent was searching for him. The story was chronological, detailed, and straight from the shoulder. I've always believed that the federal judge, R. L. Williams, before whom he appeared, believed he was the real Raymond. The two imposters who appeared in his court were tried and convicted, while he apparently never thought of having this last claimant arrested.

The question still lingers in the minds of many as to why Reverend Davis Jackson claimed the dead hobo as his son and disclaimed the last claimant, if indeed he was his son. There are two schools of thought on this subject. There are those who hold to the belief that the father had become so deeply involved that he was afraid to tell the truth. After a time, when his son had failed to reappear, he conveyed the title to the property to himself as the nearest heir. Then, too, he had never filed a full and complete report as guardian of his son. Oklahoma law requires of guardians an annual report, or at any time if some interested person asks for it. The probate judge may, on his own motion, order reports at any time. What became of the vast sums of money accumulated during the minority of the allottee? Who knows? Much of the court's record is as silent as King Tut's tomb. Why did not the mother testify in the multiplicity of actions involving this estate? Well, I happen to know that the old wife of an old freedman, like the old wife of an aged Indian, does what her man tells her to do. It would be a conservative guess to say that this allotment has produced millions of dollars in oil and gas. If there were shortages in guardian Davis' reports, or if there had been embezzlement of the ward's money, all speculation ended when the guardian proved that the dead hobo was his son, Raymond Jackson.

———

I had tired of the many long trips between my offices and was glad they were at an end. I'd learned every shortcut between the two offices but was never able to shorten the distance. And, for the first time in the twenty-odd years of our marriage, we had reached a financial standing that would allow us to enjoy some respite and surcease from stint and grinding toil. Toil continued, but of a more pleasurable kind. I continued to keep busy and so did my wife. Aside from looking after my practice, I was overseeing the completion of an apartment at 312 N. Greenwood, upon a piece of real estate we had purchased from the Reverend James Johnson. It was located between my office at 107½ N. Greenwood and my home at 338 N. Frankfort Place. Some evenings—not often, however—after office hours, my wife would drop in at the office and we would walk leisurely home, stopping at the apartment. We both were justifiably proud of this structure, the erection of which had represented enforced absence from each other, many personal sacrifices, many anxieties, prayers and tears. The two older children, Mozella and B. C., Jr., were in college, and the younger two, Anne and John, were in high school.

My wife had many activities besides her home and church duties. She canvassed the colored section of the city and took a census to ascertain the approximate number of working mothers with small children. She found appalling conditions in their homes. This moved her to establish the first Negro day nursery, thus freeing mothers who were compelled to earn money to help feed their infants. And so she sold the idea to the members of her own club, the Mary Bethune, of which she was president, and to the members of the other local Colored Women's Federated Clubs, Eunice Jackson,

Mildred P. Williams, Eva Small, Doshea Burns, Alma Berry, Maude Waynes, Katie Duckery, Corinne Ramsey, Sarah Mann, Ruby Rolly, Juanita and Josephine Wheeler. To ensure sufficient capital for the operation of the nursery, the clubs agreed with Mrs. Franklin to commence an effort to secure the services of the famous Fisk Men's Glee Club. In this effort they were ably and effectively supported by B. C. Franklin, Jr., who was then an upperclassman of the famed institution, business manager of the *Greater Fisk Herald*, and one of the outstanding members of the Glee Club. Tickets for the occasion were a sellout and Convention Hall was packed to a standing-room-only capacity.

During the administration of Dr. Mary F. Waring as the national president of the Colored Federated Women's Clubs, Mrs. Franklin was elected national recording secretary, and upon her annual visits to the clubs throughout the country, Dr. Waring was a guest in our home. My wife was the strong right arm of this charming and able woman of international renown, whom I learned to respect for what she was, a truly great woman.

My wife often engaged in many other outside activities. Often with Reverend Spencer Cary or Reverend R. A. King, and sometimes alone, she would go to business houses downtown and talk with the proprietors about jobs for some worthy Negro boys or girls. Some would heed her plea. A job or two would be opened for a colored woman or girl as helper or assistant clerk in a dry goods store or a millinery shop; or for a colored man on a delivery truck. The employees never knew how they got their jobs. As a result of these quiet crusades, many more jobs were opened for Negroes. I know of one instance where a store would sell to a colored person some merchandise, but would not permit him or her to try it on to see if it would fit. After persuasive arguments, sometimes heated, the proprietor agreed to discontinue his inhumane practice. His business increased in volume, he became a great friend of my wife, and the episode was never mentioned. She tried literally to carry out the motto of the Club: "Lifting as We Climb."

On page 8 of the 1951 summer issue of *The Sooner Woman*, a publication of the State Federation of Colored Women's Clubs, appears the following article:

> Mrs. Molly Franklin established the first day nursery in North Tulsa, and it was very much needed as an aid to working mothers. Mrs. Franklin also

presented the Fisk Singers as a benefit for the nursery and a car was raffled off and thus a large sum of money was realized from the effort. Thus we came to the long time service record and ten years of labor, sacrifice, and achievement from Mildred P. Williams, our president emeritus who not only wanted a club house, but had the courage to fight to get one and see it through.

Long weary hours of waiting in our down town offices for an audience with the Mayor and city officials with her committee headed by the late Frances Don Smith who did much to help promote the project from 1936 to 1937, a nest egg of money was secured and the home at 2001 North Peoria was secured and it was our receiving home for delinquent colored girls.

I think that the Federated Colored Women's Clubs of Tulsa stand second only to the churches in human uplift work, and on the state level, the state clubs follow the churches in human betterment.

Another great force that has done much to uplift and advance the race in Oklahoma has been the St. John Grand Lodge of Masons. Blessed from its inception in the state with able and enlightened leadership, composed of Grand Master Curran, former territorial representative from Kingfisher County, R. Emmett Stewart, twice elected county clerk of Logan County; with such members as merchant prince Clem Taliaferro of Perry, a host of lawyers, ministers, and teachers, as well as trained and dedicated members of the Oklahoma Order of the Eastern Star, its influence was great and sustained. But, it was left to attorney Amos T. Hall, the present grand master, to broaden and enlarge the base and operation of this great organization and give it greater meaning and purpose within the limits of its ancient "Land Marks." Under his administration "charity," the very soul of the order, has reverted to its original definition and purpose. His new program, and what it means, has extended beyond the jurisdiction of Oklahoma and has elevated him to national prominence within the national order.

———

Back in early April, 1921, I was working in my office on a petition to be filed in court the following morning. It had just been signed and verified by my client, when a woman of mixed Indian and Negro blood entered. Her hair was disheveled, her scanty garment was tattered, and her face appeared not to have been washed for many days. She was so intoxicated that she staggered into a nearby chair and sat down heavily. She commenced by talking incoherently. "I am Lete Kolvin. Every lawyer in the state knows me; but none of them believe what I am about to tell you."

Sitting sidewise to her at my desk, I wheeled around to face her. She looked the picture of an abandoned and deserted figure, like the scores I'd seen in my lifetime in the Territory, and I figured that she would tell me the same story that others like her had told me. I'd disciplined myself to listen to anyone who came to me for counsel and advice, and so I asked her, "What's your story?"

She asked me if I'd ever been to Oklahoma City by way of Drumright, and when I said I had, she told me that all the oil wells just before reaching Drumright were on her allotment. Plaintively, she related her story, producing a tattered photostat page from the allotment record of the last enrollment of the Creek tribe, showing the name of Lete Kolvin, with the numerals 8092 preceding the name. I'd been over that road many times and there flashed before me a vision of the scores of oil and gas wells on the left-hand side of the road, with the familiar sound of the pumps at work. "All these wells are mine," she said, "I've traveled everywhere trying to get a lawyer to take my case and recover my land for me; but none of them believe that I'm Lete, and I've never gotten one cent from the proceeds of my wells."

I asked her why she had waited so long to claim her land. "Why didn't you move on the property when you selected it for your allotment?"

"That was the beginning of my trouble. You see, Chitto Harjo was the only Indian many of us recognized as our leader, and he believed, as he told his followers, that the government could not allot lands to us unless we agreed. He refused to select an allotment, and his followers followed his advice. I never selected my own allotment, and the Dawes Commission selected it for me, and it was many years before I knew that had been done. Then it took some time to locate it. By that time it was all messed up."

"Where are your people," I asked.

"I don't have any, not a living soul," she almost moaned.

"Neither mother nor father, brothers or sisters?" I asked.

"No. I never knew my parents. The only home I ever knew was Chitto Harjo's. I left there when I was around thirteen and just moved around. I had several husbands, just took up with them; but Joe Stevens was the only one

I was ever married to." He was her Negro husband, whom I was to know almost ten years later. She talked on and on; finally I got rid of her by telling her I would come to see her and Joe in their shack in the 300 block on Hartford as soon as I could. But that time did not come, not then.

Following Lete's first trip to my office, I visited Chitto Harjo's old home and made a scanty investigation to see if I could secure some information that would justify me in the belief that she was indeed Lete Kolvin. I spent a full day in following up rumors and hearsay, but nothing that could be used as legal evidence to support her claim. I learned there was a half-breed baby girl who had been brought up in Harjo's home many years before but had left home in her early teens. My informant, an aged colored freedwoman, knew this child only as "Dot," which I assumed was a nickname for daughter, and "Sis," which I guessed was short for sister.

My informant directed me to call upon two full-blood Creeks. She told me that Chitto himself had not lived in the old home for years; that he had dropped out of sight and she was afraid that I could get no information from the Indians; that, while the white people had named him "Crazy Snake," he was by no means crazy; that he could cite almost by heart every treaty his people had made with the government as far back as the treaty of 1866; and that the full bloods held him in high reverence. I proceeded to the homes of the Indians as directed, but I could get nothing from either of them. Knowing Indians as I did, however, especially the full bloods, I knew they could have given me very valuable information.

On my return to Tulsa, I fell to thinking about some of the remarks of the aged colored woman, particularly the fact that the child she knew was of mixed breed, and the woman I had met was a half-breed. How could she be enrolled as a full blood, if she was not? Of course, I understood very well. That was the mistake of the Dawes Commission, a mistake that could not be corrected. I had personally known many such cases. I remember two such incidents very well. Two Chickasaw freedmen families who did not have one drop of Indian blood in their veins were yet placed on the full-blood Chickasaw Indian Roll. By the act of Congress creating the Dawes Commission, that body was made a quasi-judicial body, and its findings as to quantum of blood were final and could not be challenged by any court or legal process.

The commission had a prodigious task to perform in surveying the millions of acres of land in the five nations, preparing the final rolls of many thousands of Indians and their freedmen in these five nations, appraising their lands, and so forth. Remember, it took them from 1893 up to and including 1905. There was nothing dishonest in the work of the commission, but they did not see personally all the people who applied for enrollment. Possibly, in some cases, these people enrolled some of their members who were absent. Perhaps an Indian enrolled an old freedman friend as an Indian. At Tishomingo in 1903, I saw an Indian appear before the commission and enroll a colored woman as his niece. Of course, this woman was very fair. This was made easy when we remember that the relationship between many full-blood Creek and Seminole Indians and their former slaves was very close—and tender.

I recall the enrollment of a myth. This case was carried all the way to the United States Supreme Court, but that court held that the enrollment record of the Dawes Commission was conclusive and impervious to both direct and collateral attack. In other words, if that tribunal found that a certain person existed, there was no way to dispute it, although no such person ever lived. On reflection, it is easy to see that the courts could make no other ruling. If title to one piece of land could be disturbed, then all could be disturbed, which could produce widespread havoc.

I never saw Lete again. Then, eight years later, when she was dead, an old friend of mine, J. I. Wallace, a retired schoolteacher, came to my office with her surviving spouse, Joe Stevens. We spent almost a half day discussing whether or not Lete Kolvin was the real McCoy. Mr. Wallace was sure she was. He had been making extensive investigations for several years. I was not convinced. Even if she had been the real Lete, how would we prove it? I had not run across any witnesses, and Mr. Wallace hadn't found any—but he had a strong lead, he thought. Finally, I had the county court appoint Mr. Wallace, with the consent of Joe Stevens, administrator of the estate of Lete Kolvin.

On the 30th day of September, 1930, I filed suit No. 17,179 in the District Court of Creek County, at Sapulpa, against Nancy Barnett and several oil companies for the cancellation of deeds and other liens against the allotment of the deceased and for accounting and so forth. Then commenced the hard work that was to extend over a period of a dozen years or more, taking depositions, looking for live witnesses, and attending the hearing in the taking of depositions by the many opposing defendants.

This entailed riding night and day in freezing weather and going without food or water for many hours. I recall once starting near nightfall from Seminole for Langston. I ran out of gas and was compelled to walk back to the nearest station, a distance of three miles. Before I could get tanked up, night had descended. As I resumed my trip, it seemed my sweat from walking these six miles had turned to ice, and I was not only hungry and thirsty, but chilled to the bone. When I reached Langston, it was well past midnight and my hands and fingers were so numb that I had a difficult time steering my car. I had not seen any fire since I left home about daylight the day before. (On this trip, I had not used my car heater because it was not safe and I feared asphyxiation from carbon monoxide.) I knocked on the door of my old friend Bill Dunmore, and he admitted me. And while I tried to warm myself, he gave me some brandy and prepared a midnight snack. I cannot say I got thoroughly warmed that night, though I crawled into bed between two heavy blankets and other covers.

On this particular trip I was on my way to attend the taking of depositions in the Lete Kolvin case, and I did not know the exact place where they would be taken, or the exact time. The "notice" was in the regular Oklahoma form, "between the hours of 10 A.M. and 2 P.M.," and the place was near the state capitol, at a private residence. I had never been there. I would have to find the street and the house number. So after a hurried breakfast I left Bill's and was on my way very early. The morning air was brisk, and the ground was blanketed with a heavy frost, glazed and resembling a young snow.

I finally located the street and the house. I knew it was in the white part of town, and the occupants had to be either white or Indian. I knew this meant I would have to wait outside until some of the white attorneys arrived. Instead of the day becoming warmer as the sun climbed, it grew progressively colder. Man's body is a peculiar mechanism, or is it his mind? It seemed to me that the cold I had suffered the night before reappeared in me and combined with that of the morning. I grew so numb all over that it would be only a short time before I could not move. My teeth began to chatter to such a degree that I could not control them.

I got out of the car clumsily and walked up and down the sidewalk to get my blood circulating. I knew I looked foolish, and that it wasn't a sane thing for a man of color to do in a white section of the city. So I stepped boldly upon the porch of the residence and rapped on the front door. An Indian woman appeared and, with the door ajar, inquired my business. I told her, and she could see I was very cold, for she invited me in. A glorious and inviting warmth embraced me as I sat down in a roomy armchair. "I don't know a thing about this," she said, as I more fully told her about my mission. "They must want to question my mother," she continued, "but she is in her bedroom very ill, and I'm sure she is too sick to answer any questions."

It was one o'clock before the other attorneys began to arrive, and it was two before they were all there, only to learn that the elderly woman would not be able to give her deposition. It was three that afternoon before I reached Langston on my return home. Bill took me to a mechanic who fixed my car heater, and I did not suffer on the remainder of my trip.

About four years after the suit had been filed, a number of intervenors were made parties to the action. Joe Stevens and his brother, Anderson Stevens, had died, leaving two nephews, Willie and Floyd Mayweather, as heirs. A woman, Izora Lee, née Izora Alexander, intervened, claiming to be a half sister of Lete. The law firm of Bailey and Holliman of Bartlesville and a local lawyer, W. B. Blair, appeared for Anderson, with Charles Rogers representing Mrs. Lee, and a Nugent of Kansas City appearing for the nephews, the Mayweathers. Except for Rogers, these lawyers came along for the ride. They took no part in the taking of the dozens of depositions and rarely appeared at the court hearings in Sapulpa. Since Wallace had been appointed as administrator of the estate, he was the official representative and was duty bound to protect it. These attorneys had consulted neither Mr. Wallace nor me before entering the case. I did not object in the record, although the administrator told the nephews, so he informed me, that they did not need counsel; that he was representing the estate, of which they were a part.

10

1929: THE BEGINNING OF PANIC

*W*hen Boulding and I closed the branch law office, we had each made and saved a very large sum of money. Boulding invested a goodly sum in the purchase of oil and gas royalties. I bought a large acreage in a 300-acre tract in McCurtain County, a large acreage in a 400-acre tract in Pushmataha County, and a large acreage in Latimer County, all in southeastern Oklahoma. At that time there was a mineral fever throughout Oklahoma. There were very few people who did not believe that under every foot of land in the state there was an oil pool. If we had not had such heavy obligations at the time, we might have bought all three tracts above referred to and then had nightly dreams of dozens of oil and gas wells ensuring inexhaustible riches beyond calculation; but we had immediate responsibilities to our children, two of whom were still at college and two more who would enter college in a very few years. But more than once we were tempted to take a chance. Why not?

It was true that President Harding had not done so well, what with the scandal that broke while Mr. Coolidge was in office. But everybody had confidence in the man who "did not choose to run again." He was clean, none of the soot had rubbed off on him from his predecessor's administration, although his partisan opposition tried hard to saddle him with what followed. Looking back, without bias, the worst that might be said about him was that he was too conservative and too stubborn. He tried to justify

219

the administration of the man whom he had succeeded. Under his administration, the Soldier's Bonus Bill became law, Byrd made it to the South Pole, Lindbergh made his solo flight across the Atlantic in his *Spirit of St. Louis*, and the Transatlantic Radio Service began. There seemed to be prosperity everywhere, and the nation was recognized as a world power everywhere. Reputable economists had said the nation was financially solid.

Coolidge's successor, Herbert Hoover, had been a member of his cabinet, was known all over the world for his love of humanity, as he had proved it by ministering to the needs of the Belgian people, and had come through without a breath of the oil scandal sticking to him. When he said that there would be a chicken in every pot and a car in every garage, the people believed him. At least I did, and I think he did too. The crash came, however, and it was worldwide. It came as a thief in the night. Savings of a lifetime were swept away overnight. Not only did our money dwindle to nearly nothing, but we were unable to pay taxes on our acreages and our farm at Rentiesville, and lost them all. We might have saved some of it by withdrawing our children from school, but we would not.

I don't blame Mr. Hoover for this greatest of all depressions, but I blame his party and many not of his party. It was due to avarice and greed by manipulators and gamblers in the stock market. He tried hard to stem the tide by causing to be enacted into law the Reconstruction Finance Corporation and other humane concerns, but he could not secure honest and proper administration of the laws. Very little help reached down to the most needy. Railroad companies, favored corporations, and certain banks and supposedly big businesses, already defunct beyond redemption, swallowed up the help that the little fellow should have received, well knowing that they had reached the point of bankruptcy where there was no return.

The first six months of 1933 were dark, scary, and uncertain. The banks were closed for general business, except for trickles of withdrawals by a favored few. The ordinary depositor was unable to cash a check on his small savings. Washington should have ordered that no one would be permitted to make any withdrawals before a bank's solvency had been established by the proper government authority. In smaller places than Tulsa, the people were harder hit. An old friend from Rentiesville told me that the banks at Checotah were tightly closed and that the price of rabbits had risen because they could be easily sold in Checotah.

These conditions lasted for many months, but it was not until the middle of 1935, more than two years after Franklin D. Roosevelt took office as president, that jobs began to open up and relief began to flow. Here, what made conditions so hard was the fact that most Negro homes had been rebuilt from the ashes of the race conflict back in the twenties, and there were still heavy mortgages against them, with threats of foreclosure. The Federal Home Loan Corporation came into being and was a godsend. By this time the many alphabetical agencies of the government had reached down and were lending a helping hand to almost every citizen. The government, in so short a time, had accomplished a marvelous, I should say miraculous, feat. I wondered how the federal government, that I had known to be cumbersome, could move so swiftly.

My wonder was dispelled when I visited Washington some time later and went through the different departments. I found a Negro, alert and highly educated, serving in many departments as adviser, who knew to the last word the nature and needs of his people; and the executive officer of each department relied implicitly upon his knowledge. Here was our government fulfilling, in a commonsense, practical way, the needs of the colored people as well as of others; conducting for the first time in its history, as far as I knew, a "government of the people, for the people, and by the people." I think that experience made the race feel as other men. If Lincoln gave the Negro his physical freedom, I think Roosevelt gave him his spiritual liberty.[1] I think that experience marked the beginning anew of his social evolution. It may not be too much to say that had he not had such an experience, he might not have advanced to the degree of accomplishment in his fight for civil rights, educational betterment, and other things to which he aspired.[2]

President Roosevelt appeared upon the American scene in the nick of time, when the country was plunging into an abyss. I don't believe that there was any other living American at the time with the imagination and boldness

1. For a detailed account of how African Americans fared under the New Deal, see John H. Kirby, *Black Americans in the Roosevelt Era: Liberalism and Race* (Knoxville, 1980). To see what happened in a specific agency, consult Nancy L. Grant, *The TVA and Black Americans: Planning for the Status Quo* (Philadelphia, 1990).

2. On this point and related matters, see Harvard Sitkoff, *A New Deal for Blacks: The Emergence of Civil Rights as a National Issue: The Depression Decade* (New York, 1978).

to save it as Roosevelt had. And even he could not have coped with the situation had not the radio been invented. In the gloom that surrounded them, he spoke over the radio to the people with authority, and they believed and followed him gladly. He was a dedicated man, bigger than his party, any party, as witnessed by his appointment of Stimson, Knox, and Hurley to policy-making positions. I cannot recall any other American president who so lightly regarded the party line when this nation was in peril.[3] He literally agreed with an ancient Greek savant, whose name I do not now recall, who wrote that the first business of any government is the care of its people. President Roosevelt and his successor, Harry S. Truman, had many beliefs in common; but the former's method of approach, his mode of operation, was different.

My daughter had graduated from Lane College with a teacher's certificate, had completed her undergraduate work at West Virginia State College with an A.B. degree, and was now teaching in the public school system in Tulsa. B. C., Jr., had graduated from Fisk University with his A.B. and was principal of a six-teacher school at Snake Creek, just south of Bixby in Tulsa County. Anne H. was an upperclasswoman at Talladega College, Alabama, and John Hope was an upperclassman at Fisk University.

Meanwhile, the most startling and pleasant surprise of my life came when I was appointed by District Court Judge Saul Yager in 1928 as master in chancery to hear and determine a church dispute between the members of the Church of God in Christ and its pastor, the Reverend William G. Strassner. On the day of the first hearing, it was I who ascended the bench instead of Judge Yager. As I came out of the judge's chamber and took my seat, there was a sea of upturned faces looking at me, including those of the reporters from the two local daily newspapers. After the bailiff had opened court in due form, I asked the attorneys for both sides if they were ready, and each announced in the affirmative. I looked at the pleadings in the case and then inquired of the attorneys if the church had exhausted every effort to settle this matter before bringing the pending action. The pleadings did not show this. I asked the

3. The author also wrote an essay entitled "Franklin Delano Roosevelt and the American Negro," which was published in the *Oklahoma Eagle*, June 30, 1960.

clerk and pastor of the church to approach the bench. The clerk had no minutes to satisfy my inquiry, and the statement of the pastor did not satisfy me.

I then addressed the attorneys to the effect that it had always been the policy of civil courts not to interfere in religious or church disputes until every remedy within church policy had been explored, and that the petition, properly verified, should disclose this fact; that I doubted if I had jurisdiction; but for purposes of settling the matter, as all agreed was urgent, I would acknowledge jurisdiction, provided petitioners would amend their petition to show they had followed the polity and laws of their church; that formal charges would have to be brought by their proper officials, proper notices to the pastor would have to be given, trial and vote of the church membership, etc. I then adjourned court to a certain day, giving sufficient time for all this to be done and for petition to be amended and answer filed.

This was the first time that a Negro lawyer had ever been appointed to such a position south of the Mason and Dixon line, and the court reporters rushed to the telephones to send in the story. Within two or three days, the Pittsburgh *Courier* wired the Tulsa *Tribune* to secure my photograph, interview me, and send the picture and interview to the *Courier*. As soon as the *Courier* had printed the story, letters began to pour into my home and office from all over the nation—letters from old schoolmates, from friends and relatives and old acquaintances, including one from the Reverend Williamson, who had officiated at my wedding on the first day of April, 1903. The case? Well, it was settled by the resignation of the Reverend Strassner after the church had legally voted him out as its pastor.

I have never claimed to be a criminal lawyer of note; but I have had many criminal cases and have been fairly successful, especially in those which had an element of racial or religious bigotry. One such case arose in 1934 in the *State of Oklahoma* v. *O. C. Foster*, the defendant having been indicted by the Tulsa County Grand Jury, for the alleged murder of a white man, Whitey Payne.

Foster was a very wealthy man, and his wife, Helen Foster, a woman of high standing and considerable business ability, owned and operated a large drugstore and conducted other businesses in her own right. Payne was known as a numbers racket man, engaged exclusively in the Negro section of the city in the policy racket business. It was the theory of the state that Foster was also engaged in such business, although it had never been proved, and that Foster had either killed Payne or had had it done because Payne had "horned in" on Foster's territory. Further, that Foster was part of a gang of gamblers, hoodlums, and murderers with headquarters in Kansas City, Missouri, that had invaded the Tulsa Negro district to take over; that Payne was in their way, and this was the motive for his murder.

To prove its theory, the state spent large sums of money employing undercover men, crack crime investigators, in Tulsa and in Kansas City. There had been other arrests of accomplices and conspirators in the alleged commission of the murder, one or two of whom were citizens of Kansas City. Meanwhile, Foster was sent to jail without bond immediately upon the return of the indictment against him.

Foster employed a white attorney to represent him, paying him a very large retainer, as I learned upon reliable information. However, as the case moved nearer to trial, this attorney left town and Mrs. Foster brought me into the case. No defense had been prepared, and I had to start from scratch. After several conferences, I became convinced that Foster had had nothing to do with the killing and didn't know anything about such a plot, if there was one. I visited the county attorney, told him I had been retained to defend Foster, and asked him when the case would be tried. He told me that he knew nothing about the case, that one of his assistants was handling it, and he directed me to him.

I found the assistant county attorney highly incensed. He told me Foster was as guilty as hell, that he intended to see that he was electrocuted for "his crime," and that I should not enter the case, as it would hurt my race. He was so unreasonable in his tirade and so consumed by anger that he would not tell me when the case would be set for trial. A complete panel of petit jurors had already been summoned for the district court sitting. After looking over the list, I, acting with the law firm of Mills and Cowen, filed a motion in the case to quash and discharge the jury panel on the ground that Foster had been discriminated against in the selection of the panel, on account of his race. At the hearing on the motion, we summoned the jury commissioners, the county sheriff, the district court clerk, and several leading colored men to prove the allegations of our motion.

Foster, seeing that his lawyer did not intend to show up for his trial, employed another firm of white lawyers to assist in representing him. I worked day and night in preparation for the trial, discovering and following leads to secure sufficient facts that would prove the innocence of my client. In doing this, I found it was necessary to make a trip to Kansas City, and I took with me two crack investigators, one white and one black, who had previously worked together in cases somewhat similar to the Foster case. I knew the state intended to use some witnesses from Kansas City, but I did not know how many or who these men were, as they had not been subpoenaed. In Kansas City we learned who they were and that they would do anything for a price. At first, I was inclined to believe that the assistant county attorney was in on this because of his attitude toward me; but we found to our complete satisfaction that neither the state nor the assistant county attorney knew anything about it. These crooks from Kansas City saw a chance to destroy Foster and either move in themselves or sell their chance to other shady characters.

As the trial neared, the state's fake witnesses were brought to Tulsa and jailed "as material witnesses." I secured a court order giving me permission to interview these men in jail. I took the court reporter with me, gave the jailer a copy of the order, and had him bring the two men to his office where I might question them. I said to them, "I don't know why the state has brought you here, and I don't know whether or not you will answer my questions truthfully; in any case, I'm convinced from provable investigation in your hometown that you know absolutely nothing about this case. I don't know what your motive is, but if you lie on the witness stand, I'll see that you are prosecuted for perjury, so help me God. I do not make this statement to intimidate you. If you tell the truth, you will have nothing to fear, for the state will protect you."

Finally, the case came to trial. The entire weight of preparing a defense had fallen upon my shoulders. I was morally certain that the defendant was not guilty, and I had done all I could to prove it, to bring out the facts—all of them—and secure a complete exoneration. The assistant county attorney had sitting beside him the wife of the deceased. She knew nothing about the murder, and it was plain that she was only present to sway the jury by gaining their sympathy. In addition, the children of the deceased romped all over the courtroom during the entire time the case was being tried, which was some three days or so.

It was plain that the assistant county attorney was grimly enjoying every minute of the sordid spectacle and the prospect of Foster's being thrown to the lions and devoured as an example to all colored men that, under no circumstances, should they ever kill a white man in Tulsa County. He said this in so many words as he delivered his final bitter and vitriolic argument. He never at any time in his two-hour harangue presented any evidence to strengthen the scanty circumstantial evidence on which the state's case was based. I could sense that the judge was incensed and agitated, not only because of the county attorney's speech, but also at the presence of the deceased's children playing in the courtroom. The attorney closed his remarks by pointing to them and the deceased's wife as helpless victims of a cruel and unfeeling world.

The courtroom was packed as I arose to address the jury. I first called attention especially to that part of the court's instructions that every defendant is presumed innocent, and that it was the duty of the state to prove him guilty "beyond a reasonable doubt." I then asked, had the state done this? I went over every shred of the circumstantial evidence presented by the state, analyzed and picked it apart to show that it did not make a case for the defendant's guilt. On this I spent considerable time, as there were several state witnesses. I excoriated the two who had been brought from Kansas City and jailed as "material witnesses." I told the jury that in order to question them, I had had to secure a court order, and after talking to them, had felt obliged to warn them that if they told lies on the witness stand I would see to it that they were prosecuted for perjury. I reminded the jury that they had heard their testimony on the stand, and that it was plain from cross-examination that these men had been in this situation before, and that they were mercenary tools.

In conclusion I lamented the fact that Mrs. Payne had been brought into court to find out that her husband had spent his time among another race of people, not to elevate them but to drag them down. That I did not condone murder, but that maybe a merciful God had chosen this way for Payne to die in order that his children would never know what sort of a father they had. I told the jury, "I know that while your hearts go out for the widow and her sweet, innocent children, you agree with me that it were better he be dead, not because he is a white man, but because any such man, whether he be white, black, or red, is totally unfit to rear a family."

Foster was acquitted. Another thing that resulted in good for the entire county was the fact that since this trial, Negroes have been summoned to serve on every jury in this county, both petit and grand.

———

Soon after the successful termination of the Foster case, and while the Lete Kolvin case was still pending, I promised my wife, after much debate, that we would pay off the mortgages on our church and parsonage if we were successful in that case. Why the debate? Well, for a long time there had been forming in the back of my mind the conviction that there was something basically wrong about churches as regards their true mission. My mind had progressed a great distance from what I had been taught about them from my mother's knee and from what I thought I had learned about them in the three mission schools I attended.

Mother had emphasized the "call" to the ministry, and the "Great Commission," and from the study at school of the three (some authorities say four) missionary tours of St. Paul, the conclusion was being fixed in my mind that the New Testament church was not being taught or practiced in the current era. I recalled how often I was thrilled by the study of the lives of Paul and the disciples, and how this feeling had worn off. Looking about me, I could see no carbon copies of the lives and works of these great evangelists in the works of the men of "the cloth" about me. I had been taught in the schools that these men dared persecution, jail, shipwreck, and even death "for the Word's sake." I was frustrated and confused, to say the least, and told my wife as much in our talks. I did not argue that I expected the clergy to use the same weapons, but I did expect them to apply old truths to new conditions by the use of new tools that the Master would place in their hands, and that they should be able to demonstrate by their lives and practices the fulfillment of the words of the Man they professed to follow: "Let this same mind be in you as in me."

My wife felt sure we would win the lawsuit or get a sizable settlement out of it by way of a compromise, and she said: "It would be a fine gesture coming from the chairman of the Trustee Board and his family if we did pay off these debts. And the act would be a monument to your mother, who joined the church almost at its birth and was its first member in the old Chickasaw Nation." She won; but I said, "It generally takes a long time to win or settle a case of this magnitude, and we both might be dead before then." She answered, prophetically, "One of us will surely survive." I solemnly agreed, remarking, "If I die first, you will see to the fulfillment of this promise." She nodded affirmatively.

Up to the fall of 1935, things moved along in the same old way, except that Mozella, my oldest daughter, had married a young college graduate, Waldo Emerson Jones, on October 27, 1934; Anne had one more year at Talladega College; and John was a graduate student at Harvard University.

Then, in the middle of October, my wife became ill, and for a while she grew progressively worse. Tulsa was blessed with top physicians, as now, and she was examined by several of them. They consulted together, but none of them seemed able to discover the cause or nature of her illness. Dr. E. E. Bowser thought she was suffering from the lack of life-giving blood (her blood pressure was subnormal), and he worked out a special diet, to be followed rigorously. I suggested to him daily exposure to fresh outdoors air, and he thought that would be a great help.

I remained at home for the rest of the autumn, and every day when the weather was agreeable, I would bundle her up and take her for a drive. I recall those Indian-summer days and our trips to Mohawk Park, a vast area just a few miles northeast of the city. It consisted of three lakes, several connecting bayous, and a wilderness of trees and shrubbery of almost every species. Entering this spacious resort, we would drive slowly, stopping now and then, to watch the fox squirrels and grey squirrels as they crossed the well-defined road or leapt from tree limb to tree limb or played and barked amid the branches. At such times, my wife inhaled deeply the fresh air and felt the thrill of a new life. She grew stronger and stronger, and felt well enough to resume her household duties, as well as her religious and social ones. The doctor said she had fully recovered.

Elsewhere in this story, I have referred to the visit of Dr. Hope in our home in February of the following year, and how Mrs. Franklin entertained him. But, after all, she had not recovered. In late summer, her old symptoms recurred, and they did not vanish. The same doctor prescribed the same treatment. In early fall, another Indian summer, we again went to Mohawk Park and lingered amid the same familiar scenes, watching the frisky squirrels storing their winter food high up in the hollows of the trees, listening in the late evenings to the call of "bob white" gathering his and his mistress' covey together for the trip to their roosting place. We repeated the trip many times, until the cold weather drove us indoors. This time, however, there was no improvement in her health, and she grew progressively weaker. Dr. Bowser told me that she was exhausted and had nothing left in her upon which to rebuild, that she was a shell of her former self. I didn't believe him. I couldn't understand how a life that should be just beginning was feebly stretching, or fading, into an ending. But as the days dragged on into weeks, and more painfully into a month, and a few more days, I was to realize how mistaken I was. And, on the early morning of November 1, 1936, she passed away surrounded by her family, except for Anne who had been delayed in her transportation from Talladega. John Hope, teaching at Fisk, arrived the night before she breathed her last. Her passing was peaceful, unlike the disturbance on the streets, created by the all-night revelry of Halloween celebrants.

There were two things that stood out, unquestionably, measuring the greatness of my wife and the degree of love and respect in which she was held. At the funeral, our old friend of thirty years, Reverend T. M. Gatewood, delivered the oration. The moderate-sized church could not contain the people who were there from every part of the state, including Mrs. Maude J. Brockway, then president of the Oklahoma Federation of the Colored Women's Clubs.

A few years back, there lived a lowly family in the alley behind our home. The mother died after a very long illness, leaving a husband, who was a good provider, and five children, all girls. My wife had spent many hours, day and night, at the home of this family, caring for these children during the illness of their mother. Now, after my wife's funeral and just before the benediction, there came a tiny tot, not more than four, down the aisle with a tiny red rose clutched in her hand. She walked to the bier, deposited the rose upon the casket, and walked back to the door and out into the street toward her hovel. That child was the baby daughter of this family, and it was her way of remembering the ministry of my wife in this family.

I thought then, and still do, that this act of the little child was a truer mark of the love and esteem and a truer index of my wife's ministry than the attendance at the funeral. It climaxed what the minister had said. That little girl had preached a more eloquent, greater sermon, than had the minister, if the reaction of the congregation could be believed. Elsewhere in this story are newspaper articles depicting the life and works of my wife. She was buried in the family plot in the Booker Washington Cemetery, with the inscription of her tombstone, "Lifting as We Climb," as she would want it, and thus ended a perfect day.

11

A PROMISE FULFILLED

*O*nly a few things, besides my wife's death, that might be considered out of my regular routine, and might deserve brief mention here, happened to me between the years 1935 and 1942.

Anne had finished her undergraduate work at Talladega College and, for a brief while, took on duties at home. Then she became a member of the faculty of the state school at Taft, Oklahoma. In his judgment, the school was not measuring up to its possibilities, and so Governor E. W. Marland created a de facto board of regents, consisting of Major McCormick, then superintendent of the Boys' Training & Industrial School at Boley; Rev. J. B. Abram; C. S. Roberts, a retired schoolteacher; and myself, to supervise the school with a view to increasing its efficiency. There was no salary connected with this appointment, but the governor paid the board's traveling expenses and per diem out of his personal funds. Since my daughter was a member of the faculty of this school, I had to first satisfy myself that no nepotism would be charged.

During this period, John Hope was teaching history at St. Augustine's College and was soon to have off the press a history of the free Negro in North Carolina between the years 1790 and 1860, and even then he was well on his way as an authority on American history. He has since compiled and had published the *Civil War Diary of James T. Ayers*, a recruiter from Illinois during the Civil War; *From Slavery to Freedom; History of American Negroes* (a standard treatise, which has gone through a second edition, has been adopted as a textbook in many states and foreign countries, and has been translated into many languages); and *The Militant South, 1800–1860*. He has contributed a chapter on Reconstruction to a book titled *Problems in American History*, edited by Richard Leopold and Arthur Link; and dozens of articles in a wide range of periodicals. Meanwhile, he had acquired the master's and doctor's degrees from Harvard University and had married his undergraduate classmate, Aurelia Whittington of Goldsboro, North Carolina, on the 11th day of June, 1940.

During all this time, the Lete Kolvin case was still pending and I had traveled literally hundreds of miles, night and day, in all kinds of weather, searching for living witnesses who might know something about the facts we so very much needed to prove our case; and occasionally taking depositions, or rather attending the taking of depositions by the opposition. The simple case had started back in the fall of 1930 with one plaintiff and a few defendants. Now, it had grown to include many intervenors, in addition to the original defendants, with everyone trying to prove he was right. At these hearings, I think I often wished that poor Lete could have come to life and sat up right in the midst of us all to refute these claims, many of which were spurious. I had serious doubts about Izora Lee being a half sister of Lete's. From what the deceased had told me, there were no living relatives.

I had softened considerably toward Izora's attorney, Rogers, and her crack evidence man, Rev. G. T. Price, who for more than seven years had worked night and day for Izora and her attorney, spending large sums of his own money and all he could borrow from his many friends, who trusted and believed in him. I had three reasons for my change of attitude toward Izora and her attorney and the Reverend. The first one was financial. During the dozen odd years I had been on this case, I had spent all the money I had available to prosecute it with diligence. Second, I was just about physically exhausted. I had become nervous to almost the breaking point, irritable and unable to sleep nights. And third, I had come to the conclusion that if Izora did prove she was Lete's half sister and entitled to share in the estate (if we won), there would be no way of eventually prejudicing the rights of the administrator who had instituted the action and who, according to law and the record, represented the entire estate, except that possibly the amount recovered might be somewhat reduced. So, as a matter of law, Izora and her lawyer were legally bound by the services the administrator had rendered for the estate.

The case finally came to trial, which lasted for more than a week, and the court rendered judgment for the nephews, Floyd Mayweather and his brother, and found that Izora was a half sister of Lete's and entitled to share in the estate. In due course, the defendants appealed the case to the state supreme court. While the case was pending, however, the oil companies submitted a compromise offer, which was finally accepted. I might add here that as I was now personally involved, I decided that it was more ethical to choose counsel to finish the case. Mr. Wallace and I chose the law firm of Hudson and Hudson. They rendered great service, and the amount received by the administrator and his attorneys was satisfactory. We might have been able to throw the case into the county court and acquire more, and then again, we might have failed. I was so completely exhausted and had heard the name of Lete being repeated so many times that I felt I never wanted to hear it again.

I cannot close this part of my story without referring again to the Reverend G. T. Price. He never got back one cent of his own investment or any of the money he had borrowed from his friends with which to carry on this litigation. Indeed, it is entirely possible that had it not been for the ready cash that enabled Rogers and Mrs. Lee to pay court costs during the period they entered the case, and covered the expenses incurred in searching for witnesses and securing their attendance at the taking of depositions and at the final trial, the case might not have been won. The reverend, not being an attorney and not having any kind of written agreement, had no way of successfully suing and recovering judgment for his expenditures. Both Mrs. Lee and her attorney knew how much money he had used to help in the case, and the number of witnesses he had secured to prove Mrs. Lee was Lete's sister, but they paid him not one cent. Mrs. Lee took her big share and moved to California to live in luxury for the rest of her life. Mr. Rogers passed soon after, before he had time to enjoy the considerable fee he had made in his earnest efforts on behalf of his client.

A short time after the settlement, I was glad to fulfill the promise I had made to my wife to discharge the debts against the church and the parsonage. On the Sabbath of the burning of the mortgages, the bishop of the Diocese, James L. Hamlett, was present, and the church made a great show of it, none of which did I enjoy. I never have relished such demonstrations. It did not comport with, and in fact was foreign to, my idea of tithing, and I regarded this gift in that light, the source of which was God, working through a very weak and unworthy steward. Here I was being extolled as a benefactor, a philanthropist, robbing Him of praise and glory, without whom there would not have been any donation, even in the material sense.

After the burning of the mortgages, I was called on for a speech. I blundered through a brief response and did not say what was in me. I had a mind to say that "this gift did not come from me. I am very poor, don't even own the breath that's in my body which keeps me alive; nor my health; nor my strength; nor my intellect; nor my existence. Every good and perfect gift comes from our Maker, who rules and super-rules all things." The entire church missed the point that Sabbath. I think the whole world misses the point on such occasions. We rob Him not only in tithes, but of His glory and praise. It was He who blessed the loaves and fishes that fed the multitudes. Job asked the significant question, "Will a man rob God?" What do you think?

After the conclusion of the Lete Kolvin case, my doctor suggested that I take a long rest. Since 1927 I had been suffering from hay fever, especially during the summer and early fall. My eyes would smart, become irritated and burn, and the sneezing and coughing made sleep impossible, so that by morning I was completely exhausted. I could find only temporary relief, and my doctor recommended rest. So in the summer of 1943, I started out to visit my absent children. B. C., Jr., had resigned his school job, enlisted in the army, and was at Camp Rucker, Dothan, Alabama. He had married Bessye Wilson, a graduate of Wiley College, Marshall, Texas, a teacher in the Tulsa public school system. Anne was attending Howard University doing postgraduate work, and John Hope was teaching history at North Carolina College in Durham. Bessye and I left Tulsa in June for Alabama to visit Buck Jr., and after a very pleasant time I left her there and proceeded to visit John in Montgomery, where he was teaching in the summer school at Alabama State College. We had fun there, visiting Dothan one night, and would have gotten lost had it not been for Aurelia, who beat us all in picking up the trail to our destination. Aurelia was a great trouper, as I was to learn by our side trips together to many points, and once as far north as New York.

We made a side trip to Tuskegee, Macon County, Alabama, a place made famous throughout the civilized world by Tuskegee Institute, which was founded by Booker T. Washington, whose work and toil, and those of George Washington Carver and other dedicated men and women, have erected a monument to farsighted and unselfish service, that will serve and bless all mankind to the end of time. And as I stood upon that hallowed spot, I couldn't help thinking of the prayers, the ceaseless toil, planning, and tears, that must have gone into the creation of this symbol of love and universal brotherhood. I seriously doubt that there is a comparable space in the world where there exists as much culture, refinement, and gentle grace as are found today in Macon County. And as I stood there in the evening shadows, I felt, as it were, a mantle of security, that had had its beginning in 1881, encompassing me. Now the area has become infamous by the advent of the Scythians and barbarians who are attempting to tear down and destroy this symbol of brotherhood, and erecting instead an emblem of bigotry, racial hate, and prejudice.[1]

Few understood the philosophy of Washington. Some thought he was a moral coward and was too frightened to stand up and be counted for what was right and just. Some thought that he only wanted to please the other race. He was a man of uncommon common sense. He knew that, in the nature of things, he must have a long-range program, and he thought that by diplomacy, his people would by gradual processes come to taste the full fruits of their rightful heritage. This philosophy is revealed in his book *The Future of the American Negro*. What would he do today, as he witnessed the disfranchisement of his people by many wicked devices, including one called "gerrymandering." In my own mind, I'm convinced he would have done something about it. And here is hoping that his successor and followers will do everything possible to right this great wrong.

On my way home I stopped off and spent some time with Anne in Washington. She had been there since her resignation from the Taft state school, doing special postgraduate work in social work, crime prevention, and crime detection, and at Harvard University, where she graduated from its school of

1. The reference here is not to those who opposed Washington's educational philosophy and methods, but to those who opposed any effort to end racial segregation and promote equality of educational opportunity in states such as Alabama.

social work. Later, after a very rigid examination, and upon her written application, she joined the Metropolitan Police Department of Washington, D.C., where she has since served with the rank of inspector.

———

Possibly the most sensational criminal case I was ever connected with grew out of the rape-murder of Panta Lou Liles, a young white defense worker, only twenty years old, in the early fall of 1945, in the 400 block of Cheyenne Avenue in Tulsa. This was one of the most revolting, brutal crimes ever committed in Tulsa. The victim was heavy with child, and the fiend, whoever he was, after raping her had bludgeoned her to death with a metal instrument of some sort. Photographs of the deceased were admitted in evidence, over the objection of defense counsel, and the sight was sickening.

The victim was at home when she was murdered some time between midnight and dawn, while the city slept and the streets were empty. Hence, there was no one to hear her screams or cries for help. Some time elapsed before the discovery of her body. For days, city and state police worked around the clock trying to find a single clue to the murder. The undergarments of the victim were dispatched to the FBI in Washington. Failing to find a likely suspect, some thought of LeRoy Benton, a Negro who had done time for an alleged rape of a white woman, and a search went out for him. Benton, upon being informed that the police wanted to see and question him about the rape-murder, voluntarily appeared at the city jail. He was immediately arrested, lodged in jail, and questioned about the murder. For several days and nights he was held incommunicado, with only brief breathing spells from the questioning. None of his acquaintances knew what had become of him until they were informed by someone who had heard that the chief of police was inquiring about LeRoy.

Meanwhile, a bogus mob had been forming in the hall within listening distance from the jail, who were threatening to lynch Benton. The prisoner became greatly frightened, whereupon the jailer told him that the only way he could be saved from the mob was to confess. In that state, the prisoner told the jailer he would confess to the murder of Mrs. Liles if he had protection from the supposed lynching party and help later on in securing a parole or pardon. Upon receiving the promise, Benton confessed to the crime.

Before the prisoner had consulted counsel, he was spirited out of the local jail and taken to the penitentiary at McAlester, presumably for safety.

It was after all these happenings that the defendant contacted attorney Amos T. Hall and told him about his experiences. Mr. Hall called me into the case and we went to see the defendant. The killing had been so savage and heartless that we both decided we would have nothing to do with the defendant unless we were convinced beyond a shadow of a doubt that he was innocent. Many times we tried to trap him, but his story was so straight and forthright, coupled with other extraneous facts, that we were convinced that LeRoy had not been near the murder scene when it happened.

As the case opened for trial on the morning of November 13, there was scarcely standing room in the court. The swinging doors were jammed and spectators were on the west side of the second floor verandah peering through the windows. Mr. Hall and I, now sure that we were representing an innocent man, sat there in the courtroom calm and certain of the final outcome.

The case moved painfully slow. It had been fought stubbornly by both sides. The defense fought bitterly the introduction of the alleged confession. Many times the jury was withdrawn from their box so that the court might hear arguments on points of law. The jury was excused from hearing evidence so that defense counsel might question witnesses in connection with the alleged confession and the action of the alleged mob, which had prompted the alleged confession, and by the time all this was done, a whole day had been consumed. But having gotten into the record our motion to suppress the alleged confession on the grounds (1) that the defendant had been detained in jail for a week without benefit of counsel; (2) that a week had transpired before he was informed; (3) that a bogus lynch mob had been formed to induce the alleged confession; (4) that an officer had promised the defendant that if he confessed, he would assist him in securing a pardon, and that if he did not confess the mob would surely get him; and (5) that the confession was secured under severe duress and was therefore void. Several federal matters had become a part of the record. After the evidence was all in, along with instructions of the court and arguments by attorneys, the case was submitted to the jury, which in time returned a verdict of guilty and assessed defendant's punishment to a term of life in the penitentiary at hard labor.

Motion for a new trial was overruled, and defendant lodged his appeal in the Criminal Court of Appeals. The high court reversed the conviction on the ground of insufficient evidence, but the state was allowed thirty days to produce further evidence of guilt. This the state failed to do, and Benton was released and discharged. The high state could have and should have reversed the case for the simple reason that the due process clauses of both the state and federal constitutions had been flagrantly violated and should have given the police department a severe tongue lashing. It has been my experience, however, that it is extremely difficult to get a high tribunal to do this.

12

CLIMBING THE LADDER OF THE LAW

*A*fter the Civil War, the American Negro found himself in a position unlike that of any other class known to history. The Jews possibly had been enslaved for a longer time in Egypt than the Negro in America, but there was a great difference between the two enslavements. When deliverance came to the Jew, his contact with his forebears had been broken for but a short time. By a miraculous incident through the slave boy Joseph, his people were reunited; then came the birth of Moses; all of which bears witness to the fact that the Israelites had nurtured their special ethnic and religious identity. It can truthfully be said that a kingdom was established within a kingdom (Gen. 45:10). Then they multiplied, grew, and became powerful until "there arose a king in Egypt that knew not Joseph."

In contrast, the American Negro was abruptly severed from his ancestors, transplanted upon a foreign soil, and for more than two centuries was taught to believe that slavery, per se, is a badge of inferiority—although the American Negro has never believed that slavery or the color of his skin makes him inferior to other human beings. There are no "Uncle Tom" or "Sambo Rastus" Negroes. The thing that has made them seem so is nothing but a fine diplomacy developed, in some cases to the nth degree, to serve as a weapon of escape from personal injury. Those who would believe otherwise, let them remember and interpret, if they can, certain verses of the old spirituals, born of bruised and crushed souls struggling through trials and tribulations for

Divine expression, such as "All God's Children Got Wings," "Steal Away to Jesus," "There Is a Balm in Gilead," etc. All attest to the fact that slavery can never be a satisfactory condition for normal, conscious human beings made in the image of God. The evolution of society (this phrase is used in its broad sense) further attests to this fact.

In a discussion of this topic, "Climbing the Ladder of the Law," I must necessarily go back to the first stumbling block placed in the path of the American Negro, that is beyond the span of my years, but from which sprang succeeding obstacles. I refer to *Dred Scott* v. *Sandford*, rendered in 1857, U.S. 19 393.

I shall not go into the history of this matter, which every schoolboy should know, other than to say that Scott, a slave, was first the property of Dr. Emerson, an army surgeon then living in Missouri, a slave state. On being transferred from Missouri, he sold his slave. Scott was thereafter taken to a free state, then another, and finally into a free territory, before being returned to Missouri. Some of his friends advised him to sue for his freedom on the ground that when he was taken to a free state, he became a free man. In the circuit court at St. Louis he prevailed, but the Supreme Court of Missouri reversed the decision. Finally, the case reached the United States Supreme Court, which then included five southerners, and seven Democrats. Chief Justice Roger Brooke Taney of Maryland was a disciple of Andrew Jackson, who as president had first appointed him attorney general, and later secretary of the treasury, when the president was engaged in a life-or-death struggle with the national banks. The Senate, however, refused to confirm the appointment, but Taney received a recess appointment and refused to transfer any money to the banks. After that fight, the president appointed Taney to the Supreme Court following the death of Chief Justice John Marshall.

For further clarification, I would point out that Taney's predecessor, Marshall, had served on the Court from 1801 to the time of his death in 1835. He was the most able jurist to have served on the Court up to that time. He gave purpose and meaning to the executive branch of the government, and established the proper "checks and balances" between the three branches of the federal government. Before his ascendancy to the Court, he had served for many years as a soldier in the Revolutionary War, including experience at Valley Forge. After the war, he boasted that when he entered the army from Virginia, he was a Virginian; but after seeing service in New Jersey, New York, and Pennsylvania, and seeing the diversities of his country, he came out an American. Taney always boasted that he was a "states' righter," whatever that means. That phrase has no real meaning in a democracy where some of the people are enfranchised and some are disfranchised.

Hence, Marshall and Taney were two different men, made so possibly by backgrounds, environments, experiences, contacts, and training. By 1857, Taney had succeeded in undoing much of the work Marshall had done. And although Jackson died in 1845, I have often wondered how much that president's influence had to do with the Scott decision.

When Andrew Jackson became president, he adopted as a part of his program the removal of the Five Civilized Tribes from certain old states to the Indian Territory. The Cherokees were stubborn and resisted removal. A policy was put into force to starve them into submission by refusing their annual stipend from the United States Treasury—money that was theirs by treaty with the government. Many of them literally died from starvation. There was another incident during Jackson's presidency: Two missionaries, the Reverend S. A. Worcester and Elizur Butler, who had rendered long and faithful service among the Cherokees, had failed to secure a license from the governor of Georgia to continue to live and work among the Indians. The state authorities arrested, prosecuted, and imprisoned them. When the case finally came before the U.S. Supreme Court on appeal, Justice John Marshall struck down the state statute on which they were tried and convicted. Jackson was reported to have said, "John Marshall has made his decision, now let him enforce it if he can."

There are many who hold that the Dred Scott decision was the only one that could have been legally rendered prior to the Civil War Amendments. They take the position, I believe, that the federal Constitution not only countenanced slavery but protected it as it would property rights. They base this assumption on custom and practice that grew up with the institution, and upon the classifications found in section 2, clause 3, dealing with apportionment and taxes, in connection with the phrase, "and excluding Indians not taxed, three fifths of all other Persons. . . ." I take the view that we live in a moral universe, notwithstanding man's inhumanity to man, and that decision was not only immoral, but violated Christian principles; all laws enacted by man must square with the Divine purpose. Taney lost the chance of a lifetime when he failed to read and interpret correctly the prophesies of Isaiah, or even the spirit of the men who authored the Declaration of Independence. It bore the message of its time and all future times. But this decision was not without value. It awoke the sleeping moral conscience of America and stirred her soul to righteous indignation. It lighted a prairie fire, and its blaze produced an *Uncle Tom's Cabin*, Underground Railways, an Elijah Lovejoy, a nationwide abolition movement, and a John Brown. Brown, they say, fired the first shot that was to drench this nation in fratricidal blood; but I contend that it was the Dred Scott decision that triggered the bloody, devastating holocaust.

Starting from a mere commodity, a mere piece of property, the Negro has had and still has a rugged, backbreaking climb ahead. It has taken generations to be elevated even to second-class citizenship. Following the end of the Civil War, the Thirteenth Amendment was enacted, then the Fourteenth and Fifteenth. In spite of these, progress has been slow and painful. The Negro was not benefited by the enactment of the first civil rights bills, three of which were declared unconstitutional. Within the scope of this story, I very much doubt the appropriateness of discussing them.

To my mind, the case of *Plessy* v. *Ferguson*, 163 U.S. 537, decided in 1896, has given the race and the nation quite as much trouble as the Scott decision. In *Scott* the Court held, in substance, that "the Negro has no rights that whites are bound to respect." The Plessy case interjected the spurious and impossible doctrine of "separate but equal accommodations." The first was bold, immoral, and un-Christian; the second was subtle, disguised, and faithless—all to hide or cover up and twist the real law. And because of its clumsy boldness, the first was more easily discovered and attacked. As lawyers would say, "These amendments were self-executing."

In the Plessy case, it seems to me that the decision went against the defendant by default. Justice Harlan, who wrote the minority opinion, based his dissent on the elemental ground of simple justice, and strange as it may seem, this minority view has grown in popularity and has since served as a beacon, in part at least, in determining kindred lawsuits based upon fairness and justice.

As far as I have been able to ascertain within my limited means of research, being now confined in my home due to paralysis, the case of *Missouri ex rel Gaines* v. *Canada*, 305 U.S. 337, decided in 1938, was the first that began to unmask the doctrine of *Plessy* v. *Ferguson*.[1] It was not a complete unmasking, but the court did hold that "the curators of a state university who are representatives of the state in its management in refusing to admit a Negro to the law school of the university must be regarded as a state action in determining whether the equal protection clause of the Fourteenth Amendment has been infringed." The following cases: *Sipuel* v. *University of Oklahoma*, 332 U.S. 631; *Fisher* v. *Hurst*, 333 U.S. 147; *McLaurin* v. *Oklahoma State Regents*, 339 U.S. 637; and *Sweatt* v. *Painter*, 339 U.S. 629, completed the job of unmasking. In *McLaurin*, the Court went all out against discrimination. In the opinion, it said that "the equal protection clause of the Fourteenth Amendment has been violated where the state, after admitting a Negro student to graduate instruction in its state university, afforded him, solely because of his race, different treatment from other students, as by requiring him to occupy a seat in a row in the classroom specified for colored students, or at a designated table in the library, or at a special table in the cafeteria."

The most devasting and conclusive decision of the United States Supreme Court in its bombardment of prejudice and racial discrimination was finally reached on the 17th day of May, 1954, in 349 U.S. 294. It involved cases from Topeka, Kansas, and from South Carolina, Virginia, and Delaware, all of which were consolidated in the Supreme Court, with another case for Respondent in No. 5. The case first came on for argument. So many questions had been raised that the Court, being very careful and finding it necessary to settle all of them—particularly historical and sociological questions—continued the case to a future date and directed the parties, meanwhile, to submit answers to the questions. This required extensive research, study, and clarification of facts in the several fields of inquiry to enable the Court to get an overall picture of the laws, facts, customs, and so forth related to the inquiry and subject under consideration. This made it necessary for the legal department of the NAACP to call in for assistance many educators. My son John Hope was one of those who furnished the Legal Defense Fund's counsel with many valuable, pertinent facts to be used in the additional arguments and briefs.

---

1. In much of this chapter, the author has provided his own documentation in the citations of cases he discusses.

The thing that has impressed and gratified me most is the manner in which the Court reached its historic and just decision. With the data available, all of which was well documented, the Court was able to accurately measure the progress made by the Negro in all fields of endeavor since the Dred Scott decision: that he was no longer illiterate, confused, and distracted from two and a half centuries of brutal and dehumanizing slavery; and that he had become alert, sensitive, and had contributed to the material and spiritual growth of his country. The decision shows that the Court believes that the law is a living, growing thing, feeding both the body and spirit of man as he moves forward in quest of higher and more satisfying goals in life; and that "the letter of the law killeth; but the spirit of the law maketh alive." I think it is the consensus of men of goodwill everywhere that the American Negro's progress has been unequaled in history. A certain senator from a certain state, high in the counsels of our government, sent me one of his pamphlets attacking the decision on the grounds that the Negroes who assisted in the research were Communists and that the decision was socialistic! Evidently he does not believe in social evolution, especially the social evolution of the Negro.

An examination of the decision, involving discrimination against the Negro in education, was conducted by Negro attorneys. I think Thurgood Marshall's first appearance was in the Gaines case, *supra*. He has been involved in other similar lawsuits, with many other able men, and almost all of them have been successful.

Another aspect of discrimination and prejudice had its genesis in the Dred Scott and Plessy decisions. The evils that these decisions birthed in twisted minds, producing false propaganda and senseless bigotry, still live on. It might be more accurate to say that these twisted minds, operating in different areas, reinforcing each other, pile obstacle on obstacle until the Negro finds them almost insuperable.

In Oklahoma, the Negro encountered black legislation early in the life of the state. The first was the Grandfather Law, so-called because it contained a clause to the effect that no one would be permitted to vote in any state election "unless he could read and write a section of the Constitution, but anyone who could vote prior to January 1, 1866, or his line descendant, could vote whether or not he could read and write." Thousands of colored citizens of the state were disfranchised—not allowed to vote for almost five years—until, in 1915, the United States Supreme Court on appeal, in the case of *Guinn* v. *The United States*, 238 U.S. 347, declared the Grandfather Clause unconstitutional. As a result of and following this decision, many citizens were arrested, prosecuted, and imprisoned for conspiracy to prevent Negroes from voting in the state. Great excitement prevailed for some time. In some counties—Wagoner, for example—the Negro was in the majority, and an able, well-liked colored man, O. H. P. Hudson, was elected as one of its county commissioners.

Meanwhile, the state legislature in special session had attempted to amend the old Grandfather Clause by enacting a law "requiring all qualified voters to register" and submitting a new constitutional amendment which limited the right to vote or register to vote to those who could read and write any section of the state constitution, with the exception of persons who had served or whose ancestors had served in the army or navy of the United States, or in Indian wars, or in the army or navy of any foreign nation. This amendment was adopted by special election in August, 1916. The vote of the Negro, by discouragement, intimidation, or indifference, was negligible. Again, the Negro lost his suffrage for a long time. In Wagoner County, however, the colored men were not so easily discouraged. Hudson filed for re-election. He had so many admirers that the opposition feared he might be reelected, and they therefore put fear on many Negroes.

There were a few who were not scared, one of whom was Lane.[2] He made a trip to Muskogee and consulted attorney Charles Chandler, an able and conscientious lawyer. The result was the filing of a proper action in the federal district court against Wilson, registrar. This was a long and costly lawsuit. Both the federal district and circuit court of appeal decided against him, but in 1939 the United States Supreme Court upheld the contention of Mr. Chandler, deciding that the registration provision of the Oklahoma statute and the adoption of the amendment to the Oklahoma constitution contravened the Constitution of the United States and were therefore void and of no force or effect whatsoever (*Lane* v. *Wilson*, 307 U.S. 268). Thus, a Negro attorney, a graduate of the Harvard School of Law, single-handed and alone, and without funds except those supplied by himself, was more than a match for certain Oklahoma politicians. It is both just and appropriate here to remark that, beginning with

2. I. W. Lane was mayor of the all-black town of Boley, Oklahoma.

the Gaines case, Negro lawyers have been successful in battering down the artificial walls of segregation, particularly on the educational front, assisted in a few instances by attorneys of goodwill of other racial groups.

But a few die-hard Oklahoma politicians were not yet satisfied, so they caused to be enacted into law a statute making it mandatory for every Negro candidate for office in both the primary and general election to have the word *Negro* inserted on the ballot behind his name (Title 26, Section 126, A.O.S. 1941).

There were several Negro candidates who had been running for various high offices, among them A. B. McDonald and Jeff McHenry. McDonald filed an action in the Federal District Court for the Western District of Oklahoma to enjoin the State Election Board from the use of such designation. He asked for several thousand dollars in damages. Some time later, when McHenry was running for the United States Senate, he filed an action to prevent the use of such description behind his name on the ballot. I filed an original action, 36673, in the state supreme court but did not ask for damages. I knew it would be futile, remembering the Guinn and Long cases.

McDonald's case moved swiftly. On the government attorney's motion, his complaint was dismissed. "Mack," as he is familiarly known, immediately appealed to the federal circuit court at Denver, Colorado. This court in no time reversed the lower court, holding that such designation constituted discrimination and was clearly in violation of the Fourteenth Amendment. The state's attorney general was compelled to immediately notify every election official throughout the state to drop the word *Negro* from the name of a colored candidate.

This victory is all the more pronounced for the reason that the Reverend (he is a minister) is *not* a lawyer and has *no* license to practice. All his pleadings in the case were signed "per se," which means for himself, or on behalf of himself. He filed his own complaint, appeared alone at the hearings, and filed his own brief in the circuit court. Of course, he is no fool. He has done much reading and studying, when not preaching or looking after his real estate business. After the disposition of Mack's case, we very naturally dropped ours. The McDonald case is reported in 224 F. 2nd 608.

In my span of years, I have lived to witness the breaking down of many other racial barriers. As I have heretofore stated, I believe that the first legislature of the state enacted separate school and separate coach (Jim Crow) laws. Harlow in his history of Oklahoma gives his reason for such action by the state; but being an Oklahoman for eighty years, and my parents for eighty-odd years prior thereto, I say those laws were passed to destroy the friendship that has existed between Indians and their former slaves throughout past generations. Particularly has this been true of Seminoles and Creeks.

The first time the Jim Crow statute of Oklahoma was tested was in the case of *McCabe* v. *A.T. & S.F.R. Co.*, 235 U.S. 151, decided in 1914. McCabe was a highly educated and cultured man who had served as assistant auditor of the Territory of Oklahoma. And while a demurrer was sustained in McCabe's appeal to the U.S. Supreme Court, it was because the complainant did not show that every state remedy had been exhausted, and was deficient in certain other particulars. The court implied that in a proper case, McCabe would have received equitable relief, carefully pointing out the defects in the appellant's complaint.

The growth of the law has fully demonstrated that it is a living entity and is becoming more and more recognized by an enlightened public. Here, though, I must say that this fact applies only in certain sections of our country. Right is slow and tardy, while wrong is aggressive; that's the only way it can survive. It carries within itself the seed of its own destruction. The strange thing about this fact is that people of common sense don't seem to understand.

What I had in mind to write about was the right of citizens, without regard to color or race, to live in any part of the country, urban or rural, wherever they see fit. See opinion in 3 ALR 2d 466; *Harmon* v. *Taylor* (1927), 273 U.S. 668; *Buchanan* v. *Warley* (1917), 245 U.S. 60: "A state or local ordinance imposing racial restrictions on the purchase or occupancy of real estate is unconstitutional under the Fourteenth Amendment." The opinion further holds that if two or more persons buy an acreage of land and enter into a written agreement not to sell to a person of a different race, that such an agreement cannot be enforced. The United States Supreme Court, in *Smith* v. *Allwright* (1944), 321 U.S. 649, held that it contravenes the U.S. Constitution to prohibit Negroes from voting in a white primary in those sections of the nation where primary elections are tantamount to a general election.

I have not attempted to cover all the areas opened to the colored people since *Gaines*. I've barely touched on the field of transportation. The recent activity of the Interstate Commerce Commission has added a great boost to this phase. And, too, hotels, inns, cafes, theaters, and the like have undergone marked changes in their treatment of the colored race. The credit for these miraculous changes has been given to the current administration in Washington. But I know better, and I'd like for the entire world to know, especially the Negro.

The changes in the attitudes of certain people toward the Negro in regard to theaters, cafes, and the like is due to the self-sacrifice and untiring effort of one lone Negro woman, Mary Church Terrell. She hired an attorney years before her death to attach charges of discrimination against her race in restaurants, hotels, and theaters in the District of Columbia. I think the plaintiff in that case was named Thompson. The case was finally won when her counsel found an old statute passed in Reconstruction days that had never been repealed. But the heroine of this story, great lover of all people, and dedicated to universal freedom and justice, died about the time the case was won, and was denied the fruits of her endless toil and sacrifice.

Just one word about this great character and her background. Bob Church, Mary's father, a mulatto, was a self-made and hardheaded businessman who spent all of his adult life in Memphis, Tennessee. He appeared to be tough, but was personally charming. He was a success at business and, according to his lifelong neighbors, a man of his word at all times. I saw him only once, but he impressed me as being what was said of him by his neighbors. He possessed a deep, burning hatred for prejudice and was said to have vowed that his children, Mary and Bob, Jr., would never be subjected to this mental illness. When Mary married Judge Terrell of Washington, her father chartered a special train to take her there.

I never met Bob Church personally, but when I lived in Ardmore, I was chairman of a committee whose function it was to invite an outstanding Negro to speak at the annual meeting of our culture society, and on one occasion, Mrs. Terrell was the speaker. I think she was the first person I had ever heard who spoke for an hour without repeating herself. Her subject was "The New Negro Woman Finding Herself." I thought then and still do that she was the greatest woman this nation has produced. Very naturally, my wife and she took to each other like ducks to water. Both of them loved the Colored Women's Clubs of America, and they continued to exchange letters up to the time of my wife's death.

13

OTHERS IN MY LIFE

$\mathcal{B}$.C., Jr., died on the 29th day of July, 1947, in the McGuire Veterans Hospital in Richmond, Virginia, of lung cancer. He was discharged from the army on March 6, 1944, because of disability, but he was not informed of the nature of his illness. On May 24, 1944, he and his wife sold their home and moved to St. Louis, Missouri. There he assumed the position of contact officer for the Veterans Administration. His health again began to fail, but no one, not even his new doctor, appeared to know the nature of his illness. He thought nothing of his ailment and continued to work. He had worked for a while in Tulsa for the War Manpower Commission, the United States Employment Service, as manager of the branch office on North Greenwood before moving to St. Louis, where he engaged in various office jobs and enrolled in the law department of St. Louis University, studying at night. He wanted so very much to become an attorney.

His health became so serious that he went to stay with his brother, John, so that Aurelia could look after him. It was impossible for Bessye, his wife, to care for him and work too, although she was the most dutiful, loving, and uncomplaining wife any husband ever had. I am sure if she had known the nature of his illness, she would never have consented to his leaving. She, like the rest of us, never dreamed that he was afflicted with such a deadly malady as cancer. This disease was comparatively unknown then, and the average layman never thought about it. Not many doctors knew much about it or, much less, its symptoms. After his death, he was brought home and buried with military honors in the family plot on August 2, 1947. I loved him very much and I thought I saw me in him.

Back in 1906, I had become acquainted with the Reverend T. M. Gatewood, who at the time was pastoring the C.M.E. church—my mother's church. This acquaintance ripened into a friendship that was to last a long time. It is difficult to describe this man. He was born in Arkansas and his education had been very limited, but he had a consuming respect and love for what had been denied him through no fault of his own. He was born a poor tenant farmboy of a large family. His parents were unlettered and had no sense of the value of education. His environment was not conducive to either inspiration or aspiration. All he could see about him was the yoke of oppression. Schools were few and far between. He grew up in servitude through childhood to manhood, and then the first light of a different condition gleamed faintly across his vision. In a roundabout way, he had heard of Bishop Lane and Lane College, which was just getting started, and he learned more about this great man and what he was trying to do for his people.

Tom Gatewood's parents, although poor and without formal education, were God-fearing and possessed the blind faith that was common in those days among the newly freed slaves. His mother taught cleanliness, a divine virtue among any people. Finally, according to the Reverend Gatewood's story, he had a vision, and this Presence told him to shake the dust from his tattered shoes and leave the place of his birth; and he was obedient to "the heavenly vision." His travels landed him in Ardmore, but in the meantime he had made contact with Bishop Lane, the school, and the Publishing Board, had joined the C.M.E. Church, had been ordained to preach, and had pastored a church or two before reaching Ardmore.

I saw in this man a complete dedication to his calling, utter selflessness, and an uncanny grasp on the larger sociological problems of the Christian religion. In a word, he was conscientious about his duty as a minister to pastor all of his people as far as he could without forgetting his own particular tenets, one of them being that there could be no substantial conflicts among different Christian denominations. He conceded that there might be many shades of differences, but he believed that all had something to contribute, and that such contributions enriched, broadened, and gave growth to the

Christian religion. He discarded the belief that Divine inspiration can come only from one special sect.

Reverend Gatewood had many lean years, in Ardmore especially. Our church was the smallest and poorest in town—away up on the spur of the Santa Fe Railroad, while all the other churches were in the thick of and surrounded by beautiful residences. Finally, I succeeded in getting Superintendent Tucker to give Tom's wife a teaching job at the school.

Tom was an exceptional man in that he had a world view and understanding of most subjects, even with his very limited formal knowledge. I saw much of him during the almost six years that we lived in Ardmore. We saw each other almost daily as well as on the Sabbath, and we worked closely together in his effort to raise "general funds" for a church that should have been classified as a mission instead of a station. When I moved to Tulsa, he was presiding elder of the Muskogee District, which included Tulsa. From then on, we saw each other only during quarterly conferences and at times at annual conferences, which I often attended, although never as a delegate. He attended and officiated at B. C. Jr.'s marriage, my wife's funeral, and B. C. Jr.'s funeral.

In later years I began to feel the effects of years of overwork and began losing myself in travels and forming new companionships. During the summer months when the courts were not in session, I had happy times at the Hamlett Resort, northwest of Denver, at the foothills of the Rocky Mountains, where the Boulder River ran nearby. There I met my good friends Chester A. Franklin and his wife. Franklin owned the Kansas City *Call*, a leading newspaper in that area. Dr. D. H. Davis and many others from every part of the country were among the visitors. O. W. Hamlett and his wife also operated the restaurant and served excellent meals, family style.

I went to Colorado also because someone had told me that the climate would cure my hay fever, but after several seasons, I got no relief. Then I switched to Saratoga Springs, New York, for several summers. Of the twenty-seven springs there, I found two waters that cured me. One came from Guizer Spring and the other from what was called the Red Water Spring. Saratoga Springs is a very famous resort and a beautiful city. There I met and enjoyed the companionship of many notable people. I lived at a hotel operated by a Mrs. J. H. Parker at 18 Cherry Street. Her niece, Helen Hayes, a schoolteacher from Brooklyn, was the entertainer, and there was never a dull moment. I especially remember two friends, L. C. Lucas, who knew something about everything, and Miss Cassie Clack, an employee of the government in Brooklyn, a woman of grace, charm, and beauty, and an interesting conversationalist on many subjects. I also enjoyed bathing in the fine bathhouses and always seemed improved when it came time for me to return home; but, while the hay fever was cured, I soon felt that my general rundown condition was not improved.

14

THE WORLD TODAY
AND MY BELIEFS

$\mathcal{I}$ can best discuss this double topic together because of the nature of my beliefs. But first, it seems to me that it is not possible to discuss "The World Today" without touching on the world yesterday and thousands of yesterdays, since it is the combination of past ages that has produced our present world. Second, I believe in a personal God, who might at different times be called Jehovah, the Divine Presence, Logos, a First Cause, or whatever else; that He is One and the same and the Creator of all things; that His beginning is incalculable, and His end infinite; that He is a Spirit in a triad; that He is good and just; that everything He created is good when used as He intended; and that He did not create sin or evil, but suffered them to exist to test man, his highest creation; but that this is a moral universe, notwithstanding, because His Divine Nature created it.

When Adam was tempted and yielded, sin for the first time, I believe, entered the world. Now, I don't know whether the name "Adam" represented an individual or the first name of a dynasty, like the name "Caesar" or the name "Ptolemy," and I don't care, because I don't think it makes any spiritual difference at all. There is conclusive evidence that following the Adamic age, sin became so widespread and the world completely out of the Creator's hands that He sent His Son (Emmanuel) into the world as a reconciler. So, I believe in the historic and the spiritual Jesus; and in the Third Person of the Trinity, whose function and mission it is "to lead us into all truths." But I do not believe in a literal burning hell. It's too foreign to His nature.

So, that's my creed in a nutshell. Naturally, there are other, various, ramifications. For instance, I firmly believe in the New Testament Church now, as when it went forth from Antioch, with its emphasis on the "Great Command," the Sermon on the Mount, and the injunction "Love thy neighbor as thyself."

I think that Providence has been especially good to America and has placed her in a position to do more toward correcting past mistakes and righting the wrongs of yesteryear than possibly any other nation on the globe. The sins and evil she has committed are not ancient, as times go, but they exist, and can be canceled out only through repentance. Personally, I think that our greatest sin has been in the mistaken belief that we are, in some mysterious way, especially favored of God, and that we will not have to account for our misdeeds. By false and misleading propaganda, we have been led to believe that we have a Simon-pure culture, the real McCoy! But is it? If the master knew of the ancient cultures, religions, and civilizations, the American slave was never told of them.

Seasoned and reliable historians now know that Egypt was the cradle of civilization (2nd edition, *From Slavery to Freedom*, by John Hope Franklin, pp. 3–10). On pages 11 to 22, the author documents the "Early Negro States of Africa." As early as the fourth century, China had invented gunpowder, painting, a form of printing, manufacture of paper, the making of silk, porcelain, and the like. In the fourth century B.C., her greatest teacher, Confucius, was teaching the soundest of moral principles, such as: "What you do not like done unto yourself, do not unto others"—centuries on centuries before the Bible's Golden Rule was written. He taught brotherhood, love of one's fellow man. Buddha, centuries before the Christian era, taught all the Christian virtues, right beliefs, right ideals, right deeds, right way of earning a living, and right meditations. He taught against "lying, slander, abusive language, and useless conversation." He taught that "drunkenness leads to insanity and is found pleasant only by the ignorant" and that "hatred never stops until it comes under the power of love."

All the culture I know anything about is preceded by some form of religion that becomes universal with each culture. I predict that Confucianism and Buddhism will never be supplanted by *Das Kapital*, the manifesto of Communism, and its hordes of followers; nor will the great Moslem believers, whose founder taught and practiced the unity of God and man, ever succumb to a mongrel herd without a common taproot so essential to produce a heritage and culture. I have known many Chinese men, and they have told me that their womenfolk teach their young the sayings of Confucius and that they live by them, except that part of the Empire that has gone over to the Communists, or claims so. What is there to these ancient cultures that is absent from our own, that does not enrich ours?

I am reliably informed by a world traveler, in whom I have implicit belief, that a starving Indian on the streets of Ceylon or Bombay or New Delhi will beg but never steal; that the visitor never locks his door and never loses anything from his hotel room. Imagine what would happen in the average American city under such circumstances. These people have a spiritual worth and value that would be well for us to nurture, cultivate, and grow. We have been sending missionaries to the Orient for centuries and have been pouring millions into our efforts. Yet we cease to make or hold the friendship of these people whom we have sought to woo. Why?

No less an authority than the late Dr. John Brown of Siloam Springs [Arkansas], great educator, builder, and world missionary, said that our chief mistake has been in sending ignorant and unprepared missionaries. Especially those who know absolutely nothing of the history and culture of the people to whom they have been sent. And our common politicians have done worse. Most of them are untrained and, worst of all, emphasize the dollar sign as a passport to acceptance and recognition. The age-old customs and culture of these people have made them downright sensitive toward such display. Often, the white American uses his skin color as an entrance into the good graces of these people without any knowledge whatsoever as to the traits and customs in their homes which they regard as sacred. While in college I learned much from some African students, two of whom were my classmates. They were of royal descent and, I thought, overdid the thing. They could trace their ancestry back to King Tut by sheer memory. Each generation before them had kept alive the memory of this legendary character, his exploits, and everything about him, and had handed down this knowledge to succeeding generations. They actually worshiped their black skins and solid, shiny white teeth, and thought them a mark of superiority over all other men.

I have said, and still say, that America is the hope of the world; but America may not be indispensable to the Divine Plan and purpose. She has sinned grievously and still sins, and must do sincere repentance for her wrong deeds. It is a waste of time and space to enumerate these sins, but they have grown and multiplied from the ignorant and wholly unscientific theory, or belief, that slavery per se is a badge of inferiority, and for centuries this belief has been fed by constant propaganda. Those who spread this falsehood have never taken the time to learn, since they are too ignorant to know already, that slavery, from the beginnings of man, has moved in cycles and that all tribes, races, and peoples, have fallen under the yoke of servitude at one time or another; that at one time, the philosophers, savants, and learned men of ancient Greece were bound by slavery to the far less cultured and civilized hordes of Roman soldiers. But when the Aryans, the Scythians, and other early barbarians enslaved other human beings, Christ had not yet come upon the earth. So when you hear someone trying to justify American slavery by insisting that racial prejudice and slavery have always existed, just say to him that the Bible was unknown in those times.

To believe that inferiority is based on the color of a man's skin is sheer ignorance. It's pure sacrilege, bordering on blasphemy, to even intimate that God created one branch of the human race, as such, superior to the other. It is timely to note that racial bias and prejudice are not innate things. Basically, they have no entities. They have unnatural, adventitious roots. They are nurtured and fed by purely extraneous foods, such as manmade traditions, false propaganda, environment, and constant teaching and training in the home. These artificial foods are aided and abetted by a certain objectivity—the color of the skin of the natural parents. The offspring never as a rule knows that color is purely incidental, even if it does date far back to climatic conditions. He does not know that no color can change his true identity. I learned in college that real beauty shines through from within, and true beauty is one of the component parts of this identity.

Going back to the question as to whether racial prejudice is innate: Take three or more children of different branches of the human race. They live and grow up together in the same environment. Will there ever be any difference between them, based on racial strains, except by outside influences?

I have an example that comes from nearer home. My mother was born in an Indian home. She grew up in it, played with Indian children, spoke the Indian tongue, ate with them, attended their churches and schools. She never knew of any racial difference until she was married and had two children, and lived in another town; nor did any of her childhood friends, until one of them came to visit her after her marriage.

American slavery was a deadly, lethal weapon. It was a two-way street, a two-edged sword, and cut forward as well as backward; it dehumanized both the master and the slave. The aftermath of the Civil War and the period of reconstruction reveals this in the scars borne by both races. The former master, as waking from a nightmare extending over two centuries or more, was frustrated and confused, and for a time clung to a glory that had departed forever. There was a "Colonel" sitting under almost every shade tree in his almost fenceless yard, sipping his mint julep and imagining vain and sometimes evil things. Too many of the young "masters" were pampered and spoiled and felt themselves above labor with their hands. Very naturally, there sprang up "plantation commissaries," known then as "grab stores," from which it was virtually impossible for the recent freedman to free himself once he became entwined in the web. He was again a virtual slave, and the federal government had to institute suits to free him from slavery to debts. There were not many of the former masters involved in these brutal transactions, but too many who, as now, shut their eyes to the evils about them for fear of being touched by them.

As regards the former slave, he was set free without bread or shelter, except in rare instances. Three hundred thousand of them, constituting the mulatto population, were left nameless. But all of them were in a helpless condition and fell easy prey to the brutality and wiles of a bankrupt oligarchy. After the surrender at the Appomattox Court House, the patriotic and brotherly advice of General Grant to the vanquished was not accepted by all of them in the spirit in which it was given.

Much has been written and masterly orations have been delivered to justify the alleged causes of the Civil War; but all the volumes in the world cannot change the facts and the deeds. Let me say here with all the emphasis possible that, in recounting just a few of the actual facts, I have no intention of trying to open old sores or "to wave the bloody shirt." My sole purpose is to relate the facts in the hope that the present generation of Americans may investigate them with open minds and come to the conclusion that the whole ignoble, sorry mess should be forgotten and that all of us should turn our attention to the future, resolved to build a better tomorrow for the America that we should all love; and that we should be determined to build here a heritage that will in the end resolve the world's ills and differences on a permanent, equitable basis.

However, let me append here that I do not believe there can ever be a peaceful coexistence with the Russian government as it is now constituted. I have studied the various developments of the Russian government and its leaders since before the time of Peter the Great. I have studied and investigated its central seat of government at Moscow, the international Comintern, from which point this atheistic spirit directs its world campaign, with the central idea "conquer through revolution." Its robots are living human beings encircling the globe, carrying the common message of divide and conquer through revolution. Peaceful coexistence! That would be laughable were there not so much ignorance in the world, and fools being born every minute.

What makes this thing so dangerous to America is the fact that so many Americans know very little about this world menace. America, until recently separated from this danger by a great ocean, living in ease, comfort, and luxury, which are calculated to make the mind less alert, cannot contemplate this great danger. Her crass materialism and Godlessness have left her open to such subtle danger; for, it should be remembered that while Communism never changes its central idea and purpose, it does change its attitudes and methods of approach.

Personally, however, I believe that the USSR will never rule the world. I have many reasons for this belief. First, I believe that the people composing this Republic are of such varieties of cultures, such a nonhomogeneous population, that the Republic would not be able to weld all of them into an aggressive fighting unit when the chips were down, and I think the Comintern knows that better than anyone else. Second, the people of the Republic as a whole do not want war; they want to live in peace with the rest of the world. Third, I still believe in miracles, on condition that we repent of our sins, live right, trust in God, and keep our powder dry. There is an advantage in being on the right side that I don't believe the world fully understands.

Man changes slowly, unless the change comes through a supernatural power. His nature remains just above his instinct—to kill and destroy. Yet, in the presence of a Divine Power, he is known to cower, to hesitate, or even to weaken, like Baal before Elijah, or Goliath before David, or Pilate before Jesus, or the entire British government in its onslaught against Gandhi, or the evil forces against Martin Luther King. In these demonstrations, the words of the Scripture, "If I am for you, who can be against you," came to full fruition. There is a trite saying that "purity creates an air that the vulgar cannot enter." Impractical? Nonsense? Foolish idealism? Maybe. But who can fathom the ways and wisdom of the Supreme Being? I think I do know that man can live on different planes, the material and the spiritual. And I do know, if the Bible is truth, that there is a physical body and a spiritual body, and that flesh and blood, as we understand the term, cannot enter into the better and more perfect life.

But I believe that if we are ever conquered and enslaved by an atheistic power, the clergy can be justly blamed for that unholy disaster. Since the first century of the Christian era, since the dispersal from Antioch, they have been hedging, giving ground, and "passing the buck," substituting and, in many instances, abdicating—as well as subsidizing in some cases. I do not charge the entire ministry with this dereliction, but too many have been guilty of the sin of omission. They knew better, but did not have the courage to stand up and be counted as different.

In making this very grave charge, I am not unmindful of the work of the great missionary schools and universities, and the numerous charity organizations; but despite these many good things, real and true Christianity has been watered down, possibly by the infiltration of materialistic elements. The minister, if called, cannot in any sense deny the fact that his mission is to save souls, and by that, I mean the whole man, his physical, mental, and economic well-being. I believe it is his Christian duty to preach and proclaim the whole gospel to the entire world; that he is still under the "Great Command" just as much as were the original disciples; and that his authority for a visa to enter a foreign country is vouchsafed by the Bible and not the State Department. Of course, he should "render unto Caesar the things that are Caesar's," but in any instance, "Caesar" should assist in making it possible for him to go where the Spirit calls him.

You have already guessed that I literally believe in the separation of Church and State. I believe that every evangelist in a foreign country, whether hostile or friendly, should be on his own and seek protection from Him who commissioned him, and not from his native country. Think what you will to the contrary; differ with me as much as you wish; but I firmly believe that, in the struggle for men's souls, convention should be ignored. I believe that the Church wars not only against little, evil-minded men, "for we wrestle not against flesh and blood, but against powers, against the rulers of the darkness of this world, against spiritual wickedness in high places." It is strengthening and edifying to read the entire sixth chapter of Ephesians.

I have not intended to condemn the entire ministry. There are literally thousands of them whose souls are sick and conscience-stricken by the prevalence of racial hate and bigotry. I know many of them personally and have talked with them, and it is their prayers, with many others', that are working upon the consciences of our country. One of these days, they may become strong enough to go on a sit-down strike in behalf of all Americans.

I have not intended to imply that the entire clergy was directly to blame for the sins and evils that beset America growing out of the race question, but I think it is plain enough from the record that if they had been zealous of their mission they might have forced a showdown and revealed the sins and evils sooner. It is doubtful that many would have awakened even now, had it not been for the self-denying and heroic efforts of the NAACP and certain strong Negro newspapers and journals in focusing the world spotlight upon the festering sore that was spreading over the body politic, and thus revealing the shameful hypocrisy of the entire nation.

It is entirely possible, of course, that the nation as a whole was not aware of this deadly, creeping illness. Now, however, that the world is one continuous neighborhood by reason of radio, television, and rapid transportation, there is no hiding place left for the evildoers. Every evil act they perform will henceforth be weighed and scrutinized by world opinion. Fortunately for the American Negro, every battle fought has been a bloodless one, fought through the courts by orderly processes, and by laws not of his own enactment. After a few more legal steps to close the gaps, I believe the NAACP can enjoy a well-deserved respite. I do not believe in this token thing, "integration," but I do want to go on record as believing in a just, gradual integration. I think it is in keeping with natural evolution, all other things being equal. This does not mean that I believe in second-class citizenship, *for I do not.* I would accept fair, open, competitive examinations for nonelective positions. I would favor a Negro for a political office only if he was better prepared for the office than a non-Negro. Booker T. Washington once said that the Negro can only help his own race if he can do a better job than the other fellow; otherwise he does his own race a distinct disservice.

I have been trying pretty much to write that part of my story that has to do with the "era," subjectively. That trait is really a part of me. In grade school and in college, especially in history classes, my teachers had a great deal of trouble in making me discuss the chapters, subjects, or topics objectively. I wanted to explore events from every conceivable angle, to see if the results were justified. I was eternally looking for a "trend," and I think I was, in part, justified.

Almost a century and a half exists between the time Thomas Jefferson wrote the immortal words, "We hold these truths to be self-evident, that all men are created equal," and when the United Nations penned the words "a common standard of achievement for all people and nations, to the end that every individual and every organ of society, keeping the . . . Declaration of Universal Human Rights." It would be inspiring if every man the world over would read and ponder that entire instrument. I have always been certain that I saw the beginning of this social trend coexisting with the preamble to the Declaration of Independence. Let's call it the trend of social evolution.

It is true that this trend led through physical torture and slavery, across a stretch of 250 years; it led through fratricidal blood saddle-skirt deep, invisible to the common eye, but plainly marked by the cross of John Brown and the stakes and gibbets of other martyrs that served as milestones along the bloody road to human freedom. And, in the thick of this terrible carnage were the prayers of tens of thousands of simple black souls bombarding a just God on His throne for reinforcement and deliverance. As to whether or not a thing is just, I think sometimes it is best to read it in reverse.

Being past eighty and having been a part of three generations, I am now in my mellowing years, looking toward the sunset of life, and holding absolutely no hate or prejudice toward any human being. I have simply jotted down the facts, "with malice toward none." And as painful as it has been to me to state certain truths, as God has given me power and memory to see them, I have written them with a single purpose in mind, and that is that we, as people of common sense, may see and face them.

The Negro, in his growing up in this country, has made many notable achievements, some of which were original. Dr. Daniel Hale Williams was the first surgeon to operate on the human heart; Booker T. Washington was the first American to give dignity to the soil and to begin a revolution in farming; George Washington Carver changed the entire method of farming and furnished food for the struggling people of the South. Dr. Charles R. Drew was the leading authority on the preservation of blood plasma and, in World War II, directed the program of providing relief for untold numbers of soldiers in desperate need of blood. Whether in sports, in the theater, in the sciences, in literature, the arts, or as historians, Negroes have acquitted themselves well. And I have mentioned only a few of many thousands.

In Oklahoma Territory, within my own memory, I have witnessed the election and performance of many highly competent Negro officials. There was R. Emmett Stewart, elected to two terms as county clerk of Logan County by a vote of all the people. Oldsters have told me that he was the best county clerk Logan County ever had. He reorganized the office and placed it on a modern basis, and it has never been changed. He was followed for one term by another able colored man, N. C. J. Johnson. I once had the pleasure of seeing J. I. Curran, another Negro, elected as a territorial representative from Kingfisher County, perform his duties on the floor with dignity and with the respect of all his fellow representatives. And after statehood, P. B. J. Hudson was elected as one of the county commissioners of Wagoner County and served the entire term with honor and distinction. He, too, was elected by all the people. The records of these public officials stand as monuments to the able discharge of their public duties.

In this story, I shall refer almost entirely to the progress or lack of progress of Negroes living in the South, and attempt to deal with their problems, which are different from those of the Negro living in the North. In the North, the Negro has the vote, the most powerful weapon in a democracy. In the South, in many places, this instrument is denied him. Hence, his most potent defense is not available to him. It's true that this heretofore impregnable wall that has separated him from real manhood has been cracked and is slowly crumbling; but only the foolish can believe that the fiat of law, or even bloodshed, can uproot centuries of custom based upon prejudice. Bloodshed is not only foolish, but unthinkable. Therefore, I have come to this conclusion:

While the Negro must ever remain alert and jealous of his God-given rights won in the courts, he must be patient, frugal, and industrious. He must always seek to improve himself in education, cleanliness, and manners. He should never watch the time clock, for a little extra overtime has its way of giving him added insurance when needed. If he has hatred, he must get rid of it and never resort to violence or bloodshed as a means of "getting even."

Violence has never worked and will never settle anything. He must seek after true, lasting values. Ninety percent or more of the values that surround him are false and fleeting. They will not last. He must have sufficient common sense to put first things first.

I have said that most of the values in America, as we know and worship them, are false, completely false. We worship thousands and thousands of false gods. We are materialistic to the nth degree. We worship Churchill far more than we do Gandhi, and it's my solemn guess that when Britain has been dead for a thousand years and Churchill's books all forgotten, Gandhi will be shining with greater luster than ever. And so will David Livingstone, Martin Luther, John Wesley, and hundreds of others now unsung, unwept for, and un-honored. I think Eternity has its own way of reckoning values in grouping the great souls who, without a murmur of complaint, spent their lives for others, even the widow with her mite. I think, too, that time has a way of bridging the gap between the lives of these countless souls and making them contem-poraries in the very Cause for which Christ gave his life. I think, too, that all the saints who died in the Roman arena, and those yet to die in atheistic lands for the sake of brotherhood under God, will be counted in that number.

I think I have a remedy for the perilous days ahead. That remedy lies in the appointment of a number of men, independent and unafraid, men of un-blurred vision and of goodwill. I would not insist on a specific number; but I would recommend that these men be thoroughly screened and not too many in number to hinder agreement and a united front. The duties of these men will demand superb abilities and talents, including an ability to answer any argument that might be advanced by the opposition. I believe that enough men of goodwill can be found in any locality.

Above all, these men should have patience, understanding, and a love for all people; they should be sympathetic but firm; they should have strength in humility and in meekness; an unwavering belief in justice, but cautious in di-rection; and they must forever teach that government by men inevitably leads to anarchy and finally no government by law for anyone. I have a deep and abiding belief, however, that such a group of "shock absorbers" cannot right the wrongs of the world unless aided by an awakened, aroused clergy.

I am personally of the opinion that the world is in its present condition because of a sleeping or unconcerned clergy, a ministry that has been dodg-ing its sacred obligations, passing the buck to fraternal societies and the like. Let me be more specific.

In the fifty-odd years that I have been actively engaged in the practice of law, I have seen but one Negro minister visit men in prison, but many Catholic priests. When I was a boy, ministers visited the sick and afflicted, even if they had to swim swollen streams on horseback. They brought prayers, the sacrament, and consolation. Then, the preacher was a special person in any community he visited. Now, he is just a common man in the community. He is addressed by his name, flat out and without a handle, and he seems overly to like this. He is one of them. But is he? Can he be? Not according to the Bible, at least. Christ not only gave to Peter the keys of the kingdom, but made him a spiritual leader. Certainly many have been called, but it is true that few have been chosen. The modern minister has become soft, easygoing, and drifts with the crowd. Certainly not all of them, but too many.

There just has been no easy road for the true minister of Christ down through a long line of dedicated, selfless souls. There is absolutely no substitute for the consecrated minister, especially when the chips are down. A wounded soldier dying in a foxhole or on a white sheet in a hospital wants to have the chaplain called. Or the convicted murderer walking the last steps to the gallows or the gas chamber feels a certain peace or solace as the priest, by his side, gently recites the twenty-third Psalm, just as the thief on the cross found solace in "This day you shall be with me in Paradise."

So the consecrated ministry must go ahead, preparing the way not only for peaceful, gradual integration, but for changing the whole pattern of life in America—the most wicked nation in the whole world, if the reports of the FBI are to be believed. Lawlessness begets lawlessness, and like a contagious disease cannot be contained within a certain area. It is a common disease—sin—with many forms and ramifications, and like any other disease, knows no color or even situation in life. It takes so many forms that it is impossible to enumerate them.

The big, the all-important, question is, can the church carry out the gigantic tasks it is faced with. The church has suffered a tremendous moral decay; it has regressed back to the brink of spiritual bankruptcy. If the church abdicates, all is lost and total eclipse will follow. The ancient cultures followed some form of religion, and however much we may differ from them, they adhered to the intangible things that could neither be seen or touched—the finer expressions of their inner selves. Our Christianity is based on faith, hope, and love, things *we* can neither see or touch. Our culture grew from these values even if somewhere along the way artificial barriers arose on our path that caused a detour, I hope a temporary one. There is a basic unity in man. The architect, before he can make the blueprint, must be able to visualize the outlines of the building he is planning. I have been told that one cannot make a chair until he sees it in his mind's eye. Dr. George Washington Carver once told me that he always prayed before he went into his laboratory, so as "to awaken and alert my inner self."

If one studies prayerfully the New Testament church and compares it with the present-day church, I think he will see the great and fundamental differences between the two. After the stoning of Stephen (Acts 7:59–60) and the dispersal of the disciples, they were all directed by the Spirit, in where to go and what to do.

The early church was democratic. All were accepted. Peter was hesitant until he had an experience with that sheet on the rooftop. Then, after his welcome in the home of a Gentile, he could proclaim, "I perceive that God is no respecter of persons." But most of the churches now blow hot and cold. In answer to such a state of affairs, John says in his message to one of the seven churches of Asia Minor, "So then because thou art lukewarm, and neither cold nor hot, I will spew thee out of my mouth" (Rev. 3:16). I believe that if the ministry will preach the whole gospel to all men everywhere, at home and in atheistic lands, eventually we will yet be able to witness a just and lasting peace under God. Certainly, many of them will suffer martyrdom, but I believe their deaths will stifle forever the wholesale killers. Somewhere it is written, "The blood of the martyrs is the seed of the church." The Scriptures say, in substance, that without the shedding of blood, there can be no redemption. I believe it means such blood as I have referred to. I don't believe that Holy Wars are out of date. I do believe that the Great Command is as important today as it was when uttered at the time of Christ's earthly visit. And I believe it is more necessary than ever to heed that Command. I personally have more faith in the meaning of the words of the song "Onward Christian Soldiers" than I have in the greatest army in the world. I am by no means a pacifist, either. I believe in first things first.

My mother was a great Bible scholar. When I was very small, she used to teach the Sunday-school class of which, at first, I must admit, I was a very reluctant member. But she had a way of making every lesson so interesting that I came to love her class. I recall particularly the lesson about the "ninety and nine" and the "good shepherd." To illustrate, she drew a picture on the board of a sheep corral, with many sheep bedded down therein; then she drew a picture of a meadow some distance away, and along its outer edge she drew the picture of a brook of fresh, clear, running water. Then away in the northwest corner of the board, she drew a mountain of brambles, rocks, and briars, in the midst of which was a lonely sheep, entangled and bleeding, unable to extricate itself. She had a cabin drawn facing east, and as the sun was rising the shepherd came from the cabin, rubbing his eyes, to inspect the fold. Then, with a long, forked instrument in His hand, he started for the mountain, and pretty soon returned to the fold with the lost and helpless lamb. Then she would explain and apply the lesson to life. She ended by emphasizing, "And he was a good shepherd." The pictures she drew and her applied explanation stand out in my mind after three-quarters of a century as clearly as if it was yesterday.

One great setback, I am afraid, to my program is the fact that white Americans know so little about the Negro, especially those in responsible positions of leadership. Hate and mistrust, I fear, are the sources of this lack of knowledge of the Negro. Someone has said that one cannot hate what he knows.

As one example of this lack of knowledge of the Negro, witness the existence of the barbarous, blasphemous Klansmen, with their burning cross. Those who engage in such acts of anarchy are Rip Van Winkles who have been asleep so long that they are out of tune with human progress. Since the Civil War, the American Negro has participated in three great wars, slept in foxholes, and seen thousands die at his feet. He has become as familiar with the flow of blood as with the water that ran down the creek back home. Hundreds of good, upright, well-meaning white Americans only know the Negro as maids or butlers, and judge the entire Negro race by them—and, no doubt, that's good as far as it goes. But these good and, no doubt, dependable people constitute only a very small fraction of the colored people of America. They might, however, represent a great inarticulate voice of a soul yearning for a decent life for their offspring and their race. And although they might be justly entitled, through their contributions to the development of this country, to a share of what white Americans take for granted, they can never express this to their employers.

I would therefore suggest that the committee I have proposed conduct seminars as often as possible and study well-documented books such as *The Negro in Our History*, by Carter G. Woodson; *Up from Slavery* and *My Larger*

Education, by Booker T. Washington; *What the Negro Thinks*, by R. R. Moton; *The Free Negro in North Carolina, 1790–1860*, and *From Slavery to Freedom*, by John Hope Franklin; *The Negro in American Life and Thought: The Nadir, 1877–1901*, by Rayford W. Logan; and *A Pictorial History of the Negro in America*, by Langston Hughes and Milton Meltzer.

In my attempted exegesis, I have not tried to set myself up as infallible; but I have sincerely tried to explore national and international conditions, in at least a limited way, and to draw certain moral and Christian conclusions that seem to me to be inescapable. How else can we account for the loss of the sanctity of the marriage vow, and home life; the problem of youth delinquency; the commission of crimes of all degrees; the barbarous slaughter on the streets and highways; and the nearly complete breakdown of laws and order in almost every stratum of our society, from the governor's mansion to the lowest hovel? Everybody knows, or should know, that by the simple enforcement of laws already on the statute books, loss of lives on the highway could be stopped in twenty-four hours by stiffer jail sentences and revoking the licenses of drunk drivers. But we have what we call democracy—a democracy gone to seed, and a spineless set of officials without the guts to enforce the law. What a disgrace! We can jail crap-shooters and drunkards, but as one wise man said, "Show me your public officials and I will tell you the kind of citizens you have."

At best, the road ahead for the American Negro is going to be rough, and there will be no way for the weak or timid to make it. Those with strength through meekness and humility, however, with creative genius, potential, and courage, faith and hope, will make it if they are willing to work hard. They will need patience, self-discipline, and self-denial; and they will need to learn how to make friends with men of goodwill, and how to evade and shun their enemies in a diplomatic way. They must learn to recognize opportunities that pass their way, and how to seize them to the best advantage. They must be clean and presentable, for outer cleanliness advertises inner cleanliness; without pretension, with sincerity and the utmost endeavor, they must try with all that's in them to advance in learning and knowledge, remembering that mediocrity is not enough. It is still true, as Ralph Waldo Emerson once remarked, in substance, that if you make a better mousetrap than the other man, people will beat a path to your door. If you live across the tracks and have something that the other fellow needs, he will come to you for it.

15

LOOSE ENDS—CONCLUSION

*T*he reader will recall that, after my conference with attorney Patchell regarding the marshaling of Dad's assets, I reported to my brothers and sisters. My brother Tom's response was different from those of the others. He simply said, in substance, that he had other pressing business to attend to, of greater importance, and he was not interested in sharing in the assets. It was years later that I came to understand the significance of his remarks; and in order for the uninformed to understand it too, it is necessary to repeat certain facts.

You will recall that I said that Mother would have been placed on the Choctaw Indian roll had she lived long enough to follow up her efforts, or had her cousin done what he had promised to do and had been paid to do. Hence, her children were finally enrolled as Choctaw freedmen. The federal appraisers had appraised all lands in the Indian Territory in value from 25 cents per acre to $5.50 per acre, with the average allottable land appraised at $3.25 per acre. No freedman therefore could allot land in excess of $130 in value. My brother Tom was allotted forty acres, the average appraised land, located in Garvin County southwest of Pauls Valley. I do not have the legal description of his allotment before me now; but his name on this acreage still appears on the township oil map and includes a small rural town named Eola.

At the time I had the conference with my brothers and sisters concerning Dad's assets, Tom had discovered that a forged mortgage had been placed against his allotment. None of us knew this at the time, except Tom. He was then trying to get the matter adjusted but was too proud and independent to tell any of us about it. It was years before I found out. This was not an uncommon thing in those days, especially against freedmen and certain unrestricted Indians. Of course, that was long before real estate mortgages and deeds were photostated before being placed on the record, and it was easy for forged instruments to be recorded as genuine. The forger always had the original instrument returned to him, which he immediately destroyed.

I can remember but three cases where the allottee was able to prove forgery. On one occasion, the real owner was able to prove conclusively that on the date shown on the forged instrument, she was in a hospital in another state. My brother Tom was a big cattle dealer, his credit was unlimited, and he thought that he could never be a victim of such forgery. Well, by carelessness and delay, he lost his court fights. This land had inexhaustible oil pools beneath it. My brother lost his health and ambition from the shock, and was never able to recover. Instead of being a millionaire, he died a pauper.

———

I am coming to the end of my story; but it does not by any means include all my past experiences. Eighty winters have passed over my head, a long time in the life of an individual, but only a drop in the ocean measured by eternity. I can remember attending my first Sunday-school class, taught by my mother. I was four. The subject of the lesson was the ninety-nine sheep, and the hundredth that strayed and became entangled in brambles and briars. I can recall my returning to the banks of old Massey, where I sat for hours looking into the "blue hole" into which I used to plunge from an overhead branch of the old oak tree, trying to decide whether to return to college. The decision had to be mine. The forests had shrunk, the plains and prairies had become smaller, and the nation was changing. Future generations of boys would be fenced in—the great open spaces were shrinking. Within three years, the Wright brothers were to launch the first airplane, pioneering the age of iron wings, as had been predicted by a great preacher.

And what great world-shaking events were just around the corner. From Kitty Hawk, North Carolina, was to go forth great wonders of science and technology, creating one world, described by Wendell Willkie, in which

America, who had long boasted of her "isolationism," was soon to lose her great oceanic barriers and stand exposed to the glare of the world, transformed from visionless complacency.

In the twinkling of an eye, the oxcart passed through the evolutionary stages of horse and wagon, the "iron horse," the automobile, into the jet age.

It seems but yesterday that, on the hottest days of July, I stood at the mouth of an ancient threshing machine, pitchfork in hand, removing the straws from the wheat. We would first cut the wheat down with a cradle, or scythe, stack it, and on horesback tread the wheat from the straw, after first spreading the wheat on wagon sheets. Later, the wheat was cut by a binding machine, and we had to "shock it" or put it in stacks. The threshing machine was improved by the addition of a carrier of straws. Now we have the great combines, making it possible for two men to do the job of ten. This is a fair example of what technology has done in business and industry. It has created a great labor surplus, and one of the pressing problems for state legislators and Congress to solve, if we are to keep our free economy and capitalistic system. Debating about a welfare state or of socialistic government is not going to settle these great human problems. How are we going to be able to prevent our great "know-how" from becoming our Frankenstein? That is a problem we will have to solve.

I have lived through two World Wars and the Korean conflict: wars that have wrung ancient nations from their hinges overnight; wars that have left desolation and ruin, mental and physical, all over the world. Ancient mores, cultures, and religions have been uprooted. The damage cannot be measured in dollars. There are as many problems as there are different tribes and nations. Therefore, each problem is human, different and delicate. Only unselfish, dedicated men and women are able to challenge these multifarious and complex human problems.

My life has been reasonably complete. Of course, I have lived through rainstorms and I have experienced sunshine and the fellowship of real friends. I have tasted the bitter with the sweet. I have learned that as life stretches toward the end, it mellows and bitterness dissolves. One of my most pleasant memories is of my seventieth birthday celebration, all of which was prepared without my least knowledge. My children were all present, and there were telegrams from all over the nation wishing me continued good health and happiness. Another very pleasant surprise was a testimonial given in my honor by the Hutcherson Branch of the Tulsa YMCA, on the 3rd day of April, 1959. I had spent sixty or more years on YMCA work, and this was the method chosen by the local branch to show appreciation for what I had tried to do for the association. By then I had had my stroke, and had to be carried up two flights; but I enjoyed every minute of the activities. Telegrams had been sent to me from all over the state from the governor down, and visitors and telegrams came from states as far away as Alabama and Missouri.

But of all the telegrams and letters I received at my testimonial dinner, I received my greatest thrill and joy from those written by my three surviving children, and I am going to record each of them in this story as a living testimonial to show the relationships possible between all parents and their children. So they are as follows:

April 3, 1959

Dear Dad:

As long as I can remember, you have worked, struggled and sacrificed to give us the comforts and security of a good home and a good life. We have shared many joys and many heart-aches together. You and our dear mother always taught us to live clean, to be honest, to fear no man, to love, to serve and, above all, to stick together. These things are a part of us.

We honor you not only this day, but every day.

Love, your first born,
Mozella

April 3, 1959

Dear Dad:

It warms my heart to be with you on such a day as this, which is the result of your service and rich contributions to your community throughout the years. You have always been an inspiration to us. We shall always cherish the rich heritage which is ours—a heritage from our darling mother and a loving dad.

Your devoted daughter,
Anne

April 3, 1959

Dear Dad:

On this day, many of your friends are joining to greet you and to pay you a much deserved tribute. We who are very close to you are happy to join with them. This is, of course, not a new expression for us. Time and again we have honored our father and our mother, knowing full well that whatever we are today we owe, in large measure, to the two of you.

This occasion gives us one more opportunity, of which we never tire, to tell you how much we owe to you and mother and how deeply grateful we are to you and her for all your sacrifices and all your expressions of love and confidence. Greetings from Aurelia, Whit and me,

Your son, John Hope

On the 16th day of July, 1959, without previous notice or solicitation from me, I received an official notice from the Oklahoma Bar Association that not only warmed my heart with strange emotions, but gave me a thrill that was hard to contain. It was the climax of over fifty years' struggle and sacrifice and devotion to a profession—my profession—to which I had dedicated myself, without thought of self, for more than one-half century. Omitting the caption, which includes the many officials of the association, the letter is as follows:

July 16, 1959

Mr. B. C. Franklin
1828 North Norfolk Avenue
Tulsa, Oklahoma

Dear Mr. Franklin:

It is a pleasure to make you a Senior Member of the Oklahoma Bar Association and to send you enclosed your 1959 Senior Membership card.

The Oklahoma Bar Association does not have a "Life" membership classification. However, as a Senior Member, you are entitled to all the rights and privileges of active membership without the necessity of paying dues. We will each year hereafter issue you your Senior Membership card.

You have lived a rich and full life. You can indeed be proud of your children and the record which you have achieved. Your record of outstanding service was well attested by your friends at the Citation Dinner last April.

You have our prayers for your ultimate recovery and our best wishes for many pleasant memories as you reflect upon a life well lived.

Cordially yours,
Kenneth Harris
Executive Secretary

————

I am not one of those who believe that the youth of today are going to the dogs. I believe that they are the products of the age in which they live. Of course, life is more complex and more complicated now than it was in my youth; but in this connection, it is well to remember that it is the elders who make, shape, and determine the kind of society in which their children shall live and grow. It's just that simple, as I see it. And that as the parents create the environment in which their offspring are to be reared, it seems plain to me that the blame for youth delinquency, if any, that exists today, rests with their elders. I do believe that parents today are raising their kids in many instances to become soft and less self-reliant. The common expression heard today is, "I don't want my child to have the hard time I experienced in growing up," which is a laudable ambition. But there are countless dangers involved, unless one is able to compare relative values and is able to discern them clearly. Much has been said against the "age of rugged individualism," and much of it is true; but rarely did I ever hear of one pioneer not coming to the rescue of another pioneer when in distress, and without thought of remuneration. Now, one pays for everything one gets.

My children, and others, who know nothing of the life of the pioneer, will be able, I hope, to compare the life of yesteryear with that of today, after reading my story. It will then be up to them to accept in part or in whole, or reject in part or in whole, the heritage of their forebears. In this age, I think I see a real problem emerging between parents and children. Most children are growing up to believe, I think, that a parent's obligation to them never ends; whereas, as a matter of fact, a parent's natural, legal, and moral obligations end after they have reared, educated, and prepared their children for life, or when they reach their majority; unless, of course, their offspring become dependent through no fault of their own. This relationship constitutes a two-way street. Both parents and children are free to pursue their own respective ways without hindrance by either party, unless, of course, one or the other becomes disabled and unproductive. After many years of obligations, the parents are entitled to rest and to pursue their business or hobbies in contentment.

For years, I have had a strong desire to write historical fiction, and had decided to stop practicing law at the end of 1957. But I have since wondered if I would have kept to my plan if I had not been stricken. I wonder!

Aside from still being paralyzed on my right side, my eyes are fast becoming weaker and weaker. I hope they will hold out until I have completed my first fling at my historical novel. The title has already been selected— "Blood Bath"—based upon the forced removal of the Cherokee Indians from Georgia to the old Indian Territory. I have hope and faith that I will be able to accomplish and make come true this long-held dream.

INDEX

Abernathy, J. H., 201
Abram, Eddie, 74
Abram, J. B., 230
African Americans: activities of, in Oklahoma Territory, 49–53, 60–63, 261; and politics, 49, 51, 112–13, 244, 245, 261; businesses of, 51, 62–63, 166, 167; as elected officials, 51, 244, 245; as lawyers, 51, 60, 63, 127, 137–40, 244–45; colleges for, 52–53, 108–10, 113–14; and Republican Party, 55, 170, 190; as judges, 61–62; as troops in Oklahoma Territory, 61–62; as U.S. marshals, 61–62; communities of, 69, 125, 166, 184; religion as profession for, 75–76; and Atlanta Baptist College, 108–109; of Atlanta, 111; of Nashville, 111–12; as teachers, 113, 146; and definition of race, 143–44; and Native Americans, 143, 186, 188; discriminatory laws against, 145–49, 175–76, 178, 182, 242–46; franchise of, 146, 148, 175–76, 178, 182, 243–44, 261; "state Negroes," 166, 166n; and World War I, 174–75, 175n, 179–80; as troops in Indian Territory, 180; and Democratic Party, 181, 190; and Grant, 182; in federal government, 221; and Great Depression, 221; and jury selection, 226; and *Dred Scott* v. *Sandborn*, 239–41, 243; progress of, 243; achievements of, 260–61, 265; in Oklahoma Territory, 261; challenges for, 262–66; whites' knowledge of, 265

Alberta, Jerry, 166, 172
Allen, Eugene, 84, 85, 86
American Baptist Home Mission Board, 76, 114
Anderson, J. A., 51
Anderson, W. E., 110
Ardmore, Oklahoma: African American lawyers of, 127, 137–40; and Franklin, 134–45; photographs of law office in, 155
Arizona, 131
Arkansas Digest, 204
Armour Packing House, 103–105
Armstrong, J. M., 51, 63
Armstrong Academy, 19
Asp, Henry, 132
Atlanta, 111–12
Atlanta Baptist Seminary, 109
Atlanta Baptist College: and Hope, 83, 97, 109–10; and Franklin, 105, 107–16,

275